S0-AZF-626

THE NATURE OF BUDDHIST ETHICS

The Nature of Buddhist Ethics

Damien Keown
Lecturer in Indian Religion
Goldsmiths' College, University of London

St. Martin's Press New York

#25131432

BJ
1289
.K44
1992

© Damien Keown 1992

All rights reserved. For information, write:
Scholarly and Reference Division,
St. Martin's Press, Inc., 175 Fifth Avenue,
New York, N.Y. 10010

First published in the United States of America in 1992

Printed in Hong Kong

ISBN 0-312-07905-2

Library of Congress Cataloging-in-Publication Data
Keown, Damien, 1951–
The nature of Buddhist ethics / Damien Keown.
p. cm.
Revision of thesis (Ph. D.)—Oxford.
Includes bibliographical references and indexes.
ISBN 0-312-07905-2
1. Buddhist ethics. I. Title.
BJ1289.K44 1992
294.3'5—dc20 91-47931
CIP

For my parents

HOLY SPIRIT LIBRARY
94-0509
CABRINI COLLEGE, RADNOR, PA.

Vijjācaraṇa-sampanno so seṭṭho devamānuse

'The one who is perfect in knowledge and conduct is supreme among gods and men'

Contents

Preface

This book is a revised version of my Oxford D.Phil dissertation. Although intended primarily as a contribution to Buddhist studies I hope it will also be of interest to students of religious ethics and comparative religious ethics. In revising the text I have tried to make it as 'user-friendly' as possible to the non-specialist in Buddhism by using English translations wherever possible for technical terms and the names of texts. In addition, Chapter 1 provides something of an overview of the particular problems in Buddhist ethics and the approaches of previous writers. This should provide orientation as well as indicating where my own position differs from the interpretations offered so far. In spite of this there remain many technical concepts and problems which are unique to Buddhist ethics and which cannot simply be 'translated away'. I can only hope that the more arcane parts of the discussion will not be too much of a deterrent to the reader who wishes to come to terms with the fundamental issues.

Readers with a background in Buddhism but not ethics may find some of the ethical concepts employed here unfamiliar, or at least a little odd in the context of Buddhism. I have therefore provided a basic exposition of the principal features of the two ethical systems which I consider as having at least a 'family resemblance' to Buddhist ethics, namely Utilitarianism (under which I include Situation Ethics) and Aristotelianism. Ethicists may find some of this discussion elementary, and if so I suggest that they pass over this material which will be found at the beginning of each of the last two chapters. My reason for including it is that in much previous work on Buddhist ethics – as may be seen in Chapter 1 – ethical terminology has been bandied around rather freely and with a lack of precision. In attempting to come to terms with the basic structure of Buddhist ethics I have found it necessary to go back to basics and distinguish the various forms of ethical theories such as Utilitarianism before attempting to determine whether such characterisations can be successfully applied to Buddhism.

This book is basically an attempt to pursue in a sustained way some problems which have hovered around the fringes of Buddhist studies for far too long. Although they have been regularly swept under the carpet they have never really gone away. Like many 'minor' questions they have in the end required a major reassessment of views which had passed into orthodoxy before their credentials were properly examined. In approaching Buddhism through its ethics I have been obliged to reassess the meaning and relationship of many basic Buddhist doctrines such as the Eightfold Path, nirvana, karma, the 'aggregates', and of the role of meditation. Even if my own reinterpretation of some of these doctrines turns out to be wide of the mark, I hope that the book will at least target the problem areas and attract serious attention to the study of Buddhist ethics.

In terms of style I have adopted the policy that words recognised by my wordprocessor – such as 'nirvana' and 'karma' – have passed into the English language. They are therefore not italicised, although their less familiar Pali counterparts (*nibbāna* and *kamma*) are. The Pali and Sanskrit forms of words are used interchangeably as the context demands, although Pali forms predominate. Translations without attribution are my own.

Finally, I would like to record my thanks to Richard Gombrich, Alexis Sanderson and Paul Williams for their unstinting help and assistance during my postgraduate studies; to my students for asking awkward questions, and to Jo for encouraging me to get the thesis into print.

List of Abbreviations

A	*Aṅguttara-Nikāya*
AA	*Aṅguttara-Nikāya-Aṭṭhakathā*
Adhs	*Abhidharmasamuccaya*
Abhs	*Abhidhammattha-saṅgaha*
Aṣṭa	*Aṣṭasahasrikā-prajñāpāramitā*
Asl	*Atthasālinī*
Bhāṣya	*Abhidharmakośa-bhāṣya*
BCA	*Bodhicaryāvatāra*
BJS	*Brahmajāla Sūtra*
Bo.Bhū	*Bodhisattva-bhūmi*
Collection	*Sīlakkhandavagga*
BPMS	*Bodhisattva-Prātimokṣa-Sūtra*
D	*Dīgha-Nikāya*
DA	*Dīgha-Nikāya-Aṭṭhakathā*
D.An	*De Anima*
Dh	*Dhammapada*
Dhs	*Dhamma-Saṅganī*
DhSam	*Dharma-Samuccaya*
Dialogues	*Dīgha-Nikāya* tr.
Dīpa	*Abhidharmadīpa*
EB	*Encyclopedia of Buddhism*
EE	*Eudemian Ethics*
HOS	Harvard Oriental Series
IHQ	*Indian Historical Quarterly*
JAAR	*Journal of the American Academy of Religion*
Jewel	*The Jewel Ornament of Liberation*
JRAS	*Journal of the Royal Asiatic Society*
JRE	*Journal of Religious Ethics*
Kośa	*Abhidharmakośa*
Kvu	*Kathāvatthu*
Laṅk	*Laṅkāvatāra-sūtra*
M	*Majjhima-Nikāya*
Matt	Matthew
MA	*Majjhima-Nikāya-Aṭṭhakathā*
M.Av	*Madhyamakāvatāra*
Madhu	*Madhuratthavilāsinī*

MCB	*Mélange Chinoise Bouddhique*
Miln	*Milindapañha*
MM	*Magna Moralia*
MPPS	*Mahā-Prajñā-Pāramitā-Śāstra*
M.Samgr	*Mahāyāna-Saṃgraha*
MSA	*Mahāyāna-Sūtrālaṃkāra*
MSB	*Mahāyāna-Saṃgraha-Bhāṣya*
MSU	*Mahāyāna-Saṃgraha-Upanibandhana*
NE	*Nicomachean Ethics*
Nett	*Netti-pakaraṇa*
Pañjikā	*Bodhicaryāvatāra-pañjikā*
PEW	*Philosophy East and West*
PTC	*Pali Tipiṭaka Concordance*
PTS	Pali Text Society
Record	*A Record of the Buddhist Religion*
RGSG	*Ratnaguṇasamcayagāthā*
S	*Saṃyutta-Nikāya*
SA	*Saṃyutta-Nikāya-Aṭṭhakathā*
Saund	*Saundarananda*
SBB	Sacred Books of the Buddhists
SBE	Sacred Books of the East
Śikṣā	*Śikṣā-Samuccaya*
Siddhi	*Vijñaptimātratāsiddhi*
SLJH	*Sri Lanka Journal of the Humanities*
Sn	*Sutta-Nipāta*
SnA	*Sutta-Nipāta-Aṭṭhakathā*
SSidhi	*Satyasiddhiśāstra*
Suhṛll	*Suhṛllekha*
Śū.Sam	*Śūraṃgama-samādhi-sūtra*
Thag	*Theragāthā*
Thig	*Therīgāthā*
tr.	translator/translation
Treasury	*Treasury of Metaphysics*
Tract	*Sīlavagga*
Ud	*Udāna*
Vin	*Vinaya*
Vism	*Visuddhimagga*
VismA	*Visudhimagga-Aṭṭhakathā*
VNS	*Vimalakīrtinirdeśasūtra*
Vyākhyā	*Sphūṭārtha-Abhidharmakośa-Vyākhyā*

1

The Study of Buddhist Ethics

What is good, what is bad? What is right, what wrong? What ought I to do or not to do? What, when I have done it, will be for a long time for my sorrow . . . or my happiness?

Lakkhaṇa-sutta (*D*.iii.157)

1. APPROACHES AND OBJECTIVES

In the face of the complexity of Buddhist metaphysics it is easy to lose sight of the fact that Buddhism is a response to what is fundamentally an ethical problem – the perennial problem of the best kind of life for man to lead. Like many philosophers Siddhattha Gotama was driven to seek the solution to this problem and the associated ethical questions it raises of the kind mentioned above. He pondered these matters over the course of many lifetimes and ultimately resolved them during his last existence. The remainder of his life was devoted to propagating the definitive solution he had discovered and encouraging others to implement it. The invitation he extended to his followers was to participate in the highest and best form of human life, to live a 'noble' life. This form of life embraces both seeing the world in the way the Buddha came to see it, and acting in it in the way he acted. The goal, then, is not simply the attainment of an intellectual vision of reality or the mastery of doctrine (although it includes these things) but primarily the *living* of a full and rounded human life.

The fact that the fundamental ethical problem has already been solved is, perhaps, one reason why ethics, as an independent philosophical discipline, has not attained in Buddhism the autonomy which it has in the West. It would seem to be largely redundant in Buddhism since the Buddha has thoughtfully provided in his teachings – or *Dhamma* – a detailed and systematic exposition of the normative ethical principles in terms of which the noble life should be led. The urgency now is for implementation rather than further speculation.[1]

Of course, no set of ethical teachings, however extensive, can define in advance all the circumstances in which ethical problems can arise. Every age faces new problems, and there is little specific guidance in Buddhist canonical sources, for instance, on the ethical dilemmas we face today as a result of the scientific and technological advances in the twentieth century. No doubt responses to these issues could be deduced from the ancient teachings, but it must be said that the Buddhist tradition throughout its long history has shown little initiative in developing and refining the tools of ethical analysis which might assist us in formulating such responses. In comparison with the Semitic religions, for instance, Buddhism has hardly made a start. The expectation in Buddhism seems to be that ethical problems will be entirely resolved or 'dissolved' in the pursuit of the religious life. To this extent Buddhist ethics is aretaic: it rests upon the cultivation of personal virtue in the expectation that as spiritual capacity expands towards the goal of enlightenment ethical choices will become clear and unproblematic.

Eschewing hypothetical speculation in ethics as in other matters the Buddha formulated his definitive normative response to ethical questions within the framework of a Path or Way (*magga*), and specifically in the Noble Eightfold Path under its first division (*khandha*) dealing with matters of moral conduct (*sīla*). My purpose in this book is to enquire into the meaning of *sīla* and its role in the scheme of the Eightfold Path: in other words, to examine the nature of the relationship between ethics and soteriology in Buddhism.[2] Our approach here has three specific objectives: (a) to enquire into the meaning and content of *sīla*; (b) to relate *sīla* to the overall scheme of human good which culminates in liberation (nirvana); (c) to put forward a hypothesis concerning the formal characterisation of the Buddhist ethical system.

The Neglect of Ethics

The study of Buddhist ethics has been neglected not just by the tradition but also by Western scholarship. Recent decades have witnessed an explosion of interest in all aspects of Buddhist studies while this fundamental dimension of the Buddhist ethos, which is of relevance across the boundaries of sect and school, has become an academic backwater. Only recently have the signs appeared that this neglect is to be remedied and the initiative has come not from Buddhist studies but from within the 'emerging and yet ill-defined area of the comparative study of religious ethics' (Little and Twiss, 1978: 251). This discipline has stimulated some useful periodical literature dealing *inter alia* with the ethics of Buddhism.[3] Much of the work on Buddhism, however, is in the form of tentative forays into the field and there has as yet been no systematic study which provides a characterisation of the formal structure of the Buddhist ethical system using the typology of philosophical ethics. In this book I put forward a candidate for this role in the hope that the attempt itself, however inadequately accomplished here, will provide the orientation for further studies by identifying at least the possible genus, if not the species, of the subject under investigation.

The Classification of Ethics

Ethics, as a branch of philosophy, has many subdivisions. For classificatory purposes the discipline may be thought of as having three aspects: (a) descriptive ethics (b) normative ethics and (c) metaethics. Broadly speaking the job of the first is to give an objective account of the moral prescriptions, norms and values of a community or group and to show how these principles or precepts ('moral action guides') are (or would be) applied in specific contexts. The scope of the enquiry here may also include empirical data which bears upon ethical matters, such as human psychology and descriptive-theoretical models of human nature (Frankena, 1973: 4). The task of normative ethics is the derivation or formulation of ethical rules and standards, the provision of justification, and a method for the validation or defence of the norms it seeks to establish. Finally, metaethics is concerned with the meaning of moral terms, moral reasoning, the logic of ethical legitimation and validation, and the overall question of the vindication of the claims of competing ethical systems. We shall be concerned here with only the first and third of these categories and no attempt is made to defend or promote Buddhist ethics in a normative sense. To help illustrate the methodology of the present work further it may be helpful to sketch out the approach of previous contributions.

Previous Research

Most of the work done so far on Buddhist ethics (which has been concerned almost exclusively with Theravāda ethics) has, as Razzino points out, been confined to the level of simple descriptive ethics:

> The bulk of the literature on Theravāda Buddhist ethics has been descriptive. Scholars have gone to the Pali Canon and have compiled, systematised and represented moral injunctions, prescriptions and anecdotes much as they occur in the texts and with no more explication than that given by the Buddha who often spoke in metaphors and parables (1981: 4).

The literature on Theravāda ethics, however, is far from extensive – indeed the total number of books on Buddhist ethics of all schools can be counted on the fingers of one hand. The originality of the topic is noted in the Preface to the first book on the subject where the author states 'So far as I know, no work is specifically devoted to the study of this single subject' (Tachibana, 1926: ix). Tachibana's contribution in his *Ethics of Buddhism* was confined to the level of simple descriptive ethics, his stated purpose being 'To explain the practical morality of Buddhism' rather than 'merely to abstract its moral idea and philosophise it' (1926: xi). A further contribution at the descriptive level was Saddhatissa's *Buddhist Ethics* (1970) which makes the Buddha's basic moral teachings available in a clear and comprehensive form and is faithful to the traditional categories and classifications. An early book which ventured beyond the Theravāda but not outside of the Small Vehicle was Poussin's *La Morale Bouddhique*. Published in 1927 this takes its data from the *Treasury of Metaphysics* (*Abhidharmakośa*) and is in large part a summary of the theories of karma held by the schools of the Sanskrit scholastic (*Abhidharma*) tradition. The debates between the Abhidharmic schools of the kind recorded in the *Treasury* are the closest Buddhism comes to the discipline of moral philosophy. However, according to N.N. Law writing in the Poussin Memorial Volume, ethics was not a field to which the great scholar felt particularly drawn. 'In his *Morale du Bouddhique*' [sic], writes Law, 'he has dealt with the ethical aspect of Buddhism – a subject in which he did not feel much interest' (1940: v).

Beyond the Theravāda

The taboo on Mahāyāna ethics was broken in 1978 by Roderick Hindery, who devoted a single chapter of his book *Comparative Ethics in Hindu and Buddhist Traditions* to the Mahāyāna schools of the Far East. He refers to a 'lacuna' or 'perhaps a total gap' in the contemporary analysis of Mahāyāna Buddhist ethics (1978: 223). A further innovation was in the style of analysis brought to the subject: in a move away from the simple descriptive level Hindery sought to understand the dynamic of the complex Mahāyāna ethos. The breakaway from the straitjacket of Theravādin sources allows a new perspective: by looking backward at the Hīnayāna from the vantage point of the Mahāyāna it is possible to detect more clearly the value-structure of the early tradition; and by looking at the response of the Mahāyāna itself it is easier to observe the ongoing process of ethical recalibration. Those writers who have confined their attention to Theravāda sources in isolation have suffered from a lack of sensitivity to the subtly shifting pattern of development within the tradition as a whole. This defect is mitigated to some extent in the most recent full-length study namely G.S.P. Misra's *Development of Buddhist Ethics* (1984). The author must be commended for broadening out the study of Buddhist ethics by including chapters on the psychological analysis of ethical data in the *Abhidharma* (ch. 3) and the moral values of the Mahāyāna *bodhisattva* (ch. 5). A final chapter (ch. 6) explores the transcendence of ethical values in the Tantric systems. The objective is as follows:

> The present work seeks to study Buddhist ethics as a developmental process not only in terms of inner dynamics inherent in its doctrinal and ethical formulations but also in terms of its response to various historical compulsions and the ensuing willingness on the part of its followers to introduce into its general framework novelties of forms and expressions (1984: ix).

Beyond Simple Descriptive Ethics

Now that a useful store of information has been accumulated through descriptive studies attention must shift from the presentation to the interrogation of textual sources. In developing a methodology for this part of the work Buddhologists have much to learn from the discipline of Comparative Religious Ethics. Attention must be directed to such matters as the logic or mode of moral reasoning found in particular sources and the overall pattern of justification exhibited by movements, schools, sects, or even collections of texts, which may be designated as ethical systems or sub-systems. This partnership of description and analysis corresponds to the expanded conception of the discipline of descriptive ethics held by Little and Twiss, for whom descriptive ethics involves 'A scientific meta-theoretical enquiry into the ethical discourse of a specified informant or group' (1978: 11). These two broad approaches are blended together in varying degrees in each of the chapters in the present work, and a descriptive account of the ethical data is either followed by or in some cases simultaneous with a theoretical analysis and interpretation. The bulk of the descriptive material will be found in Chapters 2 and 6, which are devoted to the ethics of the Small and Large Vehicles respectively. Chapter 4 provides a critique of a specific conception of the soteriological role of meritorious moral action (*kamma*) proposed by King and Spiro: my claim here is, in essence, that they have misdescribed the role of ethics in relation to nirvana. In Chapter 5 an attempt is made to provide a more satisfactory account of this relationship in terms of the Eightfold Path, and also to clarify the meaning of *kamma* and the key ethical terms *kusala* and *puñña*. In Chapters 7 and 8 I examine the theoretical basis of Buddhist Ethics by considering it in the light of two Western ethical models: Utilitarianism and Aristotelianism. To some degree this constitutes a venture into the field of Comparative Ethics, but alternative theoretical models are introduced here only in so far as they are relevant to the understanding of Buddhism.

Asking the Right Questions

To obtain meaningful answers from the material unearthed in the descriptive stage it is important to formulate the right questions. A useful start was made in 1964 when Winston King, referring to 'the almost total lack of contemporary material on Buddhist ethics in English' (1964: 5) published his *In the Hope of Nibbāna*. King specified his interest in six aspects of Theravāda Buddhist ethics. (1) What is the relation of ethics to the total structure of Buddhist doctrine and practice? (2) How does Buddhist ethics relate itself to Buddhist psychology? (3) What is the effect of the *Nibbāna-Kamma* (*Nirvana-Karma*) polarity of emphasis upon ethical values? (4) How does Buddhism practically and specifically analyse ethical goodness and badness in the sphere of concrete action? (5) Is there a genuine social ethic in Buddhism? (6) What, if any, new ethical developments are to be found in contemporary Theravāda Buddhism? (1964: v.f.). These are some of the fundamental questions which any serious enquiry into Buddhist ethics must address. In this book I do not consider either Buddhist social ethics or contemporary developments, but a response to the first four of King's questions will be made.

More specific questions about the nature of Buddhist ethics have been formulated by Jayatilleke. 'Is it', he asks, 'egotistic or altruistic? Is it relativistic or absolutistic? Is it objective or subjective? Is it deontological or teleological? Is it naturalistic or non-naturalistic?' (1970: 194). In a well-balanced discussion P.D. Premasiri, too, refers to the kind of theoretical issues which have occupied ethicists in the Western tradition of philosophy, questions such as 'Are moral judgements subjective or objective?' 'Is "good" definable in terms of some natural property or is it a non-natural property to be appreciated by intuition?' 'What is the logical relationship between statements of fact and statements of value?' (1975: 31). Responding to his own metaethical queries Jayatilleke is of the opinion that the Buddhist ethic is 'a form of enlightened egoism or enlightened altruism, which could best be characterised as an ethical universalism'. In terms of this framework (somewhat paradoxically) 'the egoist must develop altruistic virtues for his own good' (1970: 195). On the relativism/absolutism question he concludes 'while denying absolutism and recognising relativism, the objectivity of moral values is not denied' (ibid.). He suggests that the ethical theory of Buddhism is 'teleological rather than deontological' in character (1970: 197), right actions being an instrumental means to procure the final good. 'What is instrumentally good to achieve this end is regarded as good as a means. They consist mainly of right actions and the other factors that help in bringing about what is ultimately good' (1970a: 262). Finally, the ethical propositions of Buddhism contain 'a factual component and an emotive-prescriptive component' (1970: 192).

Premasiri, after a detailed consideration of evidence from the Pali Canon, concludes that Buddhist ethics is objectivist and naturalist.

> In conclusion it may be said that the implication of the moral discussion recorded in the Pali canonical literature is that early Buddhism considered ethically evaluative statements as involving genuine judgements, which can be found to be true or false. In morals there is genuine knowledge to be acquired and this knowledge rests largely on empirical facts. In maintaining this position early Buddhism stands with the position taken by the naturalist philosophers (1975: 44).

In the course of the discussion he rejects (rightly, I believe) the possibilities of Emotivism, Prescriptivism, and Intuitionism as appropriate characterisations of Buddhist ethics.

Soteriological Structure

All of the above questions are interesting and highly relevant to understanding the nature of Buddhist ethics. However, in my view, the fundamental issue which any enquiry into Buddhist ethics must address initially is the one specified in King's first question concerning the relationship of ethics to the structure of Buddhist doctrine and practice. I would formulate this problem in terms of the relationship between three things: ethics, knowledge, and the *summum bonum*; or in Buddhist terminology: *sīla*, *paññā*, and *nibbāna*. The question then is: how do moral and intellectual goods relate to one another within the framework of Buddhist soteriology? A more familiar way of expressing the problem might be in terms of the connection between the three divisions of the Eightfold Path, *Sīla*, *Samādhi*, and *Paññā*, and their relation to *nibbāna*.

There are several ways in which these elements of Buddhist soteriology can be related, but three in particular stand out. By far the most common is the view that regards ethics (*sīla*) as instrumental to knowledge (*paññā*) and then identifies the latter with *nibbāna*. *Nibbāna* is thus essentially the possession of a certain kind of knowledge and becomes an intellectual goal. In terms of the Eightfold Path this view assumes a linear soteriology in which morality is a preliminary stage or stepping-stone to the intellectual goal of knowledge; thus Morality (*sīla*) leads to Meditation (*samādhi*) which leads in turn to Knowledge or Insight (*paññā*). Wijesekera provides a good example of this view:

> This path is said to consist of three stages or parts . . . The first of these stages is *sīla* or ethical conduct, and practical morals have a meaning for the disciple only till such time as he arrives at the next stage of the Path, namely, concentration (*samādhi*). But the goal is not reached even then, and a still higher stage of development must be gone through and this is technically known as *paññā* (wisdom) (1971: 62).

Here, ethics plays only a provisional and subsidiary role in the attainment of knowledge, and ethical values are often thought to be 'transcended' in the attainment of *nibbāna*, which is then characterised as a state 'beyond good and evil'. This view has a long pedigree and the thesis of ethical transcendence was suggested by E.J. Thomas in 1914:

> But though the process is largely ethical, the end is not so. The end is entire detachment from the world of birth and death, and the ethical character remains only so far as right conduct is considered essential for attaining it (1914: 343).

A second possibility is that while ethical values are instrumental to knowledge in the pre-enlightenment condition they are subsequently reinstated in an authentic form in the post-enlightenment state. Now it is the enlightenment experience which marks not the end but the beginning of moral potential by removing the afflictions of ignorance which fatally prejudice authentic moral conduct. True moral action becomes the prerogative of the *Arahat*, one which he is free to exercise or not as he wishes. 'Thus', writes R.H. Jones, 'the basic path required by Theravāda Buddhism is non-moral in leading to *nibbāna*, but moral activity may be opted for in the enlightened way of life' (1979: 371). This view too has been around for some time and a similar position was articulated some seventy years earlier by Dahlke:

> This, briefly, is the primal source of the whole of Buddhism. Gautama, who later became the Buddha, does not begin his career as a saviour of the world . . . Nothing lies farther from his mind than the welfare of others. He seeks his own salvation, and that only. It is a purely egoistical impulse, but what more natural than that one who suddenly finds himself in a burning house should seek first of all to save himself? However, after he has

> attained this salvation, after he has worked his own way out of the sea of sorrow to the shore of safety, after he has reached the blest apprehension 'I am saved', his mind turns back to his suffering fellowmen, and only now in this retrospective motion do we see love emerge in the shape of that compassion which comprehends (1908: 130).

A variant of this view is expressed by Stephenson with reference to karma and nirvana:

> In the first place, we submit that the concepts of *Karma* and *Nirvana* are antitheses. In no way are the two alike either in form or in content. *Nirvana* is amoral or supramoral. *Nirvana* is experienced either above or below morality in the senses of thought, word and deed (1970: 109).

These first two views can be grouped together since they share the common characteristic of making ethics dependent upon and subservient to knowledge. A third possibility is that ethics and knowledge are in some sense both present together in the final goal. Razzino (1981: 94) quotes the following statement by Rahula, which expresses a view central to her thesis and to my own:

> For a man to be perfect there are two qualities that he should develop equally: compassion (*karuṇā*) on one side and wisdom (*paññā*) on the other. Here compassion represents love, charity, kindness, tolerance, and such noble qualities on the emotional side, or qualities of the heart, while wisdom would stand for the intellectual side or qualities of the mind. If one develops only the emotional neglecting the intellectual, one may become a good-hearted fool; while to develop only the intellectual side neglecting the emotional may turn one into a hard-headed intellect without feeling for others. Therefore, to be perfect one has to develop both equally. That is the aim of the Buddhist way of life: in it wisdom and compassion are inseparably linked together (1978: 46).

The three possibilities outlined above represent very different visions of the role of ethics in the Buddhist soteriological programme. In the first two cases, which I have bracketed together, ethics is extrinsic to *nibbāna*, dispensable, and subsidiary to *paññā*.

In the third it is intrinsic to *nibbāna*, essential, and equal in value to *paññā*. Both viewpoints have their supporters and number distinguished scholars amongst their adherents. Yet how can two such incompatible interpretations have quietly co-existed for so many years, as they have? I think the answer lies in part in the fact that there are features of Buddhism which allow it to be interpreted in both of these ways. Looked at from different perspectives, and given an appropriate selection of textual material, either interpretation can fit. And until they are forced into confrontation they will continue to allow one another elbow-room. Given the general neglect of Buddhist ethics no-one has bothered to press the matter to the point where one view is discredited. Nor is this an easy thing to do, since it concerns not single issues but the interrelationship of a number of complex doctrines, and ultimately the adoption of a particular vision of Buddhism. It is a matter which is to be decided on the balance of probabilities rather than demonstrated by simple knock-down arguments. I hope to show in this book that one of these interpretations makes better overall sense than the other in that it is more coherent, consistent, and faithful to Buddhist sources. I concede that there is evidence against my interpretation and a case for the competing view could still be made out. I believe, however, that this would be ultimately at the price of fitting Buddhism into a Procrustean bed. Bearing in mind the three broad approaches to Buddhist soteriology I have indentified above we may now consider how the nature of Buddhist ethics has been characterised and defined in the secondary literature.

2. THEORIES OF THE NATURE OF BUDDHIST ETHICS

Of the small number of scholars who have studied the subject few have put forward detailed hypotheses as to the formal structure of Budhist ethics. One senses a reluctance amongst commentators, who readily acknowledge the centrality of ethics, to define its role with precision in terms of Buddhist soteriology. The importance of ethics in Buddhism is frequently stressed. Wijesekera claims boldly: 'It is universally recognised that Buddhism can claim to be the most ethical of all religio-philosophical systems of the world' (1971: 49). Saddhatissa, in the subtitle to his *Buddhist Ethics* (1970), characterises ethics as the 'Essence of Buddhism'. Poussin affirms that 'Buddhism is, in its essence, an ethical discipline' (1927: viii), while

Mrs Rhys Davids states in her introduction to the *Enumeration of Elements (Dhamma-Saṅganī)* 'Buddhist philosophy is ethical first and last – this is beyond dispute' (xxii). In the full-length studies referred to earlier we find no attempt by Tachibana (1926), Poussin (1927), or Saddhatissa (1970) to define the structural form of the system. King (1964) after posing the key ethical questions mentioned above seems to suggest that answers to them may be difficult to find since:

> 'Ethics' for Buddhism is psychological analysis and mind control, not the search for a foundation of ethical principles, a hierarchical arrangement of ethical values, or an enquiry into their objectivity (1964: 4f.).

He does, however, at a number of points move towards a discussion of theoretical matters. He considers somewhat inconclusively the issues of relativism and absolutism (1964: 70–9) and the tension between them in Buddhist cultures. Thus, on the one hand, in view of the doctrine of karma, 'We seem to be led towards a relativist and instrumentalist conception of ethical good, characterised by hedonistic overtones'. Yet on the other hand most Theravādin Buddhists affirm that the Five Precepts 'embody universally valid moral principles' (1964: 72f.). King also discusses the relation of *Nibbāna* to ethical values (1964: 88–106) but is hampered by a misconception of the relationship between *kamma* and *nibbāna*, which I discuss more fully in Chapter 4.

The case for the complete dislocation of ethics from nirvana has been made by Gudmunsen (1972, 1973) arguing that 'Ethics Gets in the Way'. He allows ethics only an instrumental role in facilitating the transition from the conditioned world to nirvana and proposes a double-decker model of Buddhist ethics comprising 'Higher Order Evaluation' (matters concerning *Nibbāna*), and 'Lower Order Evaluation' (matters concerning *Sīla*). The distinction in turn rests upon a posited 'absolute logical and ontological gulf between *Nibbāna* and the conditioned world' (1973: 16f.), such that the concerns of ethics proper to the latter can find no foothold in the former. Given this dichotomy, *sīla* becomes merely 'the first part of the way to *Nibbāna* to be "got over"' (1973:2).[4] Misra, too, seems to follow the transcendency thesis.

> The *Dhamma* of Buddha was practical and dynamic, it was also mystical. True to its mystical form, it presented an intermixture

> of religion and ethics as an inseparable pair, the latter being not an end in itself but a means leading to a higher stage which was a state of complete transcendence (1984: 30).

Two pages earlier, however, he seems to differ from the above view when he quotes (in fact, misquotes) Anesaki with approval on the *non*-instrumental relationship between *sīla* and *paññā*:

> Conduct and intuition are inseparably united; they form an essential pair, each performing its specific part with the help of the other. 'Morality', remarks M. Anesaki, 'is [sc. not] merely a means to perfection . . . it is an integral part of the perfection . . . (1984: 28).

Also supporting the notion that ethics is transcended by knowledge is Wang's article 'Can Man go beyond Ethics?' in which she argues (unpersuasively) against the background of Tantric Buddhism that 'Nothing is forbidden those giants of transcendental wisdom' (1975: 150). And although 'Buddhism does possess a set of ethics in the Ten Precepts . . . these were intended to be binding on the unenlightened, i.e. the mental children' (1975: 142). In short, 'Buddhism arrived at relativism and situational ethics before the common era' (ibid.). In contrast to this view it may be thought that 'megalomaniac immorality' is perhaps a more sober assessment of the behaviour of these 'lawless *siddhas*'.[5] The view of ethics as preliminary or instrumental usually involves an understanding of karma as a mechanism for personal reward or retribution, which tends to corrode the framework of morality which is by nature interpersonal. Thus Dahlke:

> That cordiality which forgets itself for others, that affection which breeds tenderness and emotion, is entirely wanting here. The whole moral scheme in Buddhism is nothing but a sum in arithmetic set down by a clear, cold egoism; as much as I give to others, as much will come again to me. *Kamma* is the most exact arithmetician in the world (1908: 130).

Expressing a similar view Dayal writes: 'The Buddhists have developed a precise quantitative view of *puñña*, which seems to convert their much-vaunted ethics into a sordid system of commercial arithmetic' (1932: 189).

Theravādin Utilitarianism

The conception of Buddhist ethics as utilitarian is especially prevalent among those versed in the Theravādin tradition, many of whom regard ethics as merely a preparatory stage on the path to enlightenment. Students of the Mahāyāna, on the other hand, seem less inclined to this view, perhaps as the result of their exposure to texts which on almost every page proclaim the importance of *karuṇā* as an essential attribute of a *bodhisattva*. In his Foreword to Horner's (1950) essay *The Basic Position of Sīla*, G.P. Malalasekera suggests that 'Buddhism has never regarded *Sīla* as an end in itself but only as a means to an end. This conception of morality is, I believe, unique to Buddhism.' The conception of ethics as instrumental to a non-moral end is not, of course, unique to Buddhism. It would, however, be unusual in the context of a system of *religious* ethics, of which I take Buddhism to be an instance,[6] and which is perhaps Malalasekera's point. Horner herself in her essay goes on to speak of moral conduct as 'no more than the beginning, the A.B.C. of the process of development which culminates in the Highest' (1950: 25). She prefaces this with the comment that in the context of morality 'it is quite inadequate to think that good is for good's sake' (1950: 24). On this note Wijesekera writes:

> In fact early Buddhism administers a warning to the aspirant to master morality but not to allow morality to get the better of him, and it is clearly laid down that even virtuous conduct has to be transcended at one stage (1971: 62).

A brief characterisation of Buddhist ethics is provided by Mrs Rhys Davids who comments:

> The Buddhist . . . was a hedonist, and hence, whether he himself would have admitted it or not, his morality was dependent or, in the phrase of British ethics, utilitarian, and not intuitionist (*Dhs*. tr.: xci).

A suggestion that her husband did not follow her in this view may be found in his reference to 'The fundamental Buddhist doctrine that good must be pursued without any ulterior motive' (*SBE*. XI: 222). Dayal, however, is in no doubt that 'Pure hedonism thus seems to be the ruling theory of Buddhist ethics' (1932: 205), while Kalupahana notes that 'The emphasis on happiness as the goal of ethical conduct seems to give the Buddhist theory a utilitarian character' (1976: 61). Describing the Buddhist ethical teachings J.B. Pratt concluded: 'This system may be classed as a form of altruistic hedonism' (1928: 20). Furthermore: 'The principle on which the good and evil forms of happiness are to be distinguished is explicitly stated. It is the principle of utilitarianism' (1928: 28). And:

> The Buddha's ethic might, then, well be called Stoic, but the principle underlying and justifying his Stoicism, to which he makes appeal when argument is needed, is his fundamental utilitarian or (altruistic) hedonism (1928: 32).

Anuruddha, speaking of 'the practicable nature of Buddhist morality and the utilitarian purpose that it serves' (1972: 355), comes to the following conclusion:

> To distinguish what is good and what is bad Buddhism puts forth two criteria such as 1 *cetanā*, the intention which drives one to act and *vipāka*, [*sic*] the results brought about by the action. Of these two Buddhism seems to have put much more emphasis on the second and therefore Buddhist ethics may be regarded as Utilitarian in character (1972: 434).

Saddhatissa (1970: 19) describes the 'ultimate ideal aim of Buddhism' as 'a supramundane state beyond good and evil' while Tachibana characterises the *Arahat* as 'not immoral' but 'supramoral' (1926: 55). Bush suggests that:

> We are thus led in the direction that the state of the *Arahat*, the goal toward which the Buddhist Middle Path tends, is not primarily concerned with the moral life, for this is past . . . The fruits of arahatship are certainly not to be found in any new service to mankind, any heightening of the love for one's neighbour, any good deeds done by a new person (1960: 196f.).

Those who hold views of the utilitarian kind above commonly make reference to the Parable of the Raft (*M*.i.134f.), which is interpreted to mean that ethical considerations are ultimately to be transcended. Thus Horner writes:

> Morality is to be left behind . . . like a raft once the crossing over has been safely accomplished. In other words, the *arahat* is above good and evil, and has ṭranscended both (1950: 11).

The implication of this viewpoint is summarised by Hindery:

> If the regulation of one's social relations is ultimately orientated to the eradication of ignorance and the attainment of 'personal' enlightenment, then some would contend that Theravāda morality is no morality at all, but a form of philosophical egoism, subjectively amoral (1978: 231).

In a brief attempt at theoretical classification Misra contrasts Intuitionism with Ideal Utilitarianism and identifies Buddhism with the former:

> It would be well to make here a brief comparison between two diametrically opposed systems of ethical thought, viz., *Intuitionism* and *Ideal Utilitarianism*, and then to see the Buddhist position in this regard. The former is identified with the Kantian system of ethics . . . Buddha would obviously belong to the Intuitionist school of ethical thought (1984: 43).

I believe that Misra is correct here in recognising the proximity of Buddhism to Kantian principles rather than to utilitarian ones. Unfortunately he does not develop this point further, and his general stance on the instrumental role of ethics seems at variance with the above conclusion. In fact the following comments, made only a few pages later, seem to suggest the reverse position, i.e. that Buddhist ethics is utilitarian:

> The perfect man is uncontaminated not only by evil or vice but also by good or virtue. Perfection knows no dualism. It is a disposition of mind in which good and evil both become equally undesirable . . . In the Buddhist texts this transcendence of *dhamma* in the final stage finds enunciation by way of the parable of Raft [*sic*] (1984: 46f.).

Finally, Dharmasiri claims that Buddhism is a form of Ideal Utilitarianism, of the rule-utilitarian sub-class. He qualifies this by adding that Buddhism embraces deontology and teleology only to eventually transcend them both (1986: 34f.). 'What all this shows', he concludes, 'is that the last stages of Buddhist ethics cannot be categorised by available analytical categories' (1986: 39).

Against Utilitarianism

Contraindications to the utilitarian presumption include the tendency among Buddhists to regard the precepts as moral absolutes, as noted by King above, and also the ideal of moral perfection as an end in itself as defined in the conduct of the enlightened and in particular the Buddha. Thus Pratt, while describing Buddhist ethics as utilitarian, also states that 'the two cardinal virtues of Buddhism are wisdom and love' (1928: 36). The question he does not address is whether wisdom and love (either together or independently) are ends or means. A view held by some scholars and practitioners of the Theravāda is that these things are ends, and such virtues are not normally identified as ends by utilitarian systems. We may recall Rahula's comment quoted above concerning the importance of the cultivation of both *paññā* and *karuṇā* on the path to perfection. This is echoed by Saddhatissa: 'Remembering the *Mahāprajñā* of the Buddhas', he points out, 'it is incumbent on one to remember their *Mahākaruṇā*' (1970: 50). The point is emphasised again later: 'What cannot be maintained', he writes, 'is that either morality or wisdom should exist independently of each other' (1970: 68). In a passing reference to this alternative conception of the role of ethics Hindery suggests the possibility that in Buddhism 'Morality is not merely a dispensable scaffold for faith, mind-culture or enlightenment. It is rather their symbolic (dual/non-dual or trans-dual) embodiment and in some sense their verification' (1978: xv). Andrea Razzino has argued that compassion (*karuṇā*) and insight (*paññā*) are central features of the Buddha's perfection and jointly constitute the final human good. However, she stops short of demonstrating how this view is to be reconciled in a systematic way with other aspects of Buddhist doctrine and is finally left in a quandary over the precise soteriological role of ethics. Sometimes she sees it as a means to an end (e.g. 1981: 44, 72, 135) and speaks of ethics in utilitarian terms (1981: 69); yet on the other hand her central claim is that *karuṇā* has a strictly non-instrumental status and is a constituent of the final good itself. Thus on the same page (1981: 95) *karuṇā* is characterised as essentially other-directed yet at the same time is said to be cultivated primarily for one's own benefit as a means to some further end.

In recent years the tide has begun to turn against the intellectualisation of Buddhism which has fostered the devaluation of ethics and its relegation to a preliminary stage of the religious life. A landmark study was Harvey Aronson's *Love and Sympathy in Theravāda Buddhism*, which stressed the Buddha's compassion rather than his knowledge. Directly or indirectly opposing the view that Theravāda Buddhism is amoral or that its ethics has only provisional status are Bastow (1969) (which prompted the rejoinder by Gudmunsen (1972) referred to above), and N.R. Reat (1980), who reveals the inaccuracies in Jones (1979). Those unhappy with the transcendency thesis and its soteriological implications would seem to include Swearer (1979: 62f.), Aronson (1979, 1980), Reynolds (1979a: 13, 17ff; cf. 1980: 139-45), N. Katz (1982) and J.R. Carter (1984).[7] In the next section I will briefly outline my own position with reference to the views of the nature of Buddhist ethics discussed so far.

3. AN ALTERNATIVE APPROACH

As I have suggested above, I believe that questions concerning the specific characterisation of Buddhist ethics can be resolved most successfully when more basic questions concerning the role of ethics in the overall strategy of Buddhist soteriology have been explored. It is only by understanding the architectonic structure of the system that answers to specific questions will be possible or even meaningful. To this extent I side with those who maintain that the study of Buddhist ethics must proceed along holistic lines (Swearer, 1979: 63f.; Childress, 1979: 4ff.; Reynolds, 1980: 130). After discerning the underlying structure we will be in a better position to respond to some of the theoretical questions raised earlier. At the same time, I do not believe that the principles of Buddhist ethics are absolutely unique or *sui generis*, nor do I accept that it must be understood exclusively in its own terms.

As has been pointed out above, practically all the research undertaken so far into Buddhist ethics has focused narrowly on the Theravāda system, and has suffered from a lack of perspective in terms of the organic relation between the Large and Small Vehicles. To counteract the dangers of such a truncated presentation, and since my conclusions are intended to reflect the value structure of Buddhism as a whole, I consider material from both Hīnayāna and Mahāyāna sources. I do not consider Tantra at all, although some aspects of Chapter 6 may be relevant to it.[8] In the course of an analysis of the data I will put forward a thesis concerning the overall structure of Buddhist ethics and its role in relationship to Buddhist soteriology. Definitions are not offered at the outset: if it be objected that the enquiry cannot commence until key terms such as 'ethics' and 'morality' are defined (cf. Little and Twiss, 1978: 1–7) then I am happy to adopt the Little and Twiss concept of a 'moral action-guide', and their definition of a moral statement as 'a statement expressing the acceptance of an action-guide that claims superiority and that is considered as legitimate, in that it is justifiable and other-regarding' (1978: 28f.). As far as Buddhist terminology is concerned I shall understand *sīla* and *paññā* primarily in the sense they have as categories of the Eightfold Path. Thus *sīla* denotes the sphere of moral excellence and may be translated by a range of more or less interchangeable English words such as 'morality', 'virtue', 'ethics' and 'good conduct' as the context demands. As an umbrella term in this sense I shall regard it as embracing the numerous individual virtues such as compassion (*karuṇā*), generosity (*dāna*), courage (*viriya*), and so forth. I will also regard the principle of moral retribution, or karma, as an aspect of *sīla*. *Paññā* I will take as denoting intellectual excellence, that is to say intellectual activity which has truth as its object. Once again a range of English terms may be appropriate, such as 'insight', 'knowledge', or 'understanding' ('wisdom' is avoided for reasons to be explained later). By 'nirvana' I understand the *summum bonum* of Buddhist soteriology. To avoid any confusion I am concerned throughout this book only with that nirvana in terms of which ethical goodness can be predicated of a human subject, namely 'nirvana in this life'. I do not address directly the problem of the apparent absence of a moral subject in the light of the no-self (*anattā*) doctrine. It seems to me that Buddhism provides sufficient criteria for personal identity to allow the identification of subjects within the moral nexus. The discipline of ethics requires only that one individual can be distinguished from another: to pursue the issue of the ultimate ontological constitution of individual natures in this context is to confuse ethics with metaphysics, and does not make for a fruitful line of enquiry.[9]

Contrary Opinion

To some extent the view which I put forward here goes 'against the current' of received thought which has developed by consistently approaching Buddhism through its doctrine and philosophy rather than through its ethics. Perhaps it is the rationalistic non-moralising tone of Buddhism in combination with the novelty and distinctiveness of its philosophical teachings which has attracted and channelled Western intellectual attention in the way it has. The bias towards a utilitarian reading of Buddhist ethics may also owe something to the image of Buddhism as progressive and enlightened, particularly when perceived against the background of a sombre moralising Christianity. Oddly enough, the emphasis on the intellectual aspects of Buddhism has produced a rather pessimistic picture of a tradition obsessed with suffering, impermanence and existential doubts about personal identity. When this imbalance is redressed, however, the picture of Buddhism which emerges is rather different from many of the standard depictions. My own impression is that when approached through *Sīla* Buddhism appears in a different light than when approached through *Paññā*: in terms of the stock characterisations it is more 'positive', 'optimistic' and 'life-affirming'. The emphasis falls upon action, commitment, responsibility and love rather than the apparently 'negative', 'pessimistic', and 'life-denying' philosophical doctrines of impermanence, suffering, and non-self. It is now the Third and Fourth Noble Truths which are accented, rather that the First and Second. It is to be hoped that by correcting the imbalance on the ethical side in Buddhist studies, future work will permit a more rounded stereoscopic perception of the tradition.

Several of the views encountered in the discussion so far have long since passed into the mythology of Buddhist studies. Like myths they gain their strength from repetition, and are frequently recited but rarely questioned. I do not deal directly in this book with all of these issues but among the views I shall reject are the following:

1. The soteriological goal is insight (*paññā*) alone.
2. Nirvana is transcendent of all moral values and those who attain it pass beyond good and evil.
3. *Paññā* is the goal of the supramundane (*lokuttara*) path and ethical perfection is the goal of the mundane (*lokiya*) path.

4. *Paññā* is pursued by monks, *Sīla* is pursued by laymen.
5. *Sīla* is merely a preparatory stage for *Samādhi*.
6. *Samādhi* is merely a preparatory stage for *Paññā*.
7. *Paññā* and *Puñña* are antithetical.
8. Nirvana is achieved through the eradication of all karma.
9. Moral acts are 'skilful' deeds.
10. Buddhist ethics is Utilitarian.
11. Buddhist ethics is Relativist.
12. Buddhist ethics is Emotivist.
13. Goodness is a non-natural quality.
14. Only the enlightened can be truly moral.
15. Ethical values are merely 'conventional'.

Aristotle and Buddhism

The view of Buddhist ethics advocated here is based on the Aristotelian model, or at least one understanding of it.[10] The parallel between Buddhist and Aristotelian ethics is, I believe, quite close in many respects. Aristotle's ethical theory appears to be the closest Western analogue to Buddhist ethics, and is an illuminating guide to an understanding of the Buddhist moral system. It is all the more valuable since the exegesis of Aristotelian ethics has reached a more sophisticated level than the study of ethics in Buddhism. The questions which have been raised and discussed within the Aristotelian tradition may be a guide to the identification and resolution of difficulties in Buddhist ethics. In adopting this strategy of proceeding from a known to an unknown I can claim the support of I.B. Horner:

> Parallels such as these are sometimes even more conducive to an understanding of the content of Buddhism than are the direct citations from the Buddhist Canon; for they enable the reader to proceed from a known to a lesser-known phraseology. It need hardly be said that for a European reader or scholar who proposes to study any Oriental religion seriously a considerable knowledge of Christian doctrine and history, and of its Greek background, is almost indispensable (1948: 29).

Previous references to Aristotle in the context of Buddhist ethics are almost non-existent,[11] although at one point Poussin intriguingly characterises it as 'eudaemonistic' (1927: 28). Stephenson rejects the possibility of any similarity:

> In looking back at the discipline of ethics we note that its enquiry into the *summum bonum* has since antiquity, in the West at least, been associated with the Aristotelian notion of happiness. Happiness in turn, again at least in the West, has been strictly associated with a positive Weltanschauung which is presupposed and placed as a burden on the ethical task as such almost before it begins. It is thus time to discard this specifically Western presupposition and let ethics do its task umimpeded (1970: 35).

Stephenson's rejection of a positive characterisation of the *summum bonum* stems from a rather gloomy view of Buddhism in terms of which nirvana is 'the natural result or the logical conclusion to an ethical system which understood all of life and existence as crushing, suffering and deceitful' (1970: 96). According to this view, 'When not in the experience of *Nirvana* one lives penultimately, anticipating *Nirvana* while caught in the web of sociopolitical misery and pain' (1970: 117). In this condition 'the human possibility in a Buddhist culture of a man being free for compassionate attitudes and loving actions before he experiences *Nirvana-Shunyata* are rather slim and grim' (1970: 157).

In contrast to this view my conclusions will be that ethical perfection is a central ingredient in the Buddhist *summum bonum*. The two basic values or categories of human good which are recognised by Buddhism are moral and intellectual excellence. The hegemony of these values is accepted throughout the tradition although there has been some variation in respect of the importance attached to each of them. In brief, early Buddhism emphasises the latter at the expense of the former while later Buddhism, particularly in some of its more exotic forms, has tended to do the opposite. The cultivation of these powers or excellences depends upon a corresponding potential in human nature in the absence of which no progress towards the goal could be made. Our enquiry will, therefore, make some reference to Buddhist psychology (Chapter 3) to establish the connection between the starting point and the goal. The passage from the latter to the former is, I shall argue, achieved through the cultivation of specific virtues which promote a structured participation in the end through its progressive incarnation in the present. In reply to the specific questions posed by Jayatilleke and in terms of the categories he makes available, my answer would be that Buddhist ethics is altruistic, a form of qualified absolutism, objectivist, naturalist, and teleological (but not consequentialist). I will summarise my reasons for these characterisations in the Conclusion, and the arguments in support of them will be deployed in the course of the text.

2
Aspects of *Sīla*

Our enquiry into *sīla* begins in one of the oldest sections of the Pali Canon with the group of thirteen discourses (*suttas*) known as the *Collection on Moral Practices* (*Sīlakkhandhavagga*).[1] This is the first of the three divisions of the thirty-four *suttas* of the *Long Discourses* (*Dīgha Nikāya*), and includes *suttas* one to thirteen.[2] These thirteen *suttas* are known as the *Collection on Moral Practices* no doubt in part because they each contain a stereotyped tract enumerating moral precepts or observances. Of the thirteen *suttas* of the *Collection*, eleven describe the progress of a monk (*bhikkhu*) to Arahatship via the cultivation of morality (*sīla*), proficiency in the trances (*jhānas*) and the development of knowledge or insight (*paññā*). The ninth *sutta*, the *Discourse to Poṭṭhapāda* follows this scheme only as far as proficiency in the trances, while the thirteenth, the *Discourse on Vedic Knowledge* (*Tevijjasutta*), records the progress of a monk as far as the four Divine Abidings (*brahmavihāra*) and stops short of Arahatship. The first of these thirteen *suttas* is the *Discourse on Brahma's Net* (*Brahmajālasutta*) and for convenience we will take this text as the basis for our discussion of the *sīlas*. In this chapter we consider (1) the *sīlas* of *Brahma's Net*; (2) the preceptual formulae derived from them; (3) the soteriological scheme of the *Collection on Moral Practices*; and (4) the benefits of *sīla*. In (5) we consider the imagery used in respect of *sīla* in sources from both the Small and Large Vehicles.

1. THE *SĪLAS* OF *BRAHMA'S NET*

The lengthy passage on *sīla* in *Brahma's Net*[3] is divided into three *Tracts* (*vaggas*) listing various observances or *sīlas* for which it is said the Enlightened One (*Tathāgata*) might be praised by a worldly person.[4] The three *Tracts* are known as the short (*cūla*), medium (*majjhima*) and long (*mahā*) *silas*, and I shall refer to them collectively as the *Tracts on Morality* (*Sīla-vagga*). They occur consecutively in order of length in all the thirteen *suttas* of the *Collection*, and since the *Collection* is one of the earliest parts of the *Long Discourses*[5] we would appear to be dealing with a stereotyped formula of some antiquity.[6] Such is the opinion of Rhys Davids, who regards the *Tracts* as an early independent work: 'The tract itself must almost certainly have existed as a separate work before the time when the discourses, in each of which it recurs, were first put together' (*Dialogues*, 1.p.3n). The three *Tracts* may be summarised as follows from Rhys Davids' translation.[7] They are abstention from all of the following:

The Short Tract

1. Taking life.
2. Taking what has not been given.
3. Unchastity.
4. Lying.
5. Slanderous speech.
6. Harsh speech.
7. Frivolous talk.
8. Causing injury to seeds or plants.
9. Eating more than once and after midday.
10. Watching shows, fairs, dancing, singing and music.
11. Ornaments, garlands, scents and unguents.
12. Use of large and lofty beds.
13. Accepting gold and silver.
14. Accepting uncooked grain.
15. Accepting raw meat.
16. Accepting women or girls.
17. Accepting bondsmen or bondswomen.
18. Accepting sheep or goats.
19. Accepting fowls or swine.
20. Accepting elephants, cattle, horses and mares.
21. Accepting cultivated fields or sites.
22. Acting as a go-between or messenger.
23. Buying and selling.
24. Cheating with scales, bronzes or measures.
25. Bribery, cheating and fraud.
26. Maiming, murdering, putting in bonds, highway robbery, dacoity and violence.

The Medium Tract

1. Injury to seedlings and plants.
2. Use of things stored up (food, drink, clothes, provisions, etc.).
3. Visiting shows (sixteen kinds specified).
4. Games and recreations (eighteen kinds specified).
5. High and large couches (twenty kinds specified).
6. Adorning and beautifying the person.
7. Low forms of discourse (e.g. stories and gossip).
8. Argumentative phrases.
9. Acting as a go-between or messenger.
10. Simony.

The Long Tract

Wrong livelihood, earned by:
1. The low arts such as palmistry.
2. Knowledge of the signs of good and bad qualities in things denoting the health or luck of their owner.
3. Soothsaying.
4. Foretelling eclipses, etc.
5. Foretelling rainfall, etc.
6. Use of charms and incantations.
7. Use of medicines and drugs.

At first sight this is a strange assortment of precepts, but the arrangement is not entirely random. Taking them in reverse order, the *Long Tract* directs its attention specifically to undesirable methods of gaining a livelihood through a variety of practices known generically as the 'low arts' (*tiracchāna-vijjā*). The *Medium Tract* lists only two additional practices not mentioned in the *Short Tract*: item 2, the use of things stored up, and item 4, games and recreations. On the other hand there are many omissions from the list in the *Short Tract*. As well as embracing many of the concerns of the *Medium Tract*, the *Short Tract* also makes reference to undesirable forms of livelihood, the topic which is the central concern of the *Long Tract*. It would seem, therefore, that the *Short Tract* has a claim to be considered as the primary one of the three, and that the *Medium* and *Long Tracts* expand on certain aspects of it. For example, the *Short Tract* prohibits attendance at shows (item 10), and the *Medium Tract* then goes on to specify sixteen kinds of shows included in the prohibition. Again, the *Short Tract* prohibits the use of high beds (item 12) and the *Medium Tract* stipulates twenty examples of the kind of beds to be avoided. Likewise, the *Short Tract* prohibits numerous kinds of wrong livelihood (13–26), and the *Long Tract* adds to this by describing various kinds of fortune-telling which should be avoided. It is as if the *Medium* and *Long Tracts* have been tagged on to add precision, plug loopholes, or resolve disputes which may have arisen over the interpretation of the *Short Tract*. The *Long Tract* perhaps has more claim to independence than the *Medium Tract* since fortune-telling and soothsaying, to which it is mainly devoted, are not specifically mentioned in the *Short Tract*.

Another reason for regarding the *Short Tract* as primary is that other lists of moral precepts in Buddhism consist largely of a reformulation of the items it contains. The twenty-six items listed there fall into four loose groupings, concerning:

1. Immoral acts of body and speech (items 1–7)
2. Austerity in lifestyle (items 8–12).
3. Offerings not to be accepted (items 13–21).
4. Commercial or criminal activity (items 22–6).

Each of these four groupings expresses normative concern primarily in respect of matters impinging on the life of a religious mendicant (*samaṇa*). Indeed, the *Tracts* as a whole take the form of a eulogy of Gotama *qua samaṇa*. The individual items are introduced by announcing them as observances of Gotama the *samaṇa*. Consider the first of the *Short Tract*: 'Putting aside the killing of living things, Gotama the *samaṇa* refrains from the destruction of life.'[8] The *Tracts* in *Brahma's Net* taken as a whole are an attempt to encapsulate the conduct of Gotama the *samaṇa*. The *Short Tract* seeks to define what is most essential in this by specifying the conduct of Gotama, while the *Medium* and *Long Tracts* distinguish the conduct of Gotama from other less worthy *Samaṇas* and *Brāhmaṇas*. Thus the latter two *Tracts* adopt the stock refrain: 'Whereas some *Samaṇas* and *Brāhmaṇas* do X, Gotama the *Samaṇa* does Y.' This may be seen in the first item of the *Long Tract*:

> Whereas some *Samaṇas* and *Brāhmaṇas*, while living off food provided by the faithful, continue attached [to such and such conduct], Gotama the *Samaṇa* refrains from this.[9]

The *Tracts* first of all describe, in the *Short Tract*, what is integral to the conduct of an ideal *samaṇa* (the Buddha), and then point out the difference between the ideal and other *religieux* who are deficient in their conduct. This is of importance since, as we shall now see, the conduct of the ideal *samaṇa* as defined in the *Short Tract* becomes the foundation for Buddhist ethics.

2. PRECEPTUAL FORMULAE

There are four major canonical formulations of moral precepts:

1. The Five Precepts (*pañcasīla*).
2. The Eight Precepts (*aṭṭhaṅgasīla*).
3. The Ten Precepts (*dasasīla*).
4. The Ten Good Paths of Action (*dasakusalakammapatha*).

There is also an important fifth formulation which is best described as 'paracanonical' (Prebish, 1980: 223) namely,

5. The *Pātimokkha*.

Let us list these formulations in turn.

The Five Precepts
The Five Precepts are an undertaking to abstain from:

1. Taking life (*pāṇātipāta*).
2. Taking what has not been given (*adinnādāna*).
3. Sexual misconduct (*kāmesu-micchācāra*).
4. Telling lies (*musāvāda*).
5. Taking intoxicants (*surā-meraya-majja-pamādaṭṭhānā*).

The Eight Precepts
These are precepts 1–5 above with the substitution of sexual abstention (*abrahmacariya*) for sexual misconduct, and additionally abstention from:

6. Eating at the wrong time (*vikāla-bhojana*).
7. Dancing, singing, music, watching shows, using garlands, perfumes, cosmetics and personal adornments (*naccagīta-vādita-visūkadassana-mālāgandha-vilepana-dhāraṇa-maṇḍana-vibhūsanaṭṭhānā*).

8. Using high seats or beds (*uccāsayana-mahāsayana*).

The Ten Precepts

The Ten Precepts are precepts 1–6 of the Eight Precepts (*aṭṭhangasīla*) plus abstention from the following:

7. Dancing, singing, music and watching shows.
8. Using garlands, perfumes and personal adornments.
9. Using high seats or beds.
10. Accepting gold or silver (*jātarūpa-rajata-paṭiggahaṇa*).

The order of the final five of the ten precepts seems to have been rather fluid among the schools of the Small Vehicle.[10]

The Ten Good Paths of Action

The Ten Good Paths of Action (*dasakusalakammapatha*) are:

1. Abstention from taking life (*pāṇātipātā-veramaṇī*).
2. Abstention from taking what has not been given (*adinnādānā-veramaṇī*).
3. Abstention from sexual misconduct (*kamesu-micchācārā-veramaṇī*).
4. Abstention from lying (*musāvādā-veramaṇī*).
5. Abstention from slanderous speech (*pisunāya-vācāya-veramaṇī*).
6. Abstention from harsh speech (*pharusāya-vācāya-veramaṇī*).
7. Abstention from idle talk (*samphappalāpā-veramaṇī*).
8. Non-covetousness (*anabhijjhā*).
9. Non-malevolence (*avyāpāda*).
10. Right views (*sammādiṭṭhi*).

The debt these formulations owe to the *Short Tract* is as follows. The first four of the Five Precepts correspond to items 1–4 of the *Short Tract*, with the substitution in the third of 'sexual misconduct' (*kāmesu-micchācāra*) for sexual abstinence (*brahmacariya*). These are supplemented by the introduction of a new item namely the fifth precept which prohibits the use of intoxicants. The Five Precepts are intended for the laity and it is therefore not surprising to find this addition. The Eight Precepts are compiled from the Five Precepts by the addition of *Short Tract* items 9, 10 and 11 combined, and 12. The Ten Precepts are compiled from the Five Precepts by the addition of *Short Tract* items 9, 10, 11, 12, and 13.

The Ten Good Paths of Action consist of the first seven items of the *Short Tract* with the addition of three new items. It is not hard to see the rationale for this addition. The seven items of the *Short Tract* can be divided into two groups: items 1–3 relate to bodily acts while items 4–7 relate to speech acts. The final supplementary group of three relates to mental attitudes and is synonymous with the three Cardinal Virtues (*kusalamūla*).[11] Buddhaghosa says that the first seven items are intentional acts (*cetanādhamma*) while the last three are 'related to intention' (*cetanā-sampayutta*), perhaps in the sense that they condition or influence it (*MA*.i.202). The Five Precepts also make reference to acts of body, speech and mind, although in a less direct way; thus items 1–3 relate to the body, item 4 to speech, and item 5 to the mind, since intoxicants cause negligence (*pamādaṭṭhāna*).

From the above we see that the major preceptual codes of Buddhism, which are common to the Small and Large Vehicles, are formulated directly on the *Short Tract*. The *Short Tract* of *Brahma's Net* is in turn based upon the conduct of Gotama the *Samaṇa*.[12] To observe the precepts, therefore, is to model one's behaviour on that of the Buddha. As the conduct of Christ provides the foundation for Christian ethics, so the conduct of the Buddha becomes the paradigm of ethical action for Buddhists. In the words of the refrain uttered by the Buddha's disciples: 'Things for us are rooted in the Lord, have the Lord as their guide and the Lord as their refuge.'[13]

The four formulations of precepts mentioned above can be regarded as attempts to compress and summarise the *Short Tract*, or to abstract from it to meet the requirements of a specific group or situation. Thus the Five Precepts are created for the layman, with the Eight or Ten Precepts, which approximate the rigours of the monastic life, as optional additional observances for holy days (*uposatha*). The purpose behind the formulation of the Ten Good Paths of Action, which were to increase in popularity, is not quite so clear. We may speculate that in view of the addition of the final three items they are an attempt to bring the basic Five Precepts into the wider framework of Buddhist doctrine. Through the inclusion of the final item (*sammādiṭṭhi*) morality is now linked to right views. Furthermore, the monastic associations of the Eight and Ten precepts are absent, which makes this formulation easier to universalise. Of the four formulations considered so far this is the most sophisticated and the most 'Buddhist'. The above formulations all compress the *Tracts*: we turn now to one which expands them.

The Pātimokkha

Another list of precepts may be found in the 227 rules of the Theravādin *Pātimokkha* which are incorporated into the monastic disciplinary code or *Vinaya*. Like the *Tracts*, the *Pātimokkha* is concerned both with morality and religious etiquette and combines the two in its function as a Rule for the regulation of monastic life. Since the goal of monastic life is individual spiritual development in the context of harmonious relations with others in the Order (*saṅgha*), the *Pātimokkha* includes both moral precepts and regulations not primarily of a moral nature. The most serious category of offences, the four 'Offences of Defeat' (*pārājika*), can be seen as a reformulation of the *Short Tract* items 1–4 in a form more pertinent to monastic life. The correspondence would then be as follows:

Pārājika

1. Sexual intercourse (*methuna dhamma*).
2. Taking what is not given (*adinnaṃ theyyasaṅkhātam ādiyeyya*).
3. Killing a human being (*manussa-viggahaṃ-jīvitā-voropeyya*).
4. Lying about spiritual accomplishments (*ajānam evaṃ āvuso avacaṃ 'jānāmi' apassam 'passāmi'*).

Short Tract

3. Unchastity (*abrahmacariya*).
2. Taking what is not given (*adinnādāna*).
1. Taking life (*pāṇātipāta*).
4. Telling lies (*musāvāda*).

Many of the *Pātimokkha* rules are without a corresponding rule in the *Tracts*. In part this is because they relate to different lifestyles – that of the wandering *samaṇa* versus that of the sedentary *bhikkhu*. Into the life of the latter additional concerns intrude such as the construction of dwellings, the wearing of robes of a standard type, relationships with the laity and other members of the Order, and so forth. Rules concerning all of these things are to be found in the *Vinaya*, reflecting the adjustment to new circumstances in the historical growth of monasticism. The difference is that whereas the *Tracts* relates to Gotama the *Samaṇa* alone, the *Vinaya* relates to the *Saṅgha* as a community.

Moral and Monastic Precepts

The suggestion that the rules of the *Pātimokkha* are a direct outgrowth of the Five Precepts (*pañcasīla*) has been put forward by Pachow. He writes:

> It would not be unreasonable to say that the code of discipline of the *Saṃgha* is but an enlarged edition of the *Pañcasīla* which have been adopted by the Buddhists and the Jains from the Brahmanical ascetics. And under various circumstances, they have developed subsidiary rules in order to meet various requirements on various occasions. This appears to us to be the line of development through which the growth of these rules could be explained (1955: 37).

The problem with this view, as Pachow recognises, is that not all the *Vinaya* rules can be directly related to the *pañcasīla*. This problem is also noted by Holt. 'If this hypothesis were absolutely sound', he writes, 'we could somehow relate all of the disciplinary rules in some way to the four *pārājikas* or to the *pañcasīla*. Unfortunately, we are not able to do this' (1981: 64). Indeed, over a third of the rules, some eighty-eight in number, resist assimilation to the *pañcasīla*. The eighty-eight discrepant rules deal with the regulation of monastic practice and are of a kind to be found in many religious orders. It is not surprising that they should be found in the *Vinaya*; nor is it strange that the *Vinaya* should concern itself with the practicalities of communal life as well as moral conduct.[14] Indeed, it would be difficult to separate these two concerns since communal life involves both moral duties (e.g. not to steal from fellow monks) as well as the voluntarily assumed sub-moral duties of ecclesiastical office (e.g. to wear the right garments).

Pachow may have met with more success had he attempted to derive the *Pātimokkha* not from the Five Precepts but from the *Short Tract* in the realisation that the latter underlies the former. It would not be surprising to find a greater correspondence here since the *Tracts*, like the *Vinaya*, are concerned with both ethics and religious etiquette, whereas the Five Precepts are purely of a moral nature. In fact a number of direct equivalents can be found between the *Short Tract* and the *Pātimokkha*. The handling of gold and silver is prohibited by *Short Tract* 13 and also by *Nissaggiya-Pācittiya* 18 and 19. Buying and selling (*kaya-vikkaya*) is prohibited by *Short Tract* 23 and *Nissaggiya-Pācittiya* 20. Acting as a go-between (*Short Tract* 22) is ruled out by *Saṅghādisesa* 5, and damaging plants (*Short Tract* 8) by *Pācittiya* 11. False speech, abusive speech and slander of a *bhikkhu* (*Short Tract* 4, 5, and 6) are prohibited by *Pācittiya* 1, 2 and 3, and a rule governing the height of beds (*Short Tract* 12) may be found at *Pācittiya* 87. Nevertheless, this is still far from establishing a single source from which the *Vinaya* is derived.

Holt rejects the theory that the *Vinaya* is derived from the *pañcasīla* and looks instead for another single principle or rationale underlying its diversity. He finds its essence in the mindfulness inculcated by, and essential to, the observance of the complex code of monastic discipline. What is significant about *Vinaya* discipline (as opposed to any other kind) is that it is thought to define the conduct exhibited by the enlightened consciousness. Holt writes: '"Disciplined behavior" is none other than a characterization of the behavioral expressions of a perfected being (*arahan*). It is the hallmark of one in whom all grasping has ceased' (1981: 4). However, this would seem to entail some intrinsic relation between enlightenment and such trivial observances as only using beds of a certain height. Furthermore, at another point it is suggested that a disciplined lifestyle is only of instrumental and provisional validity: 'The raft that has aided one should be discarded. Thus, discipline itself is not to be retained ultimately. It is only a means to an undisclosed end, *nibbāna*' (1981: 16). It is difficult to see how discipline can both characterise the behaviour of an *Arahat* and yet not be retained ultimately. This conflict results fundamentally from an instrumentalist conception of *kamma* and the failure to locate moral action in its proper soteriological context, a problem which will be dealt with more fully in Chapter 4. Also problematic in this context is the view expressed in *Milinda's Questions* (*Miln.* 266f.) that while *Arahats* will never infringe moral precepts (here the Ten Good Paths of Action are mentioned) they may inadvertently breach *Vinaya* rules. This suggests that it is moral rules rather than *Vinaya* rules which are a direct manifestation of their state of consciousness, thus weakening the claim that monastic discipline is in some way intrinsically related to enlightenment. Overall, there seems no reason to assume that the *Vinaya* is either derived from a simpler set of moral principles or founded upon a single underlying principle or rationale.

So far we have looked at the most basic meaning of *sīla*, namely as a moral precept, and the combination of individual precepts into preceptual formulae. We turn now to consider *sīla* as a category (*khandha*) in the overall programme of Buddhist soteriology.

3. MORALITY, MEDITATION AND INSIGHT IN THE *COLLECTION*

The second *sutta* of the *Collection*, the *Fruits of the Religious Life* (*Sāmaññaphalasutta*), incorporates the *sīlas* of the first (*Brahma's Net*) into an overall scheme or way of life directed towards the soteriological goal of *nibbāna*. We find there a sequence of thirteen stages leading through the *sīlas* to the practice of the four absorptions (*jhānas*) and thence to perfection (Arahatship) with the destruction of the defilements known as 'outflows' (*āsavas*).[15] These three broad divisions of Morality, Meditation and Insight, correspond to those of the Eightfold Path which is first mentioned in the sixth *sutta* and again in the eighth as follows:

1. Right Views (*sammā diṭṭhi*).
2. Right Resolve (*sammā saṅkappa*).
3. Right Speech (*sammā vācā*).
4. Right Action (*sammā kammanta*).
5. Right Livelihood (*sammā ājīva*).
6. Right Effort (*sammā vāyāma*)
7. Right Mindfulness (*sammā sati*).
8. Right Meditation (*sammā samādhi*).

In none of the *suttas* of the *Collection* is there a division of the Eightfold Path in accordance with the three categories (*khandhas*) of Morality (*sīla*), Meditation (*samādhi*), and Insight (*paññā*) which is found elsewhere.[16] The division of the thirteen stages into three sections can be seen evolving in the *Collection* in the following manner. The first *sutta* of the *Long Discourses* (*Brahma's Net*) lists the *sīlas* in their three *Tracts*; the second, the *Fruits of the Religious Life*, includes the *sīlas* in its scheme of the thirteen stages towards enlightenment; and the third, the *Discourse to Ambaṭṭha* introduces a threefold classification of the (by now sixteen) stages. The *Discourse to Ambaṭṭha* speaks first of all of perfection in two dimensions, namely knowledge (*vijjā*) and conduct (*caraṇa*). 'The one who is perfect in knowledge and conduct', says the Buddha, 'is supreme among gods and men' (*D*.i.99). However, when

Ambaṭṭha asks him to expand on the nature of that knowledge and conduct the Buddha introduces a threefold classification into Morality (*sīla*), Conduct (*caraṇa*) and Knowledge (*vijjā*). The *Sīla* section contains only the *Tracts*, the Conduct section culminates in the four absorptions (*jhānas*), and the Knowledge (*vijjā*) section with Arahatship.

The fourth *sutta* is different again. This time it is Soṇadaṇḍa the Brahman who asks the Buddha for clarification in respect of the two categories of *Sīla* and *Paññā* which it has been established are essential in a true Brahman. The classification of the stages to enlightenment is once again given as twofold, this time with *Paññā* including the stages beginning with the *jhānas* and ending in Arahatship (*D*.i.124). The fifth *sutta*, the *Discourse to Kūṭadanta* lists the scheme but without interposing either a twofold or threefold division, while the sixth *sutta*, the *Discourse to Mahāli* mentions the Eightfold Path for the first time. This first reference to the Eightfold Path (*D*.i.157) is followed immediately by the seventh *sutta*, the *Discourse to Jāliya* which recounts the scheme of progress of the *Fruits*, as if by way of amplification of the eight stages of the path.

The Eightfold Path is mentioned again in the eighth *sutta*, the *Lion's Roar to Kassapa* (*D*.i.165) and a threefold division of the stages to enlightenment is also given (*D*.i.171–3). Here the division is into Morality (*sīla*), Mind (*citta*) and Insight (*paññā*). The ninth *sutta*, the *Discourse to Poṭṭhapāda*, lists the stages only as far as the attainment of the *jhānas*, while the tenth, the short *Discourse to Subha* spells out the division of the *Fruits* for the first time into the three stages of *Sīla*, *Samādhi* and *Paññā*. This *sutta* is recited by Ānanda shortly after the death of the Buddha (*D*.i.204), and its analysis of the stages of the *Fruits* in accordance with the scheme of *Sīla*, *Samādhi* and *Paññā* may be evidence for its relative lateness (Pande, 1983: 91). The eleventh *sutta*, the *Discourse to Kevaddha*, contents itself with quoting from the scheme of the *Fruits* without classifying it into stages, and so does the twelfth, the *Discourse to Lohicca*. The final *sutta* of the *Collection*, the *Discourse on Vedic Knowledge* (*Tevijja-sutta*), describes the scheme of progress only as far as the Divine Abidings (*brahma-vihāra*).[17]

The Divisions of the Path

Let us list these twofold and threefold divisions of the soteriological Path showing the number of the *sutta* in which they occur in brackets:

Twofold

Caraṇa and *Vijjā* (III)
Sīla and *Paññā* (IV)

Threefold

Sīla, Caraṇa, Vijjā (III)
Sīla, Citta, Paññā (VIII)
Sīla, Samādhi, Paññā (X)

It will be seen that of the thirteen *suttas* of the *Collection* only four (*sutta* III occurs twice in the above list) offer any classification of the stages to Arahatship, and there is no uniformity of terminology in the classification of the stages. In particular the nomenclature of the middle stage when specified is different in each case. There is also disagreement as to the number of stages involved. It is noteworthy that while eleven of the thirteen *suttas* describe the stages towards Arahatship in detail, and the remaining two describe the stages up to the trances (IX) and the Divine Abidings (XIII), nine of them are silent as far as the classification of the stages is concerned. Far from agreement on the divisions of the Path there is not even an opinion in the majority of cases.

The Eightfold Path with its three categories of *Sīla, Samādhi,* and *Paññā,* is itself is a shortened version of the scheme of progress to enlightenment which is first enunciated in the *Fruits* and followed throughout the *Collection*. In the *Discourse to Ambaṭṭha* (*sutta* III) and the *Lion's Roar to Kassapa* (*sutta* VIII) the thirteen stages of the scheme are already subsumed under three categories paving the way for the shorter, more manageable, formula of the Eightfold Path. Apparently, the individual factors of the Path are not so important as the general categories which contain them. This may be seen from the *Lesser Discourse of the Miscellany* (*Cūḷavedallasutta*) in the conversation between the nun Dhammadinnā, who speaks in the presence of and with the approval of the Buddha, and the layfollower Visākha.

> But, lady, is the Noble Eightfold Path composite or incomposite? The Noble Eightfold Path, friend Visākha, is composite. Now, lady, are the three categories arranged in accordance with the Noble Eightfold Path or is the Noble Eightfold Path arranged in

> accordance with the three categories? Friend Visākha, the three categories are not arranged in accordance with the Noble Eightfold Path, but the Noble Eightfold Path is arranged in accordance with the three categories.[18]

It would seem, then, that it is the broad categories of the Path which are of primary importance rather than the number or precise definition of their individual contents. The categories indicate the areas in which development is required while their contents sharpen the picture by pinpointing specific practices or prohibitions. Similarly, the path to Arahatship in thirteen stages described in the *Collection* can be conceived of as personal development in certain key areas. In the settled formulation these are three – Morality (*sīla*), Meditation (*samādhi*) and Insight (*paññā*) – but it is also possible to regard these spheres of perfection as binary, that is to say as founded upon Knowledge (*vijjā*) and Conduct (*caraṇa*), or Morality (*sīla*) and Insight (*paññā*). The ambiguity centres on the middle section, Meditation (*samādhi*), and I suggest that this is because meditation is primarily a means for the promotion of and participation in the basic goods of morality and knowledge. The position I shall adopt throughout this book is that the final perfection to be attained by those who follow the path to Arahatship is best understood in terms of a binary model, that is to say as the perfection of morality (*sīla*) together with the perfection of insight (*paññā*). Meditation (*samādhi*) is a technique for the cultivation of these faculties, and I will argue that in terms of value-structure the tripartite scheme of *Sīla*, *Samādhi* and *Paññā* can be collapsed into the binary one in the manner described, for instance, in the *Discourse to Soṇadaṇḍa*.

The *Discourse to Soṇadaṇḍa*

The *Discourse to Soṇadaṇḍa* (*sutta* IV) helps to clarify the content of the final good and also describes the symbiotic relationship between *sīla* and *paññā*. Soṇadaṇḍa the Brahman has been led by the Buddha to define the essential qualities of a true Brahman, and concludes that there are only two such qualities, namely virtue (*sīla*) and understanding (*paññā*) (*D*.i.123). The Buddha then inquires whether a man will still be a Brahman if either of these two qualities is left out. Soṇadaṇḍa replies as follows:

Indeed not, Gotama! For understanding, Gotama, is washed around with virtue, and virtue is washed around with understanding. Where there is virtue there is understanding, and where there is understanding there is virtue. Those who have virtue possess understanding, and those who have understanding possess virtue, and virtue and understanding are declared to be the best things in the world. Just as, Gotama, one hand might wash the other or one foot wash the other, even so Gotama, is understanding washed around with virtue and virtue washed around with understanding.[19]

The Buddha signifies his assent to this and repeats the first part of Soṇadaṇḍa's statement almost verbatim. He then specifies in what virtue and understanding consist, namely in following the path to Arahatship described throughout the *Collection* which is here divided into the two components of *sīla* and *paññā*. These are the necessary and sufficient conditions of a true Brahman. The conclusion to be drawn from the passage from the *Discourse to Soṇadaṇḍa* is that moral excellence is an essential dimension of human perfection. This needs emphasising since it is usually overlooked and almost always made secondary to intellectual development. A second point to note is that the Buddha does not stipulate *samādhi* in his conception of the essential qualities of true Brahman, or as we would say 'a good man'. He includes it as part of the path, but does not specify it as part of the end.

The *Discourse to Lohicca*

Support for the notion of final perfection as binary may be found in the XIIth *sutta*, the *Discourse to Lohicca,* which in the text makes no reference to a division of any kind, but on closer examination may be seen to presuppose the twofold model. The story concerns Lohicca the Brahman who was inclined to the following wicked view:

> If a *Samaṇa* or *Brāhmaṇa* attains something good (*kusala dhamma*), then once he attains it he should tell no-one else about it – for what can one man do for another? To do so would be like escaping from an old bond only to create a new one. This would have the same result, and I say it is a kind of craving – for what can one man do for another?[20]

The contrast drawn here is between one's own interests and the interests of others, but it may be characterised more precisely as a clash between moral and intellectual values. The postulated *Samaṇa* or *Brāhmaṇa* has achieved 'something good', which I take to refer to the widely sought-after goal of realisation through mystical knowledge. Since this achievement could be kept entirely secret, it would seem to be essentially a private intellectual or cognitive experience of the kind involving intuition, insight or understanding. It thus falls within the ambit of *paññā*. Once this state of illumination has been achieved, in the opinion of Lohicca, it should be kept secret and not revealed to others. To share the benefit of this experience with others would be merely a form of attachment, he alleges.

We may note that this opinion of Lohicca is at once described as an evil view (*pāpaka diṭṭhi*) and is roundly condemned by the Buddha.[21] A person who held it, it is said, would be selfish and inconsiderate of the needs of others. Not considering the welfare of others (*ahitānukampī*) his heart (*citta*) would not be well disposed towards them (*paccupaṭṭhita*) but full of enmity and the result of this would be rebirth as an animal or in hell. A person who held such a view would be a hindrance (*antarāya-karo*) to the progress of others and be out of sympathy with their welfare, in other words deficient in moral concern. Buddhaghosa comments that Lohicca's view is wrongful (*lāmaka*) because of its absence of concern for others.[22] We may conclude from the Buddha's condemnation of Lohicca's view that his own conception of human perfection (of which he is the embodiment) is not one-sided but requires the fulfilment of both intellectual and moral potential. Indeed, elsewhere he explicitly links teaching to sentiments of love and compassion.[23]

The Buddha goes on to illustrate the importance of bilateral development in these twin spheres by describing three sorts of teachers (*satthar*) who fail to develop them in tandem. Each of them is worthy of reproach (*codanāraha*), and such reproach would be 'right and proper, in accordance with the truth and not improper'.[24] The first teacher has not attained the goal of samanaship (*sāmaññāttho ananuppatto*) yet teaches a doctrine to his followers (*sāvakānam dhammam deseti*). His followers do not profit from his teaching, cease to listen to him and eventually depart. The second teacher has also failed to reach the goal of samanaship yet his followers listen, profit from his words, and remain. The third teacher has attained the goal of samanaship yet as in the first case his followers cease to listen and depart.

What is it about these three teachers that makes them unsatisfactory? And in particular, why should the third teacher who has attained to personal realisation be criticised? This presents something of a problem for those who see the aim of Buddhism mainly in terms of religious gnosis. The answer to these questions is not spelt out in the text but we may deduce that they are unsatisfactory because they are deficient either morally or intellectually or both. The first teacher is deficient in both: he teaches without understanding and with no appreciation of the needs of his followers, which is why they abandon him. He communicates nothing of value to them either intellectually or as a moral exemplar. We might say that he can neither see nor act.

The second teacher is likewise intellectually deficient but has forged a bond between himself and his followers which is why they do not depart. He is at least in tune with the needs of others even if unable to satisfy them completely. He functions in the moral dimension but not the intellectual one. We might say that he can act but not see. The third teacher is intellectually sound but morally deficient. He is not alive to the needs of others, and while having attained the goal himself is unable or unwilling to communicate effectively with others who have not. This is the condition of the Private Buddha (*paccekabuddha*). He is intellectually clear but morally out of focus; he can see but not act.[25]

The conclusion to be drawn from this condemnation of the three teachers would seem to be that neither cognitive realisation nor moral perfection are adequate in isolation. At this point Lohicca asks the Buddha if there is any teacher in the world not worthy of reproach. The Buddha replies that indeed there is, and this teacher is the one who has followed the path to Arahatship described throughout the *Collection*, a path which, we must conclude, ensures the combination of intellectual and moral perfection lacking in the other teachers.

The Buddha's Hesitation

The Buddha himself, of course, is one such teacher who has followed this path to perfection in *sīla* and *paññā*. He too had been a *samaṇa* who had achieved a state of realisation on the banks of the Nerañjarā and he too, according to tradition, had personally faced this dilemma in respect of teaching or remaining silent. According to the version of the story in the *Long Discourses*, all six of the

Buddhas prior to Gotama, beginning with Vipassi, faced this choice.[26] The fact of the Buddha's hesitation suggests that although the Buddha was moved to teach, teaching is not entailed by the intellectual realisation attained through *paññā*. Lohicca's opinion also suggests that the option is there to remain silent. In the course of a discussion on the significance of the 'Great Hesitation', Wiltshire suggests that the Buddha's initial hesitation emphasises the distinct and supererogatory nature of the subsequent decision to teach:

> If he had taught automatically and without hesitation as the natural consequence of his enlightenment, then the act of teaching would not have been seen as *distinct achievement*. As it was, by representing a state of affairs in which it was possible to make a negative choice, the Buddha's decision to teach would be seen as a definite act of compassion (1983: 17 emphasis in original).

According to the *Vinaya* account (*Vin*.i.6) it is only when asked for the third time that the Buddha 'surveys the world with his Buddha-eye out of compassion (*kāruññatā*) for beings'. This initial hesitation and subsequent decision by the founder of the tradition to teach can be seen as emblematic of the new scale of values introduced by Buddhism into the contemporary religious scene. It is a precedential action which establishes a new ideal of human perfection: mystical knowledge by itself is no longer enough but must henceforth be coupled with action inspired by a consciousness of moral good. By his hesitation the Buddha signals his recognition of alternative conceptions of human good, and by his choice he indicates his evaluation of one of them as superior. The reverberations of this paradigmatic choice were felt throughout the tradition, and the twin ideals of insight and teaching as a manifestation of moral concern seem to have been emulated by the Buddha's immediate disciples. Katz marshalls evidence to show that teaching is integral to the state of perfection of an *Arahat* and concludes: 'An *arahant* does in fact teach, and does so for the same reasons as does the Buddha' (1982: 197).[27] We have made reference above to a class of enlightened beings who do not teach, namely the Private Buddhas (*paccekabuddha*), whose significance in the Buddhist tradition is far from clear. Their status, however, is recognised by all schools of Buddhism as being inferior to that of the Perfect Buddha (*sammāsambuddha*) who is distinguished by the greater moral perfection manifested in his compassionate teaching mission. In devaluing the status of the Private Buddha by substituting a higher ideal, the Buddha redefined the notion of human perfection by making space for moral as well as intellectual goods.

Buddhist Synthesis

Returning to the Eightfold Path, its tripartite division may have crystallised under the influence of existing Brahminical categories. This suggestion is made by Richard Gombrich (1984). He draws attention to the similarities between the Buddhist scheme of *Sīla, Samādhi* and *Panna,* and the Hindu soteriological strategies of Action (*karma-yoga*), Austerities (*tapas* or *yoga*), and Knowledge (*jñāna-yoga*). He writes: 'Thus the Buddhist sequence of *sīla, samādhi* and *paññā* was very like the Hindu sequence of *karma, yoga* and *jñāna*. I refer of course to the formal structure, not to the content' (1984: 98). In the Hindu tradition the ways of action and knowledge are alternative paths – this is stated as early as the *Chāndogya Upaniṣad* (v.10.1–7) – but in Buddhism they are both essential facets of the path towards, and the experience of, enlightenment itself. Gombrich writes:

> The Buddhist view is in stark contrast to the Hindu view that the disciplines of work and gnosis are hierarchically related alternatives. The Buddha is denying both that they are hierarchically related and that they are alternatives (1984: 98).

We may speculate that one of the reasons the threefold classification of the Eightfold Path became popular was due to its power to embrace and transform competing modes of thought: it includes the available alternatives and by synthesising them sets the seal of Buddhist superiority upon them. In both traditions, however, for Hinduism as much as for Buddhism, it remains true that the basic dimensions of human good are binary, namely wordly action and salvific knowledge. While neither austerities (*tapas*) nor mental and physical discipline (*yoga*) are ends in themselves, both traditions recognise the importance of these techniques in the religious life. Professor Gombrich puts it as follows:

> The Buddha declared ritual valueless; the kind of *karma* he recognised was purely ethical. On the other hand even this ethical *karma* was powerless by itself to achieve the goal of liberation; that depended on gnosis, *paññā*, the Buddhist equivalent of Hindu *jñāna*. For the Buddhists as for the Hindus, to attain the salvific gnosis one had to practise the discipline of meditation – the discipline which in Hinduism grew out of archaic austerities (*tapas*) into meditative *yoga* (1984: 98).

While endorsing this I would wish to go even further, and in the next chapter I will suggest that the function of *samādhi* is not only to attain salvific gnosis but to promote human good in a wider sphere.

4. THE BENEFITS OF *SĪLA*

While *sīla* and *paññā* jointly constitute the final end, it is not uncommon to find either of them specified independently as worthwhile goals in their own right. In this section we consider the benefits and consequences of the pursuit of moral perfection as described in sources from both the Small and Large Vehicles. Buddhaghosa describes *sīla* as the 'root of all success' (*sabbasampattimūlam hi sīlam*) and a stage which, when consolidated, will lead to *nibbāna* (*Vism*.1.159). Ideally, virtue and knowledge should be cultivated together, but if there is a choice to be made it is better, says Buddhaghosa following the *Incremental Discourses* (*A*.ii.7f.), to choose virtue:

> Now if a man has little learning and is careless of his virtue they censure him on both accounts for lack of virtue and of learning.
>
> But if he is of little learning yet he is careful of his virtue, they praise him for his virtue, so it is as though he also had learning.
>
> And if he is of ample learning yet is careless of his virtue, they blame him for his virtue so it is as though he had no learning.[28]

A view contrary to the above is taken by the *Catuḥśataka* (v.286) which maintains that it is better to fail in morality (*śīla*) than in doctrine (*dṛṣṭi*). Buddhaghosa illustrates the interrelation of *sīla* and *paññā* by the image of a man trapped in a dense jungle of bamboo: he escapes by standing firm on the ground of *sīla* (*sīla pathaviyaṃ patiṭṭhāya*) and cutting his way out with the knife of insight (*Vism*.1.7)

In his analysis of *sīla* in the *Path of Purification*, Buddhaghosa inquires as to the benefits (*ānisaṃsa*) derived from it (*Vism*.I.16). He summarises these from the *Nikāyas* as follows (I.23):

1. Absence of remorse (*avippaṭisāra*).
2. For laymen:
   a) A large fortune produced through diligence (*appamādādhikaraṇam mahantaṃ bhogakkhandhaṃ*).
   b) A good reputation (*kalyāṇo kittisaddo*).
   c) Entering confident and untroubled into any assembly (*visārado upasaṅkamati amankubhūto*).
   d) An unconfused death (*asammūḷho kālaṃ karoti*).[29]
   e) A happy rebirth in heaven (*sugatiṃ saggam lokaṃ upapajjati*).
3. The affection and respect of fellow monks.

The benefits collated above are found scattered throughout Buddhist literature of all schools. In connection with the reference to death at 2 (d) above the *Lamp of Metaphysics* (*Abhidharmadīpa*) (*Dīpa*.230) states that 'The acme of *sīla* is said to be not abandoning one's control even at the point of death.'[30] The commentary (*Vṛtti*) adds that when a man who is dying does not flinch from the precepts he can be said to have truly fulfilled the perfection of morality.

A Happy Rebirth

In respect of heavenly rebirth the *Treasury of Metaphysics* and commentary (*Vyākhyā*) (IV.124ab) declare that the primary effect of *śīla* is the attainment of heaven (*śīlam prādhānyena svargāya bhavati*). The commentary to the *Lamp* states that *śīla* results in both prosperity and *moksa*.[31] That heaven is the reward of *śīla* is stated emphatically in the *Compendium of the Law* (*Dharmasamuccaya*). Chapters 22–7 deal with the Six Perfections (*pāramitās*) in turn and the section on morality (*śīlavarga*) is easily the longest containing eighty-six stanzas. Of these, forty-nine refer to the ends attained by *śīla* and in forty cases this is given as heaven (*svarga*). Two stanzas say that *śīla* promotes *dhyāna* and the remaining seven describe other effects.[32] As examples of the last category the reward (*phala*) of *śīla* is said (v.26) to be without comparison and indescribable (*anupama anirdeśya*); v.35 describes it as countless pleassures (*asamkhyāni ca saukhyāni*); and v.64 says that it gains nirvana.

Śīla is frequently associated with the production of merit (*puñña*) and occurs as a component part in the three 'Meritorious Actions' (*puññakiriyavatthu*) namely, generosity (*dāna*), morality (*sīla*) and mental culture (*bhāvanā*). The effects of the first two are described in the *Incremental Discourses* (*A*.iv.241). The man who practises *dāna* and *sīla* on a small scale (*paritta*), it is said, is reborn among men of low fortune (*dobhagga*) such as trappers and cartwrights. Someone who practises them to a greater degree (*mattaso*) is reborn among men of good fortune (*sobhagga*) such as one of the twice-born castes. And someone who practises them on a high scale (*adhimatta*) is reborn among the gods. By practising *dāna* and *sīla* it is said that the gods can be surpassed in ten ways; in divine life, beauty, happiness, pomp and power, divine shapes, sounds, perfumes, taste and touch. Harivarman comments that different combinations of the three Meritorious Actions produce different results. Thus *śīla* may be practised in conjunction with generosity (*dāna*) with consequent rebirth in the sensory realm (*kāmadhātu*). If *śīla* is practised along with *samādhi* rebirth in the material realm (*rūpadhātu*) is secured.[33] Likewise, emphasis on the different components of the Eightfold Path produces a different result. By concentrating on *sīla* one becomes a Streamwinner (*sotāpanna*) or a Once-Returner (*sakadāgāmī*), and by concentrating on *sīla* and *samādhi* a Non-Returner (*anāgāmī*). Only by practising all three perfectly does one become a Perfected One (*arahat*).[34] The *Compendium of the Law* says that one who has *dāna* and *śīla* and is compassionate to all beings realises all his desires.[35] The *Prātimokṣa* of the Dharmaguptakas states that a monk who guards the precepts receives the triple benefit of a good reputation, alms from the faithful, and a rebirth in heaven if he has not attained Arahatship (Wieger, 1910: 259). The *Cullavagga* is of the opinion that even animals who keep the five precepts will be reborn in heaven (161).

The benefits of morality are extolled in the short story of Sīlavat which occurs in the *Elders' Verses* (*Thag*.) (608–19). It is said that *sīla* brings success of every kind (*sabbasampattiṃ upanāmeti*), which the commentary interprets to mean as a man, as a god, or in *nibbāna*. It produces a threefold happiness: a good name, worldly goods, and the joys of heaven. The moral man (*sīlavā*) wins many friends, fame (*vaṇṇa*), renown (*kitti*), and praise (*pasaṃsā*). In the *Path of Purification* (*Vism.*I.24) *sīla* is described both as a stair that leads to heaven (*saggārohana-sopāna*) and a gate into the city of *nibbāna* (*dvāraṃ va pana nibbāna-nagarassa pavesane*).

The Dangers of Sīla

There is a danger in obsessive attachment to *sīla* just as there is in excessive devotion to *paññā*. Undue emphasis on either will lead to imbalance and fixation rather than progress towards the goal. If intellectual development is favoured at the expense of moral development there will be a tendency to cling to theoretical notions (*diṭṭhi*) such as the sixty-two speculative views listed in *Brahma's Net*, or become obsessed with the kind of learning mentioned in the *Discourse on Vedic Knowledge*. And if moral development is favoured at the expense of intellectual development there will be a tendency to become obsessed with external forms of conduct such as rules, rituals and rites. The Buddha tells Māgandiyā that neither of these alternatives is satisfactory: 'Purity is not attained through views (*diṭṭhi*), learning or knowledge, nor through rules and rituals [the Lord] said.'[36]

On the contrary, the man who stands on *dhamma*, speaks the truth and is held dear is the man who has perfected *both* morality and insight (*dassana*).[37] If too much emphasis is placed on morality there is danger of falling into the error of 'attachment to rules and rituals' (*sīlabbataparāmāsa*). This the third of the Ten Fetters (*saṃyojana*), and according to the *Path of Purification* (*Vism.*XVII.243) is one of the four kinds of clinging (*upādāna*). Buddhaghosa says that the reason for the false belief that rules and rituals will produce purification is twofold: (a) due to craving (*taṇhā*), i.e. in the hope that the rite will produce a desired result such as rebirth as a god or; (b) due to a false view (*diṭṭhi*) about the means of purification, namely that it can be achieved by ritual practices alone (*Vism.*I.29). According to *M.*i.67 attachment to rules and rituals is wrong because it has its roots in *taṇhā*.

Attachment to rules and rituals is also one of five false views and is listed as such at *Treasury*, V.7. It is said to include false views such that suicide will result in a heavenly rebirth, a criticism perhaps directed at the Jains, or that Prajāpati is the creator of the world. Such beliefs are condemned along with the view that morality and ascetic practices by themselves (*śīlavratamātraka*) can lead to liberation. The commentary (*Vṛtti*) on the *Lamp* 271 instances attachment to rules and rituals as the lifelong practice of the *agnihotra* sacrifice, while Harivarman defines it as the taking of ritual baths and other such observances in the hope of purification by one who is not concerned with understanding. He adds that purity is attained by *prajñā* but that morality is the basis of the faculty of wisdom.[38]

The danger of following rules mechanically is obvious and in complete contradiction to the Buddha's emphasis on mindfulness and correct motivation. He was concerned to avoid the excesses of Brahmanism with its attachment to ritual observances, and specified six ineffectual methods of purification clearly drawn from the sphere of Brahmanic ritual (*A*.v.263). In another place he describes these forms of behaviour as follows:

> Such ways as fasting, crouching on the ground, bathing at dawn, reciting of the Three [Vedas], wearing rough hides, and matted hair . . . chanting and empty rites and penances . . . washings, ablutions, rinsing of the mouth . . . (*S*.iv.118 PTS tr.).

Horner suggests that the category of 'clinging to rules and rituals' was introduced specifically as a safeguard against the influence of such Brahmanical practices (1936: 273). If followed mechanically or obsessively moral observances can have a stultifying effect on soteriological progress, as can an excessive fascination with speculative views and opinions (*diṭṭhi*). The Buddha's strategy was to steer between both extremes and pursue the even-handed cultivation of morality and insight. To conclude this chapter we now turn to a survey of the imagery which is used to describe *sīla* in the literature of both the Small and Large Vehicles.

5. THE IMAGERY OF *SĪLA*

The various aspects of *sīla* are illustrated by many different types of imagery. For convenience these images can be divided into five main groups as follows:

1. Images of a basis or foundation.

2. Images of protection.
3. Images of motion or ascent.
4. Images of purification.
5. Images of precious objects.

Before considering each of these groups in turn below we may look briefly at the etymologies of *sīla* which are also informative in respect of imagery and metaphor.

Etymology

Buddhaghosa proposes three etymologies for *sīla*, firstly his own and then two alternatives. His own etymology relates *sīla* to *sīlana* in the sense of 'composing', which is in turn defined as 'coordinating' (*samādhāna*) or 'upholding' (*upadhāraṇa*):

> It is virtue (*sīla*) in the sense of composing. What is this composing? It is either a coordinating, meaning non-inconsistency of bodily actions, etc. due to virtue; or it is an upholding, in the sense of being a basis owing to its serving as a foundation for profitable states. These are the two meanings accepted by etymologists. Others, however, comment on the meaning along the lines 'The meaning of virtue (*sīla*) is the meaning of "head" (*siras*), the meaning of virtue is the meaning of "cool" (*sītala*).'[39]

Buddhaghosa also gives *sīlana* as the defining characteristic (*lakkhaṇa*) of *sīla* (*Vism*.I.20) and indicates how *sīla* can have the associated meaning of 'character', 'nature', or 'disposition' (*pakati*).

> But in common usage the character of such and such beings is called their 'nature' (*sīla*), of which they say 'This person is good-natured (*sukha-sīla*), that one is miserable, this one is a troublemaker, that one is ostentatious.[40]

Other sources tend to favour Buddhaghosa's second and third etymologies. Vasubandhu derives *śīla* from the root *śī* in the sense of 'refreshing' and alludes to its cooling effect: 'The taking up of morality is pleasant; because of that the body does not burn'.[41] The *Book of Options* (*Vibhāṣā*) lists two of the meanings of *śīla* as coolness and refreshment.[42] The *Ornament of Mahāyāna Sūtras* states that 'Coolness (*śaitya*) is gained through morality since one is not burnt by the defilements' (*MSA*.XVI.15). The *Introduction to Madhyamaka* interprets the meaning as follows:

> Morality, or *śīla*, because it is cool (*śītala*), appeasing the fire of remorse of the mind through resistance to the passions and the non-production of sin; or because being the cause of happiness it is taken as a point of support by the good (*M.Av*.II.1a tr. Poussin).

sGam po pa states that *sīla* (*tshul khrims*) is so called because it leads to coolness (*Jewel*, 1970: 150). Much of the imagery used in respect of *sīla* is based upon these etymologies, as we may now see.

A. Morality as a basis or foundation

This is the most common image used to represent *sīla*. It occurs in three main forms: organic, physical and abstract.

Organic Buddhaghosa describes *sīla* as the 'root of all success' (*sabbasampatti-mūla*) (*Vism*.I.159) of which *nibbāna* is the 'fruit'. And in *Milinda's Questions*, *sīla* is compared to a seed which will yield the fruit of the religious life:

> As, Sire, a seed, even though small, if sown in a fertile field, and receiving good rainfall, will yield abundant fruit, even so, Sire, morality (*sīla*) if practised by the yogin, the earnest student of yoga, will yield the whole fruit of the religious life, thus it should be rightly practised.[43]

Continuing the organic metaphor there are many images of *sīla* as the Earth. Thus *Miln*. 33:

> As, Sire, whatever seeds and plants come to growth, increase and maturity, all do so in dependence upon the earth, established on the earth; even so, Sire, does the earnest student of yoga, depending on morality and based on morality, develop the five faculties of faith, energy, mindfulness, concentration and wisdom.[44]

According to Aśvaghoṣa, the shoots of the vices are unable to take root and grow in *śīla*, just as seeds fail to germinate in the wrong season (*Saund*.XVI.34).

In *Milinda's Questions* this metaphor is modified such that those established in the religious life are likened to a tree with roots of virtue (*kusalamūla*), trunk of *samādhi*, pith of *dhamma*, branches of *sīla*, and bearing the flowers of freedom (*vimutti*) and the fruit of the religious life (*sāmaññaphala*).

Physical Other images emphasise the earth as a physical foundation rather than its fecundity. For example *Miln*. 34:

> As, Sire, a town planner, when he wants to build a city, first has the site cleared, the stumps of the trees and thorns removed, and the site levelled. Then he builds the city after planning the streets, squares and junctions – even so, Sire, does the earnest student of yoga, depending on morality and based on morality, develop the five faculties (*indriya*).[45]

Also:

> As, Sire, an acrobat who wants to show his craft has the ground dug, the grit and gravel removed and the ground levelled, and then displays his skill on the soft ground, even so, Sire, . . . etc.[46]

The *Letter to a Friend* states that morality is the support of everything valuable, just as the earth is the support for the animate and inanimate. Mi Pham comments that *śīla* is the support for an elevated existence and liberation (Kawamura, 1975: 11f.). Just as the Earth is the foundation for all kinds of activity so *sīla* is the foundation for the cultivation of all the limbs of enlightenment (*bojjhaṅga*):

> Just as, monks, whoever adopts the four postures, now going, now standing still, now sitting, now lying, does so in dependence on the earth, established on the earth; even so monks, dependent on virtue, supported by virtue, does a monk cultivate the seven limbs of enlightenment.[47]

Aśvaghoṣa uses the simile of *śīla* and the earth in *Nanda the Fair* (*Saund*.XIII.21)

> For by taking your stand on morality all actions take place in the sphere of the supreme good, just as standing and other actions of the body are performed by taking your stand on the earth.[48]

Milinda's Questions says that just as an archer plants his feet firmly on the ground before making a shot, so must the yogin plant his feet on the ground of *sīla* before loosing the shaft of knowledge (*ñāṇanārāca*).

Abstract The final category here is *sīla* as a soteriological foundation. The *Elders' Verses* (*Thag*.612) describes *sīla* as the support of all good things (*sīlam patiṭṭhā ca kalyāṇānam*). In the *Clarifier of the Sweet Meaning* it is said:

> *Sīla* is the foundation of all virtuous qualities. Founded on *sīla* one does not deteriorate in respect of virtuous qualities, but acquires all the mundane and supermundane attributes.[49]

And at *Miln*. 32:

> *Sīla*, Sire, has as its distinguishing mark that it is the basis of all good things; . . . In one who is established on *sīla*, Sire, none of these good things decreases.[50]

Buddhaghosa defines the characteristic (*lakkhaṇa*) of *sīla* in terms of 'the coordination of bodily action and the foundation of all good states'.[51] The *Ornament of Mahāyāna Sūtras* listing six benefits of *śīla* describes it as the basis of all good qualities.[52] It also says (*MSA*. IV.4) that the thought of enlightenment (*cittopāda*) rests upon *śīla*. Aśvaghoṣa declares that morality is the foundation for yoga and meditation, a point which is echoed by Kamalaśīla who says that the yogin must be supported (*āśrita*) by pure morality (*śīlaviśuddhi*) (Demieville, 1952: 338). The *Śrāvakabhūmi* states that *śīla* is the foundation (*mūla*) for meditation and insight (Wayman, 1961: 70). sGam po pa quotes several sources to the effect that *śīla* is the foundation for meditation and enlightenment and mundane and spiritual success (*Jewel*, 1970: 163–71). Finally, as already mentioned above, Buddhaghosa employs the image of a man standing firm on the ground of *sīla* and cutting his way through the tangle of *saṃsāra* with the knife of insight.

B. Images of Protection

The second group of images stress the protective power of *sīla*. In the *Elders' Verses* (*Thag*. 614), *sīla* is described as 'a wonderful coat of mail' (*sīlam kavacam abbhutam*). The same image occurs in the *Clarifier of the Sweet Meaning* (*Madhu*. 269) where there is a reference to 'moral armour' (*sīla-kañcuka*). It adds that *sīla* is 'a shelter, a cave and a succour for one who has come into *saṃsāra*'.[53] *Milinda's Questions* describes *sīla* as an umbrella to hold off the rain of the defilements (*Miln.* 416). It also suggests that like an ant constructs a shelter for itself the yogin should construct a roof or covering (*chādana*) of moral restraint before he wanders for alms (*Miln.* 392). The *Fruits of the Religious Life* (*D*.i.69) compares the monk who has mastered the *sīlas* to a powerful monarch who has beaten down his enemies on all sides and is confident that there is no further danger. Aśvaghoṣa in *Nanda the Fair* likens *śīla* to a guide in the wilderness (*kāntār'iva daiśika*) (*Saund.* XIII.28) and says that *śīla* goes in front as the foremost (*śīlam nayaty agram*). He describes it as a refuge (*śaraṇa*), a friend (*mitra*), a kinsman (*bandhu*) and a protector (*rakṣā*) (*Saund.* XIII.28). According to the *Introduction to Madhyamaka* the Buddha taught morality for the safeguarding (*avipranāśa*) of good qualities (*guṇa*) such as generosity (*dāna*) (*M.Av.* 41.5–8). A number of medical images also occur. *Milinda's Questions* says that *sīla* is an antidote for destroying the poison of the *kilesas* and a healing balm for allaying the sickness of the defilements (*kilesas*) in beings (*Miln.* 195). The *Teachings of Vimalakīrti* describes it as an antidote to convert beings of opposite (immoral) tendencies (*VNS.* 29).

C. Images of motion or ascent

In this connection the *Path of Purification* asks: 'Where can such another stair be found that climbs, as *sīla* does, to heaven? Or yet another gate that gives onto the city of *nibbāna*?'[54] Moving horizontally this time the *Elders' Verses* (*Thag.* 613) compares *sīla* to a strand (*tittha*) for all the Buddhas which, according to the commentary, means the place from which the Buddhas ford the sea of *nibbāna*. The verse following this describes *sīla* as a 'mighty causeway' (*setu mahesakkho*). Continuing the nautical metaphor, *Milinda's Questions* (*Miln.* 195) says the moral man (*sīlavā*) is like a ship (*navasamo*) for beings to go beyond the four floods of sense-pleasures, becoming, wrong views and ignorance. The same man is like a caravan leader (*satthāvaho*) for leading beings across the desert of births, a teacher (*ācariya*) and a guide (*sudesika*). Morality is frequently compared to the feet which make movement towards the destination possible. The *Prātimokṣa* of the Dharmaguptakas states that just as a man without feet cannot walk, so one who lives without the precepts cannot be reborn as a god in heaven. It adds that one who has violated the precepts will be, at the hour of death, like a coachman about to cross a dangerous pass who notices that he has lost the bolt from a wheel or that his axle has a crack in it (Wieger, 1910: 213).

D. *Images of Purification*

The *Path of Purification* (*Vism*. I.24), says that only the water of virtue (*sīlajala*) can wash out the stain (*mala*) in beings. According to the opening verse of Chapter 24 of the *Lamp*, *śīla* destroys the *kleśas* such as deceit and jealousy just as a fire cooks food. *Milinda's Questions* compares the possession of morality to water that carries off the dirt and dust of the *kilesas*,[55] and to a wind (*vata*) that extinguishes the three fierce fires of greed, hatred and delusion in beings. According to S.i.183 the *Dhamma* is compared to a lake with virtue as a strand for bathing; after being purified in it one passes over to the beyond.

E. *Images of Precious Objects*

This fifth and final category is the most disparate and includes many precious objects which please the senses. Perfume (*gandha*) is extremely common: virtue smells fragrant[56] whereas evil has an unpleasant smell.[57] *Milinda's Questions* compares the precepts to the Lord's 'perfume shop' (*gandhāpaṇa*) and describes how the perfume of *sīla* is more pervasive even than that of flowers or incense.[58] The imagery of jewels or treasures is frequently encountered.[59] *The Guide* (*Nett*. 56) compares *sīla* to an ornament (*alaṃkāra*), a treasure (*nidhāna*) riches (*dhañña*) a mirror (*ādāso*) and a palace (*pāsādo*). *Milinda's Questions* (*Miln*. 400) says that *sīla* adorns the yogin like a beautiful mane adorns a lion. The *Śrāvakabhūmi* speaks of *śīla* as an ornament (*alaṃkāra*), as ointment (*anulepana*) and as perfume (*gandha*) (Wayman, 1961: 70). The image of cloth also occurs at *Path of Purification*, I.43 not in the sense of being a valuable possession but as an illustration of *sīla* as a complex web of observances which can easily be damaged or torn.[60] According to the *Prātimokṣa* of the Dharmaguptakas the precepts of the *prātimokṣa* are more precious than treasure (Wieger, 1910: 213). It also states that the bimensual recital of the *prātimokṣa* is like a mirror held up before the face which causes one to rejoice or grieve at the beauty or ugliness of the reflection (ibid.).

Summary

In this chapter we have seen that *sīla* circumscribes the conduct of the Buddha, and that the condensed description of his behaviour encapsulated in the *sīlas* of *Brahma's Net*, particularly the *Short Tract*, becomes the blueprint for Buddhist preceptual formulae.

The Buddha's *sīla*, or moral perfection, becomes an essential goal for all who aspire to his status, and in the thirteen *suttas* of the *Collection*, *sīla* is incorporated into the foundations of the Buddhist soteriological programme. The settled formulation of this emerges in the form of the three divisions (*khandhas*) of the Eightfold Path. Of these three I have suggested that *sīla* and *paññā* constitute the primary dimensions of perfection with *samādhi* providing the impetus for their full development. I will give my reasons for this more fully in the following chapter. If *sīla* and *paññā* are cultivated asymmetrically a psychological imbalance will emerge in the form of intellectual or legalistic fixation instead of insightful knowledge and compassionate moral concern.

The five groups of imagery found in Buddhist literature in respect of *sīla* illustrate its many facets; when they are considered together a picture of *sīla* is built up as a complex quality or state with both static and dynamic dimensions. We see from group (A) that it is a starting point, and from group (C) that it is also a way forward; it conserves what has been achieved (B) and also seeks further development and transformation (D). As well as being a support, *sīla* provides protection for whatever good qualities are developed. It is an impermeable defence against evil of all kinds, but also takes on an offensive role against the *kilesas* by engaging and overwhelming them, with the result that vice is transformed into virtue. *Sīla* provides the impetus and dynamism without which liberation cannot be reached: it is the feet which make travel along the road possible in cooperation with the eyes which seek the correct destination. Finally, whatever stage of the path has been reached, *sīla* is an intrinsically valuable and desirable quality. The good is analogous to the beautiful, and the language of aesthetics is commonly invoked to describe *sīla* as seen in section (E).

Sīla is precious, valuable and pleasant in itself, and at the same time is the necessary foundation for the entire spiritual project envisaged by Buddhism. In one respect *sīla* provides a static platform for the establishment and cultivation of good qualities of all kinds, especially the intellectual virtues of meditation and insight; and in another it is a source of dynamic potential which contains within itself the seed of flourishing and growth in respect of moral qualities. Thus it is the sphere of moral cultivation and at the same time a precondition for proper intellectual development. It is important to bear in mind these twin functions of *sīla* through which it stands in both a direct and an oblique relation to *nibbāna*. It stands in a direct relationship to *nibbāna* since it is itself part of the final good; and it stands in an oblique relationship to *nibbāna* as the basis for the development of knowledge. To put it another way we may say that *sīla* is dynamic in respect of moral development and passive in respect of intellectual development. All too often the second, oblique, aspect of *sīla* is taken to be the primary one and morality is regarded as merely a means to knowledge. This leads to great difficulty in unravelling the role of ethics in Buddhist soteriology. In the following chapter I consider more fully the antagonism between *sīla* and the *kilesas* in the context of Buddhist scholasticism, and explore the role of *samādhi* in the soteriological Path.

3
Ethics and Psychology

Our moral appreciation is extraordinarily sensitive to our desires and passions, which should not surprise us since it is not exaggerating very greatly to say that our moral appreciation can only exist in the absence of our selfish desires, in the absence of exclusive love of self.

R. Beehler, Moral Life

Of the voluntary acts of every man, the object is some good to himself.

Hobbes, Leviathan

In the first part of this chapter we explore the relationship between ethics and psychology as described in Buddhist scholasticism (*Abhidharma*). As our primary source here we rely on the *Treasury of Metaphysics* rather than the Theravādin *Abhidhamma* in order to broaden the range of the enquiry and avoid the inadvertent 'curve fitting' of our conclusions to the data of a single school. In the second part we consider the nature of the relationship between moral and intellectual virtue and its psychological basis. Part 3 examines the role of the affective faculties in the moral life and focuses on the compassion of the Buddha, and the concluding section 4 explores the role of Buddhist meditation techniques in the perfection of morality and insight.

1. *DHARMAS* AND VIRTUES

In terms of Buddhist psychology the basic problem of salvation can be summed up as the need to purify the mind of evil. In Buddhist scholasticism the problem is analysed in terms of the mind (*citta*) and its modes or concomitant states (*caitta*), and one of the central concerns of this analysis is to identify those states which are conducive to the overthrow of greed, hatred and delusion. At the core of the Abhidharmic system lies the theory of *dharmas*. In terms of Buddhist philosophy, *dharmas* are the basic constituents or elements of reality; they are ultimate reals or ontologically grounded existents which cannot be further subdivided or analysed. *Dharmas* are the point at which analysis stops: they exist in the most fundamental sense (*dravyasat*) and provide the framework across which the web of conceptual reality (*prajñapti*) is woven. The goal of the *Abhidharma* is to pick away at the subtle threads of the world of *prajñapti* and to uncover the world of real existents or *dharmas* which lies beneath. In this way it is hoped to come face-to-face with reality 'as it really is' (*yathā-bhūta*). It should be pointed out that although these *dharmas* are real they are not in any sense permanent: if they were there could be no scope for change or personal development.

In adopting a strategy of rigorous analysis and classification the Abhidharmikas regarded themselves as faithfully continuing the methodology of the Buddha, and not without justification claim the Buddha as the originator of the *Abhidharma* tradition itself (*Asl*, 34f.). The Buddha was the first to unravel the skein of false consciousness within which the notions of permanence and self-hood were fostered. The theory of the *skandhas* was the first step in this process of critical analysis, exposing the illusory 'self' as a projection onto these underlying mental and physical 'aggregates'. The categories of the *Abhidharma*, which are essentially based on the *skandhas*, represent the continuation of this analytical critique and an extension of its application beyond the human subject to reality as a whole.

The Relevance of the Abhidharma

The nearest thing to a theoretical approach to moral philosophy within the Buddhist tradition is to be found in the *Abhidharma*, and it is worthwhile to direct our attention to its analytical framework. An opinion contrary to the above is held by Winston King (1964), who maintains that in an enquiry into Buddhist ethics the *Abhidharma* is best dispensed with. He writes:

> It is doubtful whether the statement of Abhidhammic ethical theory would be of much use or significance to the Westerner. Attempts in this direction up to the present are not particularly promising. The usual result seems to be a vocabulary and system of distinctions almost completely foreign and meaningless to the

Western mind, in which the ethical element, in the Western sense, is lost sight of in an unfamiliar maze of Buddhist psychological terminology (1964: 5).

I disagree with this view. Although we cannot embark on a major analysis of the *Abhidharma* here, its basic categories can shed useful light on the nature of Buddhist ethics. That the terminology is unfamiliar can hardly be pleaded as a reason for neglecting what the tradition itself regards as a summary of its key elements. Part of my argument in the remainder of this section will be to the effect that far from being 'almost completely foreign and meaningless to the Western mind', the Abhidharmic ethical classifications are readily intelligible in terms of one of the oldest and most influential concepts in Western ethics – the concept of a virtue.

The soteriological purpose of the *dharma*-theory is to identify and facilitate the elimination of those factors which impede enlightenment, namely the defilements (*kleśa*). To this end the *dharma*-theory is indispensable, as is stated in the *Treasury*:

There is no way of removing the defilements apart from the analysis of *dharmas*. It is because of the defilements that the world wanders in the sea of existence.[1]

According to the *Abhidharma*, enlightenment is achieved by purifying the personal continuum (*santāna*) of all defilements (*kleśa*). Good qualities (*kuśala-dharma*) bring about this purification and evil qualities (*akuśala/kleśa*) oppose it. Due to the presence of the defiling elements the *santāna* is polluted (*sāsrava*) and the whole stream is brought into a state of instability and disquiet. The goal, therefore, is to neutralise the destabilising elements and bring the *santāna* into a state of quiescence.

It is difficult to overlook the ethical significance of the *Abhidharma*. The first book of the Theravādin *Abhidhamma*, the *Enumeration of Elements*, embarks upon an extremely ambitious ethical programme, namely a classification of the whole of reality in terms of ethical predicates. In her introduction to the translation of the text Mrs Rhys Davids describes the import of the work as mainly ethical:

Its subject is ethics, but . . . the enquiry is conducted from a psychological standpoint, and, indeed, is in great part an

> analysis of the psychological and psycho-physical data of ethics (*Dhs*. xxxii).

This close connection between ethics and psychology is also noted by De Silva who comments 'A close study of Buddhist ethics would show that it betrays a significant link with psychology' (1979: 3). The *Enumeration of Elements* systematises the raw data of Buddhist ethics and provides an evaluative classification of reality in terms of Buddhist soteriology. However, one looks there in vain for the articulation of a theoretical structure in terms of which this data may be interpreted, and King is correct to the extent that it bears no resemblance to what would be regarded in the West as a treatise on ethics or moral philosophy.[2] Yet we must not be intimidated by this unfamiliar moral landscape which is familiar territory to those within the tradition. In the *Path of Purification* Buddhaghosa begins his analysis of *sīla* by describing it as 'the states beginning with volition (*centanādayo dhammā*) present in one who abstains from killing living things, etc.' (*Vism*. I.17) Here he is defining *sīla* by reference to the list of fifty-two mental qualities or states (*cetasika-dhamma*) specified in the *Abhidhamma* of the Theravāda school, and without an understanding of the ethical function of these *dhammas* it is impossible to provide an analysis of *sīla* at its most basic level. *Sīla* itself is not a *dhamma* since it is reducible or analysable into component parts, namely the individual mental states identified by the *Abhidhamma*. Rather, it is a category which embraces different kinds of virtuous consciousness. As we saw in Chapter 1, Buddhaghosa says that *sīla* has the sense of 'composing' (*sīlana*) or 'coordinating' (*samādhāna*), and that this embraces all virtuous states just as visibility is a common feature of diverse colours.[3] We might say that in this sense *sīla* is a collective term denoting the organisation or structuring of the good mental states (*dhamma*) identified in the Abhidhammic system.

The Mind (*citta*)

The mind (*citta*) and mental states (*caitta*) are at the heart of the Abhidharmic ethical analysis. In the taxonomy of the Sarvāstivāda[4] school, of the seventy-five *dharmas* of their system forty-seven are of a psychological nature. The Sarvāstivāda *dharma*-system differs from that of the Theravāda in the range of its taxonomical categories, the number and occasionally the specification of the *dharmas* comprising each category and sub-category. Other schools have formulations which are different again but such variations are only of minor importance for our present purposes. Despite the variations in detail all schools acknowledge similar basic classificatory rubrics. The standard classification is a fourfold one into matter (*rūpa*), mind (*citta*), mental forces (*caitta*) and the unconditioned (nirvana).[5] Only the third of these categories contains elements which are ethically productive. We are, accordingly, concerned here mainly with this third category of morally related forces, elements or states (*caitta*) but our discussion will also make reference to the closely related category of mind (*citta*).

Citta, mind or psyche, is the common denominator of mental and emotional operations and the centre around which the constellation of psychic events (*caitta*) revolves. *Citta* is defined in the *Expositor* (*Asl*. 63) as 'that which thinks of its object, that which knows'.[6] And later as follows:

> The distinctive characteristic of *citta* is knowing; its function is to precede; its manifestation is connecting; and its proximate cause is mind and body.[7]

Citta and its concomitants (*caitta/cetasika*) are invariably connected. According to the *Compendium of Metaphysics* (*Abhidharmasamuccaya*) they arise and perish together (*ekuppādanirodha*) and share a common object and a common basis (*ekālambhanavatthuka*) (*Adhs*. 2.1). Buddhaghosa compares *citta* to a king who arrives with a retinue of over fifty attendants, namely the *cetasikas* (*Asl*. 67). Yaśomitra states that *citta* and *caitta* share the same basis (*āśraya*), object (*ālambhana*), form (*ākāra*), time (*kāla*) and substance (*dravya*) (*Vyākhyā*. II.49, 14–50, 15). *Citta* is the personal mental or psychic centre. 'Judged by its general usage in the Pali *Nikāyas*', writes Karunaratna, '*citta* appears basically to refer to the centre and focus of man's emotional nature as well as to the seat and organ of thought in its active dynamic aspect.' And again, '*Citta* is viewed as an arsenal of dispositional properties which take the form of mental predispositions, proclivities, tendencies and dormant and latent forces which activate themselves at the subliminal level of consciousness.'[8] *Citta* is the centre of subjective consciousness. Johansson describes its most typical meaning as 'a personal psychological factor responsible for the unity and continuity of the human being' (1979: 158). It is 'a centre for conscious activity' and 'corresponds fairly closely to "mind"' (1979: 161). Again it is 'a conscious centre of activity, purposiveness, continuity and emotionality', including not only momentary conscious processes but also 'the continuous, unconscious background, e.g. all the moral traits which are not manifest in every moment but are latent, prepared to influence thoughts and behaviour as soon as the opportunity is given' (1979: 161). Piyananda comments that 'the Pali *citta* primarily pertains to the sensorily perceptual and emotional functions of the active consciousness of mind' (1974: 18).

Various translations for *citta* have been proposed: Karunaratna lists 'mind, thought, heart, conception, consciousness, mood, emotion, spirit, idea and attitude'.[9] While 'mind' captures the operation of the conscious processes 'psyche' is preferable as a translation since it embraces intellectual and emotional life, the conscious as well as unconscious activity of the mind, and encompasses better the dimension of moral traits, dispositions and character. *Citta* is encountered in the many states or modes of subjective consciousness, its total potential at any one time being roughly equivalent to a person's mood or general state of mind. In this sense *citta* is the aggregate of mental forces (*caitta*) and resonates, so to speak, according to the pitch and tone of the dynamic psychic energies (*caitta*) in operation at any given moment. To understand the pattern of primary mental energies, therefore, we must turn our attention to the category of basic mental forces, or *caitta*.

Mental Forces *(caitta)*

If we narrow our search down to faculties (*dharma*) which have a bearing on ethics, we find that from the Sarvāstivādin list of forty-six *caitta-dharmas*, there are twenty-eight which are significant. Specifically, we find a list of ten good qualities (*kuśala-mahābhūmika-dharma*) contrasted with eighteen bad ones. The good qualities begin with faith (*śraddhā*), zeal (*vīrya*), and equanimity (*apekṣā*), and the bad ones with ignorance (*moha*), heedlessness (*pramāda*), and torpor (*kausīdya*).[10] These lists of moral and immoral items are reminiscent of the lists of virtues and vices compiled in other scholastic traditions, such as Christianity. And just as in Christianity all good qualities have their origins in the Christian Cardinal Virtues of Faith, Hope and Charity, so too in Buddhism all good qualities have their origins in the three Buddhist Cardinal

Virtues of Liberality (*arāga*), Benevolence (*adosa*), and Understanding (*amoha*).[11] Conversely, all evil qualities stem from the negation of these things. We thus find a structured opposition between embedded psychological traits which stand in an intimate relation to the soteriological goal. These good and evil qualities (*dharmas*) are perhaps best understood as corresponding to the Western notion of virtues and vices. The concept of a virtue will be discussed more fully in Chapter 8 but for the moment we may take the following as our definition of a virtue:

> In ethics, virtue is moral excellence, a settled attitude which conduces to habitually good action in some respect. The virtues have been variously classified. The intellectual virtues (e.g. wisdom) are distinguished from the practical virtues (e.g. courage), the former being associated with the life of contemplation, the latter with the life of action.[12]

As pointed out here, virtues and vices may be either cognitive or non-cognitive. Aristotle, for instance, as we shall see in Chapter 8, distinguishes between the intellectual virtues (*aretai dianoetikai*) such as insight (*sophia*) and practical wisdom (*phronesis*); and the moral virtues or virtues of character (*aretai ethikai*) such as generosity and courage. I shall argue in the next section that this distinction may be seen in Buddhism in the form of an opposition between the intellectual vices rooted in *moha*, and the moral vices rooted in *rāga* and *dosa*. Another point about the virtues is that it is their nature to be counteractive, to overcome the weakness and deficiency which is vice. This point is made by Phillipa Foot in her essay 'Virtues and Vices':

> I shall now turn to another thesis about the virtues, which I might express by saying that they are *corrective*, each one standing at a point at which there is some temptation to be resisted or deficiency of motivation to be made good. As Aristotle put it, virtues are about what is difficult for men (1978: 8).

In the context of Buddhist soteriology it is not difficult to see why *dharmas* such as delusion (*moha*), anger (*krodha*) and jealousy (*īrṣyā*) should count as vices; they are those factors deemed antithetical to the state of final perfection which is the Buddhist ideal. It is the task of the virtuous qualities to overcome these things, and

Buddhist sources constantly stress the need for mindfulness, diligence, exertion, and self-control if spiritual progress is to be made.

One important conclusion to be drawn from the Abhidharmic analysis is that virtues and vices – since they are *dharmas* – are objective and real. They are not part of the realm of mental construction (*prajñapti*), but are actually 'found' within the psyche. This means that Buddhist ethics is naturalistic: good and bad are not abstractions to be apprehended by observers according to their various intuitions and sensibilities. Nor can morals be reduced to questions of taste or personal preference, as suggested by Emotivism. A final implication of this objectivisation of ethics is that relativism is ruled out: what is to count ultimately as good and bad is not determined by accidental factors but grounded in the reality of human nature. Since human nature is everywhere the same the moral teachings of Buddhism are of universal extent and will hold good at all times and in all places. The corollary of this is that Buddhist ethics cannot be a self-contained system which is intelligible only in its own terms or within its own frame of reference.

2. MORAL AND INTELLECTUAL VIRTUE

I would like now to focus more closely on the distinction between intellectual and moral virtues and vices. I suggested above that this may be seen in the formulation of the Cardinal Virtues and we may illustrate this binary distinction as follows, using the three opposing vices of greed (*rāga* or *lobha*), hatred (*dosa*) and delusion (*moha*).

INTELLECTUAL VICE	*MORAL VICE*
	LOBHA
MOHA	|
	DOSA

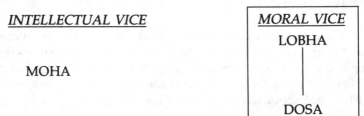

Intellectual vice is a form of cognitive error and is epitomised by *moha*. The moral vices, on the other hand, are forms of non-cognitive error; they are inappropriate emotional propensities or responses which may be located at the polar extremes of the emotional continuum marked by craving *lobha* and hatred (*dosa*). Lama Govinda observes that '*lobha* and dosa are only two sides of the same force, i.e. *taṇhā*' (1974: 54). And according to De Silva: 'Man's desires influence his cognitive powers and his cognitions have an impact on his desires. There is both a cognitive and an emotional component to man's suffering, and these arise from his craving and ignorance' (1979: 29). Emphasis may be placed upon either craving or ignorance as causes of the arising of suffering. In the scheme of the Four Noble Truths it is the emotional aspect of attachment and clinging (*taṇhā*) which is specified under the Second Noble Truth. And in the formula of Dependent Origination (*paṭiccasamuppāda*) it is ignorance (*avijjā*) which is given as the first link in the chain with *taṇhā* figuring as the eighth. *Taṇhā* often does duty for all three of the 'roots of evil' (*akusalamūlani*) as the primal cause of suffering:

> Whatever suffering arises, all that is because of *taṇhā*.[13]
>
> The world is led by *taṇhā* and dragged about by it. All have come under the sway of this one thing called *taṇhā*.[14]
>
> From *taṇhā* arises grief, from *taṇhā* arises fear. For him who is totally free from *taṇhā* there is no grief, let alone fear.[15]

The Triangle of *Taṇhā*

Taṇhā and *avijjā* overlap, and as Johansson points out *avijjā* involves both cognitive deficiency and an 'unfavourable attitude' or 'prejudice'. He states that '*avijjā* is a dynamic term, involving lack of motivation for Buddhist pursuits' (1979: 137). Linked together the three root vices form what we might term 'the triangle of *taṇhā*', as the sum of intellectual and moral deficiency and the cause for the arising of suffering.

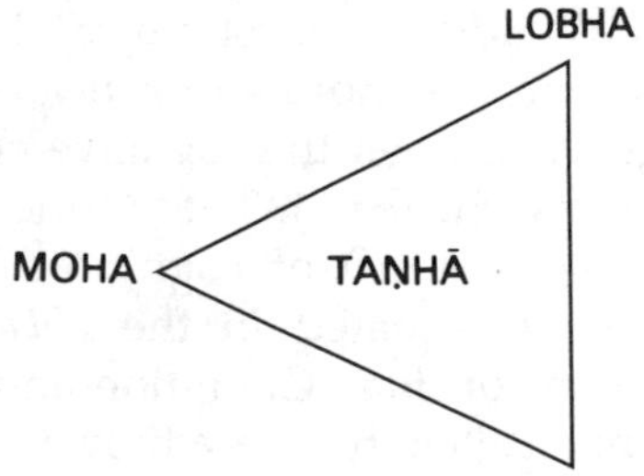

Although these two categories of vice may be logically abstracted they cannot in the final analysis be disentangled and isolated within the psyche. The current of *taṇhā* flows around all three sides of the triangle: *taṇhā* involves both a misconception of the good through a failure to perceive and understand rightly, and an emotional attachment or fixation in respect of that misconception. False views could quickly be replaced by right views through a process of reasoning and analysis were it not for the stubborn emotional attachment (*lobha*) to the wrong view and fear of and aversion (*dosa*) to the right view. The three *akusalamūlāni* are mutually reinforcing in respect of what is bad and the three *kusalamūlāni* in respect of what is good. Ñāṇapoṇika writes:

> In their positive aspects, non-greed and non-hate are likewise strong motives of good actions. They supply the non-rational, volitional or emotional motives, while non-delusion represents the rational motive of a good thought or action (1965: 79).

In its simplest terms the problem concerns the interrelation of reason and emotion in the human psyche. Reason and emotion cannot be disentangled and they cannot be perfected in isolation without resulting in psychic disequilibrium. They are 'washed around together' and must be perfected in conjunction. I am not suggesting that enlightenment can be achieved merely through the elimination of moral vice; what I hope to show is that moral perfection no less than intellectual perfection is an integral ingredient in the Buddhist ideal because the capacity for moral sentiment is an integral part of human nature.

The Buddhist View of Human Nature

How is this distinction between the affective and the cognitive expressed in terms of Buddhist psychology? Both the mind–body (*nāma-rūpa*) analysis and the more sophisticated categories of the *Abhidhamma* distinguish between the cognitive and affective powers or dimensions of the psyche (*citta*). These functions are subsumed under the categories (*khandhas*) of cognition (*saññā*) and feeling (*vedanā*) respectively. It is stated in the *Nikāyas* that these are dimensions or functions of *citta*: 'Cognition and feeling are mental processes dependent on *citta*: therefore they are called functions of *citta*.'[16] However, the exact nature of the relationship between the categories on the psychological side of the mind–body analysis is difficult to state with precision, as is pointed out in the *Greater Discourse on the Miscellany* (*Mahāvedallasutta*):

> That which is feeling, your reverence, that which is cognition, and that which is consciousness – these states are associated not dissociated, and it is not easy to make a distinction between these states even after repeated analysis. Your reverence, whatever one feels, that one cognises; whatever one cognises, that one is variously aware of.[17]

Milinda's Question says that it is very difficult to disentangle mental states such as *vedanā, saññā,* and *viññāna* whose nature it is to co-exist (*ekatobhāvan-gata*). It compares the problem to the difficulty of separating the ingredients of a sauce once it has been prepared by a chef,[18] or of tasting the water in the ocean and determining which of the great rivers it had come from.[19] In broad terms, however, it may be helpful to regard the categories of *saññā* and *vedanā* respectively as denoting the cognitive and non-cognitive dimensions of psychic life. The functions of *saññā* and *vedanā* may be logically distinguished but do not correspond to any real division in the structure of the human subject. Each is merely a power of the psyche: yet as the function of each is different so is its respective virtue or excellence. The virtue of the cognitive aspect (*saññā*) is to understand and discriminate correctly; its vice is delusion and error. The virtue of the non-rational part of the psyche is to sense, feel, and respond affectively in an appropriate manner; its vice is to swing to the extremes of craving (*rāga*) and aversion (*dosa*).

The malfunction of *vedanā* and *saññā*, which is *taṇhā*, is the basic soteriological problem of Buddhism. Here one is both deluded as to what is the case (*moha*), and emotionally attached (*rāga*) to the misconception or averse (*dosa*) to the truth. Immoral conduct is not simply the result of ignorance or emotional maladjustment alone: it comes about through a misapprehension of the facts (most fundamentally involving the belief in a self) together with an emotional investment made on the basis of that factual error (attachment to the imputed self). It is commonly assumed in connection with Buddhism that the fundamental problem is a simple lack of knowledge. This underestimates the power of the emotions to dominate and manipulate reason, to 'drag it around like a slave', as Plato puts it. The Buddha recognised the power of greed and hatred, and the practice of the Eightfold Path cultivates a middle course between them:

> Herein, Brethren, greed is evil and hatred is evil, and for the abandoning of greed and hatred there is the Middle Path which makes for vision, knowledge and leads to tranquillity, to awakening and to *nibbāna*. And what, Brethren, is this Middle Path . . .? It is this Noble Eightfold Path.[20]

The commentary explains how metaphysical views are themselves conditioned by the emotional polarisation between *rāga* and *dosa*:

> Greed is one extreme and hatred is one extreme, but the Path does not go near, does not approach the two extremes. It is free from these two extremes, which is why it is called the Middle Path. It is 'Middle' because it is between them, and a 'Path' because it is to be followed. One extreme is ... eternalism and another is annihilationism.[21]

Feeling *(Vedanā)*

Let us look at the functions of *vedanā* and *saññā* in more detail, beginning with *vedanā*. The Pali Text Society Dictionary gives two meanings for *vedanā*, namely, 'feeling' and 'sensation'. Various classifications of *vedanā* are given in the *Nikāyas*, the most basic being a threefold one into feelings which are pleasant, unpleasant or neutral: 'It feels, monks, therefore it is called feeling. What does it feel? It feels pleasure, pain, and that which is neither pleasure-nor-pain.'[22]

This is expanded into a fivefold one by making a distinction between bodily and mental feelings which are pleasant, unpleasant and neutral, and a sixfold one by reference to the six 'sense-doors'. The *Expositor* defines *vedanā* as follows:

> Feeling is that which feels. It has feeling as characteristic, either experiencing or the enjoyment of something desired as function, the relishing of mental states as manifestation, and calmness as proximate cause.[23]

Vedanā is a basic psychological process and its function cannot be further reduced or expressed in terms of any other psychic operation. Each of the aggregates is irreducible and five must be the minimum number or else the Buddha's analysis would have proceeded further. The *Expositor* compares *vedanā* to a king who alone tastes the food prepared by his many attendants and alone experiences its flavour (*Asl*. 109f.). According to De Silva, '*vedanā* may be considered as the basic concept for affective experience' (1979: 77). In its most fundamental sense the category (*khandha*) of *vedanā* represents the human capacity for affective response: it is 'the feeling component of our experience' (De Silva, 1979: 18). Its function is limited and specific: Lama Govinda states that '*Vedanā* covers only the hedonic aspect of feeling and emotion' (1974: 117). However, insofar as the affective response may be positive or negative, *vedanā* may be said to perform an evaluative function. Thus Guenther defines *vedanā* as:

> A basic psychological function which imparts to every conscious content . . . a definite value in the sense of acceptance ('like') or rejection ('dislike') or indifference . . . Thus, feeling is a kind of judging, although it does not establish an intellectual connection but merely sets up a subjective criterion of acceptance, rejection or indifference (1976: 37).

'What affirmation and negation are in thinking', says Aristotle, 'pursuit and avoidance are in desire' (*NE*. VI.8, 1139a22). Johansson states that *vedanā* 'is defined in terms of feeling and clearly refers to an evaluating function' (1979: 87). Any affective 'evaluation' carried out by *vedanā* is preconceptual and non-cognitive; the cognitive function of the psyche is designated by the *khandha* of *saññā*.

Cognition *(saññā)*

Whereas the paradigm function of *vedanā* is to feel, the role of *saññā* is to cognise: 'It cognises, it cognises . . . which is why it is called cognition. And what does it cognise? It cognises blue, yellow, red, white.'[24]

The *Treasury* and *Bhāṣya* explain cognition as follows:

> Cognition (*saṃjñā*) consists in the apprehension of characteristics. The apprehension of different natures – noticing that it is

blue, yellow, long, short, man, woman, friend, enemy, pleasant or unpleasant, etc.: this is the faculty of cognition.[25]

Cognition may be of external objects (*paṭigha-saññā*) or of ideas, images or concepts (*adhivacana-saññā*) may mean simply 'an idea': 'One idea (*saññā*) arose in me: the end of becoming is *nibbāna*.'[27]

Although its paradigm function is to cognise the attributes of an object, *saññā* also refers in a broader sense to intellectual activity in general. On the problem of translating the term Mrs Rhys Davids comments: 'The apparently capricious way in which the intension of the term *saññā* is varied in the *Piṭakas* makes it difficult to assign any one adequate English rendering.' She notes that 'Some experts . . . prefer the rendering "conception"' (*Dhs*. tr: 6f.n.). De Silva relates *saññā* to 'sense-impressions, images, ideas, concepts' (1979: 16). Johansson states that 'mental representations of all the sense-modalities are then called *saññā*, including memories and imaginations' (1979: 93). Accordingly he translates *saññā* as 'ideation'.[28] *Saññā* may thus be said to include the cognition of external and internal objects and the power of conceptual thought in general. *Vedanā* and *saññā* operate closely in conjunction. As we have seen, both are basic and irreducible functions of *citta* and the human predicament may be expressed in terms of a malfunction of these powers which manifests itself in the form of the root vices of attachment, aversion, and delusion. This is the cause of the formation of psychic complexes or *saṅkhāras*.

Complexes *(saṅkhāras)*

Buddhist psychology provides an explanation of how the operation of these two psychic faculties may be disturbed with the result that complexes (*saṅkhāra*) are formed leading to suffering and rebirth. The two input channels for the formation of *saṅkhāras* are craving (*taṇhā*) and ignorance (*avijjā*).[29] In the scheme of Dependent Origination the second link, *saṅkhāra*, is conditioned in dependence on ignorance (*avijjā*) (*M*.i.67). *S*.iii.96 describes how *saṅkhāras* are formed out of ignorance and craving: 'From sensation that is born in association with ignorance, craving arises in the untutored common man. From that is born this *saṅkhāra*.'[30]

In the *Discourse of the Honey-Ball* (*Madhupiṇḍika-sutta*) Mahākaccāyana explains the role of feeling (*vedanā*) and cognition (*saññā*) in the formation of these complexes which assail the individual:

> In dependence on the eye and forms, O Brethren, arises visual consciousness; the meeting of the three is contact; because of contact arises feeling (*vedanā*); what one feels one cognises (*sañjānāti*); what one cognises one reasons about; what one reasons about one proliferates conceptually; what one proliferates conceptually is the origin of the host of ideas and notions which assail a man in regard to the forms discerned by visual consciousness, past, present, and future.[31]

According to Yaśomitra, *vedanā* experiences (*anubhavati*), *saṃjñā* discriminates (*paricchinatti*), and *cetanā* accumulates (*abhisaṃṣkaroti*) (*Vyākhayā* II.50 2–4). We have noted that *vedanā* and *saññā* are themselves described as *saṅkhāras*, and in this sense the term has no pejorative connotations. The various virtues, too, are also technically *saṅkhāras*. More commonly, however, the term *saṅkhāra* has a negative connotation not dissimilar to the contemporary sense of 'complex' in a psychological context. These things are the product of an inappropriate interaction of thought and feeling which compels patterned forms of behaviour and produces suffering. This is the manner in which the process occurs in a worldly person under the sway of *taṇhā*. For the enlightened there is no *taṇhā*, no *papañca*,[32] and no *saṅkhāra*-formation, and the faculties of feeling and thought no longer give rise to the formation of complexes. According to *S*.ii.82 one free from ignorance produces no *saṅkhāras* either good, bad, or neutral. Despite the fact that no new *saṅkhāras* are produced the *Arahat* retains all five *khandhas* until he dies: 'The five aggregates being well understood continue to remain although their roots are cut off'.[33] On the night of his enlightenment the Buddha declared himself to be free of *saṅkhāras* and *taṇhā*: 'My mind is free of *saṅkhāras*. I attained the extinction of all forms of *taṇhā*.'[34]

However, the Buddha was not left without the capacity to feel or think, as we shall see in a moment, and the eradication of *saṅkhāras* means only that the affective and cognitive faculties operate perfectly and without hindrance, such that 'in the seen there is just the seen' (*Ud*.8).

Psychology and Moral Philosophy

I suggested above a connection between morality and the emotions by which emotional disequilibrium manifests itself in the polar vices of *lobha* and *dosa*. That there exists a relationship between morality and the emotions has long been recognised by moral philosophers although the nature of the relationship has been disputed. Some, for instance Hobbes and Hume, have sought to account for morality entirely in terms of the emotions while others, such as Kant, have attempted to ground morality in reason alone and in a refusal to accede to the emotions. Buddhism is commonly identified with the Socratic position which holds that virtue is reducible to knowledge;[35] this is a view I challenge in this book on the grounds that just as neither *vedanā* nor *saññā* are reducible to one another, so neither of the two basic values of Buddhism, *sīla* and *paññā*, is reducible to the other. An alternative approach is to view the reason-emotion bifurcation as artificial and seek a 'middle way' between them: this is the position of the Aristotelian tradition and the view most congenial to Buddhism. For both, reason and feeling are complementary rather than disjunctive. The argument I am putting forward here, therefore, is not innovative or radical in the context of moral philosophy although it has not previously been applied to Buddhism. In speaking of the emotions here I am referring to that non-rational dimension of psychic life which manifests itself across a spectrum or continuum of non-cognitive responses ranging from aversion, hostility, anger and wrath, etc. (encapsulated by *dosa*), to attachment, craving, longing and lust, etc. (encapsulated by *lobha*). These are the extremes; the middle range of this continuum embraces attitudes such as benevolence, kindness, affection and sympathy. Katz (1979) describes these as the 'nibbānic' emotions. What, then, in the context of Buddhism, is the evidence for a link between morality and the emotions? To answer this question we can do no better than turn to the Buddhist paragon of moral perfection – Siddhattha Gotama.

3. THE BUDDHA'S COMPASSION

What we are seeking to discover is whether the Buddha's ethical perfection was underpinned by a sentiment of moral concern. By 'moral concern' I mean non-self-referential concern for the well-being of others. By 'sentiment' I mean a non-cognitive state as distinct from the intellectual understanding or acceptance of the validity or rationality of a set of moral rules or principles. It is this sentiment which animates moral life and its absence which reduces morality to prudentialism or self-interest.[36] On the view put forward here, moral appreciation means caring about others and the effects one's acts or omissions will have upon them. As noted by Beehler (1978: 26), this caring about or regard for other persons is what in the Eighteenth Century was spoken of as 'natural affection', but perhaps may best be characterised as a form of love. In the absence of this sentiment there can be no motive for true moral action since the needs of others will fail to make any claim upon us. One's actions can, of course, mimic those inspired by moral concern, but the motivation of the counterfeiter will inevitably be self-interest. Is there any evidence, then, of such an other-regarding sentiment at the root of Buddhist ethics?

That precisely such a sentiment underlies the conduct of the Buddha and his disciples has been demonstrated by Harvey Aronson (1980). The Buddha's moral concern is found in his sympathy (*anukampā*) for all beings. This is how Aronson describes the Buddha's ethical motivation:

> Gotama Buddha was a sympathetic teacher as is clear from the numerous references to Gotama's sympathy in the Theravāda discourses. Etymologically, 'sympathy' (*anukampā*) can be understood as the condition of 'being moved' (*kampa*) 'in accordance with [others],' or 'in response to [others]' (*anu*). Though not defined in Buddha's discourses, there are definitions in the commentaries – 'the preliminary level of love' (*mettāya-pubbabhāga, DA*.ii.456), or 'the state of having a tender mind' (*muducittatā SA*.ii.169). Similarly it is said to be synonymous with 'tender care' (*anuddayā, SA*.ii.169) and 'simple compassion' (*kāruñña, SA*.ii.169) (1980: 3).[37]

The Buddha's moral concern was not a consequence of his enlightenment: it preceded it and, indeed, motivated it.[38] 'Gotama's fundamental motive in arising and coming to be', says Aronson, 'was his concern for others' welfare.' He quotes the Buddha's own words in support:

> Monks, there is one individual who arose and came to be for the welfare of the multitudes, for the happiness of the multitudes, out of sympathy for the world; for the benefit, welfare, and happiness of gods and humans. Who is that one individual? The Harmonious One, the Perfectly Enlightened One (1980: 3).

The Buddha often describes his motivation in terms of sympathy and affection. As Aronson points out, 'He uses the term "sympathy" and its etymological relatives at least twenty times in connection with himself as in describing his motivation for arising and coming to be. He also uses it to motivate the monks to go out and teach others' (1980: 15). The Buddha is described as 'concerned for the welfare of his fellow man' (*bahujana-hitānukampī*) (*Sn*.693) and as 'sympathetic to all creatures' (*sabbabhūtānukampī*) (*A*.ii.9). And it is said of the Buddha at *S*.i.206: 'If with joyous heart he teaches others it is not from duty, but out of compassion and sympathy.'[39]

Ethical Motivation

In the face of what has been said above it is difficult to take seriously two suggestions noted in Chapter 1: first, that true moral conduct is only possible after enlightenment; and second, that Buddhist ethics is motivated basically by the self-interested pursuit of karmic merit. These views stem from a misunderstanding of the doctrine of karma, and the practice of some individuals in Buddhist countries (or perhaps the rationalisation of their practice when pressed for an explanation by anthropologists). The fact that sub-moral self-interest is displayed by some Buddhists is not in itself any more an argument for the claim that Buddhist ethics is 'egotistical' than is the fact that because some Christians keep the commandments in the hope of going to heaven Christian morality is merely enlightened self-interest. It should be clear by now that the contrary is the case, and that the fundamental inspiration for the Buddhist moral life is concern for others.

There can be no ulterior motive for ethical action in Buddhism in the sense that one can ask for and be given a non-moral reason for such action, for instance in terms of karmic benefits. To require such an incentive already indicates a lack of moral concern. Sympathy is not a reason in this sense: it is a non-rational sentiment which *precedes* the formulation of moral objectives. One cannot become sympathetic by formulating the wish to do so because sympathy does not lie in the power of the will. A sentiment of sympathy or concern is given: it cannot be engendered by a cognitive act. Moral concern is not the same as rationalisation, which is why there can be no such thing as a prudential motive for morality. If the motive is prudential and performed for personal gain, then the action is not inspired by *anukampā*. We see from the conduct of the Buddha, who lived an exemplary moral life with nothing to gain thereby, that morality is not a means to an end but an end in itself. It is not a means to enlightenment but a *part* of enlightenment. It cannot be chosen as a means to anything because it is impossible to *choose* to care or not to care about others. A choice to care about others as a means to furthering one's own karmic ends would be simply an affirmation of self-interest whereby others become once again means instead of ends. In Buddhism the moral life cannot be adopted as a means to an end because *anukampā* cannot be 'adopted' by a simple rational decision. It involves a gradual emotional realignment and must be cultivated slowly. As the claims of self lower on one side of the scale so fraternal concern will rise on the other.

The Cultivation of Moral Concern

Moral concern is not the prerogative of the religious virtuoso. 'Sympathy', writes Aronson, 'is the fraternal concern that is present in an individual and does not require cultivation or meditative development' (1980: 16). At the same time, it is possible for this sympathy to be cultivated and deepened, and *anukampā*, as noted above, is defined as the *preliminary* level of bevenolence or love (*mettā*) (*DA*.ii.456). The cultivation of feelings of concern for others is closely linked to the practice of the Divine Abidings in *samatha* meditation, and it is interesting to note that the Divine Abidings are particularly effective in counteracting those *dharmas* identified above as moral vices (*kleśa*). Thus love (*mettā*) is said by the Buddha to be unique in its power to counteract anger by preventing its arising and dissipating it once arisen (*A*.i.4). The elimination of anger is produced by 'freedom of the mind through love' (*mettā cetovimutti*). Buddhaghosa reaffirms the effectiveness of *mettā* in counteracting hatred (*Vism*. IX.10) and describes the other three Divine Abidings as efficacious in eliminating other vices. Compassion (*karuṇā*) counteracts harmfulness, sympathetic joy (*muditā*) counteracts displeasure, and equanimity (*upekkhā*) counteracts lust (*rāga*).[40] He tells us elsewhere that the Buddha assigns the appropriate meditation subject to correct any imbalance: thus for one in whom hate is prevalent (*dosa-caritassa*) he assigns meditation on *mettā*.[41] According to the *Path of Purification* (*Vism*. IX.106) the Divine Abidings are the correct attitudes to adopt towards beings-in other words correct moral attitudes – and we may regard them as reflecting the content of the enlightened moral consciousness.

The states or dispositions cultivated through the Divine Abidings in *samatha* meditation also occur in waking consciousness in the course of daily life – they are not exclusive to meditation or to the meditator. The technique of transic meditation (*jhāna*), however, is a powerful device for accelerating their cultivation and pervasion of the psyche. Love (*mettā*) and compassion (*karuṇā*) are frequently spoken of as 'liberation of the mind' (*cettovimutti*), a condition in which the psyche is entirely permeated with these qualities. The Buddha himself says:

> Monks, I see no other single cause [*dhamma*] by which hatred which has not yet arisen does not arise, or once arisen passes away, as freedom of the mind through love.[42]

In the course of the above discussion I referred to the Divine Abidings as a technique of meditation for fostering the basic sentiment of *anukampā*. I also stated in Chapter 2 that meditation (*samādhi*) stands between and unites the two basic values of ethics (*sīla*) and insight (*paññā*). I will conclude this chapter by pursuing further the role of meditation as a soteriological ethical technique.

4. VIRTUE AND MEDITATION

In the scheme of the Eightfold Path, *samādhi* stands between *sīla* and *paññā* and supplements them both.[43] It is a powerful technique for the acceleration of ethical and intellectual development towards their perfection in *nibbāna*. An image in *Milinda's Questions* illustrates nicely how meditation is the focal point and support of all virtuous qualities (*kusaladhamma*):

> The King said: Reverend Nāgasena, what is the distinguishing mark of meditation?
> – The distinguishing mark of meditation, Sire, is being the chief. All virtuous qualities have meditation as the chief; they lean, tend and incline towards it.
> – Make a simile.
> – As, Sire, in a pitched roof, all the rafters go to the ridge-board, lean towards it and join it, and the ridge-board is said to be their

chief – even so, Sire, all virtuous qualities have meditation as the chief; they lean, tend and incline towards it.[44]

Since progress in the religious life is made on two fronts, there exist two kinds of meditation techniques. I wish to suggest that 'calming meditation' (*samatha-bhāvanā*) cultivates moral virtue and 'insight meditation' (*vipassanā-bhāvanā*) develops knowledge or insight. The existence of two meditation techniques within the one tradition has been regarded as problematic. Paul Griffiths speaks of the 'unsatisfactory combination' of these two soteriological techniques, and finds evidence of uncertainty within the tradition as to their relative importance. He summarises the essentials of the problem as follows:

> There are presented in the canonical and commentarial texts of Theravāda Buddhism two radically different types of meditative practice which have different psychological effects and issue in different soteriological goals (1981: 618).

For Griffiths these facts are problematic but in terms of the thesis set out here they are not. Indeed, they are exactly as we should expect. Griffiths' difficulty arises from the suppressed premise of his argument that the unique soteriological objective of Buddhism is knowledge (*paññā*). Any soteriological technique which does not issue in *paññā* is therefore redundant and its existence puzzling. If *nibbāna* is defined exclusively in terms of *paññā* then *vipassanā* will quite naturally appear to be essential while *samatha* remains a curious anomaly.

Calming Meditation *(samatha)*

The technique of *samatha* meditation exists to enrich and deepen the capacity for human sympathy which exists in all to some degree and which reached its perfection in the personality of the Buddha. Central to *samatha* practice are the *jhānas* or stages of trance, and immersion in the *jhānas* leads directly to the elimination of discursive thought. In this the technique contrasts sharply with *vipassanā* where discriminating awareness is a *sine qua non* for propositional knowledge of the *paññā* kind. In *samatha* meditation, reasoning (*vitakka*) and discursive thought (*vicāra*) are left behind after the first *jhāna* (*Vism.* IV.146) and in the higher stages the intellectual functions are progressively reduced until they 'wink out' (Griffiths' phrase) altogether in the state known as 'the cessation of cognition and feeling' (*saññā-vedayita-nirodha*). The suppression of intellectual activity in *samatha* practice is a specialised technique for gaining access to the non-rational, emotional dimension of the psyche. It is a means of penetrating the deeper layers of consciousness and restructuring them in accordance with virtue rather than vice. According to De Silva access to the consciousness-continuum (*viññāṇa-sota*), the level at which this restructuring would take place, is only within the reach of those who practice meditation, and is achieved by entry into the third *jhāna* (1979: 76). And Michael Carrithers is quite correct when he states that the purpose of *samatha* is 'to cultivate an attitude, not to learn a doctrine' (1983: 225).[45] Even in the first *jhāna* there occurs a correction of emotional imbalance in the form of the suppression (*vikkhambhana-pahāna*) of sensuous desire (*kāmacchanda*) and ill-will (*vyāpāda*) (*A*.iv.437), two synonyms for *rāga* and *dosa*. The suppression and dissolution of these negative tendencies brings about a transformation in attitude towards others: the elimination of ill-will (*vyāpāda*) is described as follows:

> Putting aside the fault of ill-will, he dwells with a heart free from ill-will, compassionate and kind to all living creatures he cleanses his heart of ill-will.[46]

The Interaction of Calming and Insight

That *samatha* and *vipassanā* have distinct objectives has been recognised by others who have considered the problem of Buddhist meditational theory. Thus Gimello:

> It is in general a twofold discipline. On the one hand, there is what might be called a psychosomatic and affective component. This consists in of arts calming and concentrating the mind-body complex of the meditator, usually by the deliberate inducement of certain rarefied states of mind . . . The purpose allegedly served by these practices is that of quelling, if not extirpating, desire, attachment, and other elements of the affective life. On the other hand, there is an intellectual or analytical component of meditation. This consists in the meditatively intensified reflec-

tion upon the basic categories of Buddhist doctrine and in the application of them to the data of meditative experience (1978: 187f).

It is not entirely clear from the above whether Gimello is suggesting that *samatha* only 'quells' or 'quells and may also extirpate' desire, attachment and so forth. Earlier in the article (181) he cites a text which suggests that *samatha* extirpates as well as quells:

> With his mind thus concentrated, *purified, cleansed, spotless, with the defilements gone*, supple, ready to act, firm and impassable [all as a result of *samatha*], he [the meditator] directs his mind to the knowledge of insight [my emphasis].

The passions will not be extirpated in the course of a single *samatha* session any more than a single session of *vipassanā* will boost *paññā* to the point of perfect illumination; both techniques are slow and gradual but each is the most appropriate in its own sphere. Griffiths comes close to acknowledging the autonomy of the two techniques in the last two paragraphs of his paper. He compares the 'radical tension' between ignorance (*avijjā*) and desire (*taṇhā*) with the 'tension' between concentrative and insight meditation.

> Clearly, if ignorance is regarded as the root of all evil for the Buddhist, then he should take steps to remedy this condition by gaining insightful knowledge. There is no better way of doing so than the practice of insight meditation . . . If, on the other hand, craving and desire are regarded as the root causes of suffering, then the Buddhist should at once take steps to rid his mind of all desire. Once again, there is no better way of doing this than the practice of concentrative meditation (1981: 619).

Griffiths regards these options as alternatives and does not consider the possibility that there exist two techniques of meditation precisely because the obstacles to enlightenment are themselves twofold, both moral *and* intellectual. The Buddha learnt the technique of *jhāna* meditation from his own teachers and practised it himself first; his genius lay in supplementing it with the method of *vipassanā*. Both have an essential function to perform and the Buddha makes this abundantly clear in a passage cited by Griffiths:

> What is the result, O monks, of the development of tranquillity [*samatha*, here equivalent to *samādhi*]? The mind is developed. What is the result of a developed mind? Passion is abandoned [*rāga*, here equivalent to *taṇhā*]. What is the result, O monks, of the development of insight [*vipassanā*]? Wisdom (*paññā*) is developed. What is the result of the development of wisdom? Ignorance (*avijjā*) is abandoned (ibid., bracketing in original).

The translation of *paññā* as 'wisdom', as in the passage above, has undoubteldy helped to bolster the notion that *paññā* is the unique goal of Buddhism. After all, what more worthy goal could there be than wisdom? However, care must be taken here since 'wisdom' connotes moral as well as intellectual maturity whereas *paññā* is essentially cognitive. Griffiths tells us what *paññā* means: 'In terms of Pali grammar it is an awareness that can be contained within a *ti* clause, a discursive and intellectual understanding' (1981: 612). In other words it is propositional knowledge, the perception of the truth of a statement in quotations such as 'all phenomena are impermanent', or '2 + 2 = 4'. Griffiths qualifies this further when he adds: 'Such awareness appears to be a kind of detached, emotionless, intuitive vision of the nature of things as a flux of causally conditioned point-instants' (614). This is echoed by Johansson:

> Basically, *paññā* seems to be a pure theoretical function of understanding, without a motivational power of its own . . . *Paññā* is referred to as a purely intellectual tool, clearly distinguishable from motivational and emotional factors (1979: 200).

But this is not what is meant by 'wisdom'. *Paññā* is essentially the knowledge of facts, but wisdom means something more than just knowledge. Mrs Rhys Davids quotes Croom Robertson to the effect that 'wisdom . . . is a term of practical import; it is not mere insight, but conduct guided by insight. Good conduct is wise; wise conduct is good' (1936: 268). Buddhism does not seek the sterile and incomplete end which *paññā* on its own represents. The goal of the Eightfold Path is indeed wisdom, but wisdom is much more than *paññā*. This is why two meditative techniques are required for the eradication of the roots of evil and the attainment of the ethical and intellectual perfection which is *nibbāna*.

That *samatha* functions as the support of ethical development is not a novel suggestion – it was pointed out over thirty years ago by Conze:

> How then does concentration as a spiritual virtue [*samatha*] differ from concentration as a condition of the intellect [*vipassanā*]? Spiritual, or transic, concentration results less from intellectual effort than from a re-birth of the whole personality, including the body, the emotions, and the will . . . Further, the change of outlook, on which it is built, can well be described as an 'ethical' one. Tradition is quite unambiguous on this point (1956: 20).

More recently the ethical connection has been noted by Gimello, who describes the input of meditative experience into ethical values in the penultimate paragraph of his article referred to earlier:

> Regarding finally the problem of the relationship between mystical experience and other human concerns, Buddhist meditation, especially as it is defined in Mahāyāna, suggests that there may be connections between them deeper than normally supposed. The point of Buddhist meditation, including the mystical experience it allows, is, as Dogen has said, 'not to obtain a certain thing' but to 'become a certain man'. Mystical experience thus has no sovereign autonomy in Buddhism. Rather it is seen to have important consequences for all areas of human life – *not the least of which is morality* – and to be judged according to those consequences. *The mystical experience affects the moral life,* Buddhists believe, and they therefore take the greatest pains in their meditative disciplines to see that its effect is the proper, just, and compassionate one. In so doing, they may offer instruction to those who examine mystical claims for antinomianism or the transcendence of good and evil, and may offer caution to those who would hold that mysticism can be a refuge from a life of moral responsibility' (1978: 194, my emphasis).

Summary

This chapter dealt with four topics. The first (1) concerned the relationship between *sīla* and the *dharma*-theory. The *Abhidharma* posits two classes of mental forces which produce either defilement or purification of the mind. I described these forces as virtues and vices in accordance with Western ethical terminology since they perform a similar role in respect of promoting or inhibiting the attainment of the final good. In part (2), again in common with the classical Western tradition, I divided these forces into two groups, intellectual and moral, and argued that *taṇhā* was the collective interaction of the vices. The eradication of this root source is synonymous with nirvana and the virtues are collectively engaged in the promotion of this condition. The intellectual virtues remove mental obscuration (*moha*) and the moral virtues counteract the emotional complexes which manifest themselves in habits of attachment and aversion and inhibit the concern for others (*anukampā*) which is fundamental to the moral life. In the words of Khantipalo:

> As *Paññā* is the cultivated intellect, so these *Brahma-Vihāras* are the cultivation of the emotions. As the intellect has to balance in development emotion, so wisdom is complemented by friendliness and compassion (1964: 78).

In part (3) we considered the compassion of the Buddha as a paradigm affective disposition. To conclude the chapter, in part (4) the results of our investigation so far were applied to a practical problem, namely the existence of two types of meditation technique which has often been thought paradoxical. It was suggested that the two techniques exist precisely because final perfection can only be achieved when both dimensions of psychic functioning, the emotional and the intellectual, are purified of vice. The notion of *sīla* has now been examined in some depth and from a number of different angles, and in the course of this examination I have put forward a thesis concerning its role in Buddhist soteriology. In the next chapter we consider an alternative conception to our own and discuss the countervailing evidence which it presents to our views.

4

The Transcendency Thesis

In the preceding chapters I have argued that moral and intellectual perfection are integral components of the Buddhist *summum bonum*. I now wish to consider the evidence for a view which runs counter to this: that morality is at best a preliminary to enlightenment and at worst an obstacle to its attainment. This proposal has been put forward independently by Winston King (1964) and Melford Spiro (1970), although, as noted in Chapter 1, other writers have adopted this general position. I am concentrating on the version of the transcendency thesis set out by King and Spiro since theirs is the most systematic, familiar and accessible. My purpose in the present chapter is twofold: (1) to examine the King–Spiro hypothesis and to offer a critique of its view of the soteriological relationship between ethics and nirvana and (2) to consider an important piece of textual evidence, the Parable of the Raft, which although not adduced directly by King and Spiro is commonly taken to support the view of Buddhist ethics they advocate.

1. THE KING–SPIRO HYPOTHESIS

Both King and Spiro have undertaken anthropological research in the field in Burma, and it may be some distinctive feature of Burmese Buddhism which has led them to their similar conclusions concerning the nature of Buddhist ethics. I doubt, however, that this is the case, and believe that their theory of the structure of Buddhist soteriology stems from a misinterpretation of their field data rather than being implicit in it. King's book on Burmese Buddhism, *A Thousand Lives Away*, was published in 1964, the same year as his volume on Theravāda Buddhist ethics *In the Hope of Nibbana*, in which he sets out in the central chapters the theory now to be considered.[1] Six years later, in his *Buddhism and Society* Spiro set out in chapters 2–6 a theory almost identical to King's. Spiro makes no reference to King's work on ethics even in the second expanded edition of his book published in 1982.

Briefly, King and Spiro allege there are two forms of Buddhism (both confine their remarks to Theravāda Buddhism), and that these two forms of Buddhism are regulated separately through the disjunctive values of nirvana and karma. They argue, moreover, that these two values are pursued by distinct sociological groups, namely laity and monks. Thus while a layman seeks to generate merit (*puñña*) through generosity (*dāna*) and morality (*sīla*) in the hope of a good rebirth, a monk seeks to eradicate all karma through mental culture (*bhāvanā*) in the hope of putting an end to rebirth by gaining nirvana. These two forms of Buddhism are termed respectively (a) 'Kammatic Buddhism' (Spiro) or 'the ethic of *kamma*' (King); and (b) 'Nibbanic Buddhism' (Spiro) or 'the ethic of *nibbāna*' or 'the ethic of equanimity' (King). The basic polarities between the two forms of Buddhism may be tabulated as follows:

Form of Buddhism	goal	pursued by	means	technique
1. Nibbānic	*Nibbāna*	Monks	destroy kamma	*bhāvanā*
2. Kammatic	good rebirth	laity	produce *puñña*	*dāna-sīla*

In the terms of this polarisation moral values are confined to the sphere of kammatic Buddhism and excluded from nibbānic Buddhism. In view of the fact that ethics (*sīla*) is intrinsic to only one of these two divisions this version of the transcendency thesis may also be characterised in terms of value disjunction or discontinuity. The version of the thesis to be examined here rests primarily upon sociological and doctrinal grounds, and I shall shortly examine the evidence for each in turn. Before doing so let us consider Spiro's own summary analysis of the situation. His claim is that the two forms of Buddhism were originally distinct and that confusion has arisen from an attempt made in the past to combine them. This is how he sets out the problem:

> It should be apparent, then, that the attempted integration of the doctrine of nirvana with the doctrine of karma has produced an inherent and complex 'double-bind.' Whereas according to the

doctrine of nirvana (in which even the blissful life of a *deva* is a detour rather than a way station on the road to salvation), *saṃsāra* and nirvana comprise two distinctive and discontinuous planes of existence, by contrast, according to the doctrine of karma they comprise one hedonistic continuum, ranging from the suffering of hell at the one pole to the nonsuffering of nirvana at the other. And whereas according to the doctrine of karma samsaric pleasure is the just and proper reward for (Buddhist) moral action, according to the doctrine of nirvana this is not only an illusion but a snare, diverting one from the quest for true salvation; hence such pleasures should not be sought, and if achieved, should not be cathected. Hence the antimonies in nibbanic Buddhism: the consequence of moral action is a pleasant rebirth which, on the one hand, it holds out as a reward (while denigrating its pursuit as unworthy of a true Buddhist), but which, on the other hand – since all samsaric existence is painful – it sees as a persistence of suffering (although it is the harvest of action which it itself requires)' (1982: 69).

I am not alone in denying that this radical discontinuity exists, and the King–Spiro hypothesis has been criticised by Nathan Katz (1982) and Harvey Aronson (1979; 1980). Both Katz and Aronson attack the discontinuity on canonical grounds either by adducing conflicting scriptural evidence (Katz) or by pointing out the misinterpretation of doctrinal formulae (Aronson). Neither, however, offers an alternative soteriological framework within which the ethical values they defend may be appropriately located. Katz redefines the discontinuity in terms of an opposition between *puñña* (Kammatic Buddhism) and *kusala* (Nibbanic Buddhism). I do not follow Katz's terminology since I shall argue in the next chapter for a rather different interpretation of these terms. Let us turn now to a consideration of the grounds upon which the transcendency thesis rests, beginning with the sociological evidence provided by Spiro.

Burmese Religious Aspirations

The confusion underlying the transcendency thesis stems from an overestimation of the significance of the distinction between lay and monastic lifestyles, a distinction which is likely to impress itself upon an anthropologist in the field. I do not wish to deny on *a priori* grounds that this sociological distinction is necessarily invalid. It could conceivably be the case that such a situation obtains in Burma, and it is an issue to be resolved by empirical research.

Let us begin with Spiro's own data. In his book Spiro questions both monks and laymen as to their soteriological aspirations. On p. 285 he tables the result of a survey in which monks were questioned concerning the functions of a Buddhist monk. Out of 20 questioned only 4 considered one of their functions as a monk to be 'to strive for nirvana'. The great majority therefore dissented from Spiro's conception as to 'the culturally stipulated end or ends for which monasticism is the culturally prescribed means'. When laymen were questioned the results were equally embarrassing for the theory. On p. 81 the results of a questionnaire are tabulated in which 159 laymen and laywomen were asked the question 'What do you desire for your next existence?' The 'overwhelming majority' replied 'nirvana'; according to Spiro's statistics 61 out of 83 males gave this answer and 104 out of 159 males and females combined. Only 3 out of 159 wanted rebirth in heaven and none wanted rebirth as a monk which, as Spiro admits, is 'more than a little surprising' (1982: 80n). So far, then, the theory does not fit the facts: monks, who are supposed to strive for nirvana, say they do not; and laymen, who are supposed to desire rebirth, seek nirvana. Faced with this falsification of the theory Spiro falls back on the auxiliary hypothesis of 'normative and rhetorical pressures' upon his respondents. Thus:

> Given the fact that 'nirvana' is a stereotypic response (and its meaning, moreover, obscure), it is at least plausible that many who offered 'nirvana' as their first choice view it as a kind of superparadise (1982: 80).

The suggestion now is that lay Burmese are unable to distinguish between nirvana and heaven, yet this is scarcely credible in a culture which supposedly acknowledges a radical distinction between the 'kammic' and the 'nibbānic'. Not only this, but Spiro himself states earlier in the book that the Burmese do *not* view nirvana as a 'superparadise' in the way he suggests above. On page 59 he writes: 'Believing (as they do) that *nirvana means extinction*, most Burmese do not view it as a desirable goal' (my emphasis). And on page 76 he seeks to have it both ways:

> Since most Burmese reject the Buddhist doctrine of suffering, there are basically two attitudes towards nirvana . . . in Burma. Those who conceive of it as total extinction reject it as a desirable goal, while those who accept it as a desirable goal have transformed it into a state of great pleasure, a kind of superheaven.

Spiro has now attributed three different attitudes concerning nirvana to Burmese lay Buddhists.

1. 'Most Burmese' believe that nirvana means extinction and do not view it as a desirable goal.
2. The 'overwhelming majority' of Burmese lay Buddhists conceive of nirvana as a superparadise and hence as a desirable goal.
3. The Burmese hold two contradictory (and heretical) views about nirvana, namely (1) and (2) above.

Points (1) and (2) are not only mutually contradictory but no evidence at all is adduced in support of them. In fact (1) is contradicted by Spiro's own survey on p. 81 which clearly shows that his respondents regard nirvana as a desirable goal. Point (2) is merely a tentative suggestion ('it is at least plausible') to support the transcendency thesis in the face of the conflicting testimony of lay Buddhists. The final point (3) simply compounds the defects of the first two. Apart from the testimony of laymen, the testimony of monks also contradicts the theory, but no attempt is made to reinterpret their evidence.

Outside Burma

Looking beyond Burma the evidence from other Theravāda Buddhist societies does not support Spiro's theory of the teleological divergence of the two social groups. According to Gombrich religious aspirations of monks and laymen in Sri Lanka coincide rather than diverge. He writes: 'Most people, monks included, devote themselves exclusively to acts of merit (*piṅkam*), the aim of which is a good rebirth in heaven or on earth' (1971: 322). The centrality of *sīla* in the lives of Sri Lankan monks is also made plain by Michael Carrithers (1983). To cite a final example, the research of Jane Bunnag in Thailand which was devoted specifically to the relations between laymen and monks reveals complementarity in respect of lay and monastic objectives. She writes:

> In practice . . . none of the Thai monks to whom I spoke appeared to consider *Nirvana* a relevant goal for which to strive; those who considered that salvation was attainable in modern times, believed that only after billions of years of tireless effort could they or their contemporaries achieve this state . . . Thus both the Buddhist *bhikkhu* and the Buddhist householder pursue the same end, though by different means; each 'seeks the secondary compensation of a prosperous rebirth' . . . by doing good and avoiding evil (1973: 19f.)[2]

We may conclude, then that the sociological-teleological aspect of the transcendency thesis is invalid. Generally speaking, both monks and laymen pursue the same proximate religious objective, usually specified as a pleasant rebirth. There is no anthropological evidence to indicate that laymen and monks as distinctive social groupings pursue antithetical soteriological goals. In fact, all the evidence is to the contrary. Buddhism does not embrace two stark and incompatible values; it would be more accurate to say that it offers proximate and remote objectives. The sociological analysis is by no means the primary one here – what constitutes progress is the degree of understanding and practice of the *Dhamma*. Indeed, according to the earliest sources, there is no reason why a layman should not become an *Arahat*, and many lay *Arahats* are mentioned in the Canon.[3]

Doctrinal: *Saṃsāra* and Nirvana

The proponents of the transcendency thesis regard the disjunction as not merely sociological but ontological. Spiro puts it as follows:

> From an ontological point of view, Buddhism postulates the existence of two planes which, like parallel lines, never meet. On the one hand there is *samsara*, the worldly (*lokiya*) plane; on the other hand there is nirvana, the otherworldly (*lokuttara*) or transcendental plane . . . These two planes, however, are not only ontologically discontinuous, they are also hedonistically dichotomous. The former is the realm of unmitigated suffering; the latter is the realm of the cessation of suffering (1982: 68).

Such is Spiro's conception of the double-decker ontology of early Buddhism. He suggests that in the course of time the Burmese have 'wittingly or unwittingly' transformed this into a one-plane continuum embracing both kammatic and nibbānic values:

> Unlike nibbanic Buddhism, in which admission to nirvana requires the extinction of merit as well as demerit, Burmese Buddhism insists that nirvana, like *samsara*, is attained by the accumulation of merit (1982: 84).

Divergent Views

King and Spiro agree that the spheres of *kamma* and *nibbāna* are distinct and can never meet. Having said that, it should be pointed out that they hold slightly different positions on the function of moral action (*kamma/puñña*). Let us outline King's position first. King holds the weaker hypothesis that *puñña* leads in the direction of *nibbāna* but must finally be discarded before *nibbāna* is attained. We may call this the 'scaffold theory' since it envisages merit as a means of raising oneself upwards towards a higher goal. King writes as follows:

> Thus in the end the ethical significance of Kamma is ambiguous. Or perhaps it is better to say that its ethical significance is relative, not absolute. For kammic evils are only temporary evils, and kammic goods only half-way houses on the way towards the truly good. Kammic goodness is the necessary but not sufficient condition for either the saintly life or the attainment of Nibbana. True perfection is transcendent of all kammic values (1964: 67).

Although *kamma* is a halfway-house on the way to *nibbāna* and a necessary condition of its attainment it is simultaneously and paradoxically a hindrance to enlightenment. King continues:

> Indeed kamma and all that it represents are a bondage and a danger to the life of the saint in the final analysis. He must kick away from under him the laboriously built ladder of kammic merit by which he has risen towards sainthood, and take to the transcendental flight on the wings of super-normal (super kammic) wisdom . . . The abundance of that good Kamma itself which raises one to such a realm, and the love even of the highest kind of goodness to be found in the realm of Kamma, no matter how much preferable to the love of evil, bind him more

subtly and dangerously than before to the realm of time and space, that is, birth death and suffering.'

Curiously, in *A Thousand Lives Away*, King adopts a different position, one not dissimilar from the interpretation I am proposing here. He speaks of *sīla* as a 'kammic good', but this time there is no reference to an antagonism between *kamma* and *nibbāna* – quite the contrary:

> One cannot say that Sila is first perfected and then left behind when one reaches Samadhi and Paññā stages - even though there is talk of rising above mere morality as one progresses in the meditative life. For even the meditating saint remains moral in his actions. Indeed his saintliness, at least in part, is the perfection of his morality, the turning from mere observance of external standards to the spontaneous exercise of inward virtues. So it is that morality is never left behind (1964a: 188).

Here progress towards enlightenment is seen quite correctly as a long gradual process of development and maturation with no sudden and abrupt leaps into the transcendent fuelled by the rejection of what has long been patiently cultivated.

Spiro's general stance is more radical than King's first position in holding that *kamma* is entirely fatal to the quest for *nibbāna*. We have already quoted Spiro to the effect that the kammic consequences of moral action are 'not only an illusion but a snare'. For him any activity other than meditation is soteriologically deleterious:

> Meditation is *the* soteriological act of nibbanic Buddhism. Any other kind of action, even moral action, is subversive of salvation, for morality produces karma, which in turn causes rebirth (1982: 93).

In other words nibbānic Buddhism specifies *paññā* without *puñña*, while kammatic Buddhism specifies *puñña* without *paññā*. Both King and Spiro seem to overlook the fact that meditation (*bhāvanā*), along with generosity (*dāna*) and morality (*sīla*), is specified in canonical sources as one of the three Meritorious Actions (*puñña-kiriya-vatthu*). The practice of meditation, then, would be as soteriologically counterproductive as any other kind of meritorious act.[4]

Two Kinds of Nirvana

Spiro's inability to appreciate how the quest for *nibbāna* can begin and end in the same continuum may be due to his failure to distinguish between *nibbāna* as an event in life (*sopādisesa-nibbāna*) and final or post-mortem *nibbāna* (*nirupādisesa-nibbāna*). According to Buddhaghosa these correspond to the extinction of the defilements (*kilesa-parinibbāna*) and the extinction of the aggregates (*khandha-parinibbāna*).[5] We have seen in Chapter 3 that the extinction of the *kilesas* is clearly an ethical objective and does not involve any kind of ontological transcendence. In the condition of *kilesa-parinibbāna* the Buddha remains a moral subject and member of the moral community. The application of moral predicates to him was unproblematic for his contemporaries and it is through their interaction with him as a moral agent that the foundation of Buddhist ethics was laid, as we saw in Chapter 2. Some, indeed, would argue that nirvana was originally understood *exclusively* as the lived experience of ethical perfection. Such was the view of Rhys Davids:

> *Nibbāna* is purely and solely an *ethical* state, to be reached in this birth by ethical practices, contemplation and insight. It is therefore not transcendental. The first and most important way to reach *Nibbāna* is by means of the Eightfold Path, and all expressions which deal with the realisation of emancipation from lust, hatred and illusion apply to *practical* habits and not to speculative thought.[6]

It is only in the state of final nirvana that ethical predication and evaluation become problematic due to the absence of an identifiable moral subject. This never became an ethical problem in Buddhism since for the Small Vehicle the Buddha's *parinibbana* in any event marks the end of all possible interaction with him. And for the Large Vehicle he remains within the community of moral agents and there is still scope for a moral relationship with him. To put it another way round, for the Theravāda final salvation consists in the termination of moral relationships whereas for the Mahāyāna it is their eternal prolongation. It is not my purpose here to enter into a discussion of the problems of nirvana and I wish only to show *contra* King and Spiro that there need be no ontological discontinuity between ethical perfection and enlightenment. In particular I wish to repudiate the claim that the attainment of perfection necessitates the transcendence or rejection of ethical values and marks the entry to a state beyond good and evil.

However, we cannot dismiss the problem Spiro poses as the result of a simple failure to distinguish between the two kinds of nirvana. Leaving the question of final nirvana completely on one side, the problem could be restated in terms of the gulf between ethical action and nirvana-in-this-life. If Spiro's theory of karma is correct, good deeds will still subvert the attainment of either kind of nirvana. Moreover, as we saw in Chapter 1, Spiro's view of ethics is shared by distinguished specialists in Buddhism who are certainly aware of the distinction between the two kinds of nirvana. Although making this distinction helps avoid greater confusion, it does not directly address the fundamental problem of the soteriological status of ethics. However, we must reserve further discussion of this problem for the following chapter which provides an account of how the ontological gulf between karma and nirvana is bridged through the medium of the Eightfold Path. For now, we consider an important canonical passage which is often cited in support of the transcendency thesis.

2. THE PARABLE OF THE RAFT

The Parable of the Raft at *M*.i.134f. is commonly interpreted to mean that the attainment of nirvana involves the transcendence of both good and evil.[7] This interpretation derives from the Buddha's remarks at the end of the parable, which are translated by Horner as follows:

> Even so, monks, is the parable of the Raft *dhamma* taught by me for crossing over, not for retaining. You, monks, by understanding the Parable of the Raft, should get rid even of (right) mental objects, all the more of wrong ones.[8]

Largely on the basis of these two sentences from the Canon the notion has gained acceptance that ethics in Buddhism has only a provisional and instrumental status and may – even must – be discarded when it has fulfilled its function of ferrying the practitioner to the further shore of enlightenment. Just as, it is suggested, no-one would be foolish enough to carry around a raft after fording a stream, so those who have crossed over leave behind the burden of the normative ethical injunctions which earlier facilitated their passage.

In Chapter 1 we cited several instances of this view spanning a period of over thirty years from when Horner expressed it concisely in 1950 as follows:

> Morality is to be left behind . . . like a raft once the crossing over has been safely accomplished. In other words, the *arahat* is above good and evil, and has transcended both (1950: 1).

The most recent example is G. Dharmasiri:

> Here one goes beyond morality. That is why an Arahant has been described as having gone beyond both good and bad. He has transcended ordinary morality (1986: 183).

So far as I am aware, this view has never been challenged by direct reference to the Raft Parable, and although the parable is known to everyone with even a slight acquaintance with Buddhism little critical attention has been paid to the text itself. More recently there has been evidence of dissatisfaction with this view of Buddhist ethics and of a desire to sort out the unsatisfactory muddle of which the words 'beyond good and evil' form the nucleus.[9] It seems to me, in brief, that the interpretation of the Parable of the Raft suggested by Horner and others is not sustainable when the passage is placed in context, nor is it compatible with the cumulative and progressive structure of the path to perfection taught by the Buddha.

Some Preliminary Reflections

Before turning to the text itself, however, let us raise some preliminary queries of a general nature about the conclusion drawn from the Parable of the Raft. Clearly it involves a claim of some magnitude which at a stroke devalues the status of ethics (upon which Buddhism at other times places great emphasis) by allocating to it only a provisional, temporary and instrumental role. However, advocates of the view repeatedly cite only one piece of scriptural evidence in support of it from the voluminous and repetitive Pali canon. If Horner's interpretation is correct it would have great significance for the understanding and practice of the Eightfold Path. Why, then, does the Buddha, who taught with an 'open hand', not make this important point explicit throughout his sermons? Is it really credible that in a teaching ministry of forty-five years he would have so little to say on such an important subject? Apart from the Buddha, the Theravāda tradition itself seems reticent on the matter, and there appears to be no evidence that it understood the parable in the way suggested. On the contrary, the evidence is that it did not. Nor do Mahāyāna sources appear to take the parable as significant in an ethical sense. We might expect it to be cited frequently by texts which seek greater moral latitude for *bodhisattvas*, but it does not appear to be used in this way. To my mind the above considerations, circumstantial though they may be, cast doubt from the outset on the prospect of Horner's interpretation being correct. A final question we might ask is whether there is any corroborating textual evidence related to the theme of 'crossing over' or the use of rafts which would support the conclusions drawn. We will return to some of these points in the discussion below, but for now let us take just the last one.

Images of 'Crossing Over'

The image of fording a stream by a raft or boat is common enough in the *Nikāyas*. The rivers and streams of North-East India must have been a frequent obstacle to travellers and mendicants like the Buddha, especially with the complication of the monsoon rains. Crossing to the further shore would at times have required perseverance and ingenuity, and it is not surprising to find it used as a metaphor for the religious life. The symbolism lends itself to adaptation in various ways, as may be seen from a selection of texts on this theme which have been conveniently compiled by Coomaraswamy and Horner herself (1982: 180–6). It seems fair to take these nine or so texts as a reasonably representative selection from the Canon. Of these, some are just single verses, which leaves about five or six passages, including the Parable of the Raft from the *Medium Discourses*. In one passage (*S*.iv.179–81) the two riverbanks are both compared to obstacles to enlightenment, and the correct course is said to be to steer between them down to the sea of *nibbāna*. In the majority of cases, however, *nibbāna* is represented by the further shore. The symbolism is helpfully spelt out in *S*.iv.174f.; the water is the 'four floods'; the near shore is belief in a self (*sakkāya*); the further shore is *nibbāna*; the raft is the Eightfold Path;[10] and the man who has crossed over is the *Arahat*.

It is noteworthy that in only one of the examples selected by Horner, namely our passage from the *Medium Discourses*, is their any mention of the raft being left behind. Moreover, two passages are cited from the *Incremental Discourses* which flatly contradict the notion that the attainment of the further shore involves the transcendence of ethics. In fact the gaining of the further shore is explicitly identified with moral perfection in the form of the Ten Good Paths of Action:

> What, Gotama, is the near and what the further shore?
> – Taking life, Brahman, is the near shore; abstaining therefrom is the further shore. Taking what is not given is the near shore; abstaining therefrom is the further shore. Sexual misconduct is the near shore; abstaining therefrom is the further shore. Falsehood . . . spiteful speech . . . harsh speech . . . idle talk . . . coveting . . . malevolence . . . wrong views . . . are the near shore and abstinence therefrom the further shore.[11]

And at *A*.v.232 the further shore symbolises the *practice* of the Eightfold Path and not its abandonment:

> What, Gotama, what is the near shore and what the further shore?
> – Wrong view, Brahman, is the near shore, right view the further shore. Wrong resolve, speech, action, livelihood effort, mindfulness, concentration, wrong knowledge and wrong release are the near shore. Right view and the rest are the further shore.[12]

It is made perfectly clear here that *sīla* along with *samādhi* and *paññā* are part of the further shore and are not left behind on the near side after enlightenment. In these passages the symbolism of the further shore is a way of life in accordance with the *Dhamma*, in other words the implementation and practice of the Buddha's teachings. Why, then, in the *Majjhima* version of the Raft Parable, does the Buddha make a reference to 'crossing over but not retaining', and speak of 'leaving behind both *dhammā* and *adhammā*'? The answer must be sought in an examination of the passage in the context in which it occurs, and this will reveal that the Buddha was using the parable to make a specific point about religious practice. I suggest that his remarks at the end of the Raft Parable should be understood not in the general sense that his ethical teachings are to be transcended, but as a critique of a particular wrong attitude *towards* his teachings, of the kind evinced by the monk Ariṭṭha and others.

The Composition of the *Alagaddūpamasutta*

The Raft Parable occurs in the *Alagaddūpamasutta* or *Discourse on the Parable of the Water Snake* (*M*.i.130–42) and I believe it is helpful to read it in this wider context which, after all, is how the tradition has chosen to present it. The text of the *Water Snake* as we have it now seems to be a composite of at least four sections:

1. *M*.1.130 – *M*.i.134.22
2. *M*.i.134.23 – *M*.i.134.29
3. *M*.i.134.30 – *M*.i.135.26
4. *M*.i.135.27 – end.

The first section tells the story of the incorrigible monk Ariṭṭha; the second is a stock passage on the danger of the mastery of scripture for the wrong ends; the third is the Raft Parable, and the final section discusses a number of false views about the self. Buddhaghosa regards the text as both a compositional and thematic unity, as we shall see below. My own view is that the text probably consists of sections which were originally separate and subsequently placed together by the compilers of the Canon on the basis of their thematic unity. If so, this will provide support for the interpretation of the Raft Parable I present below. I am not concerned here to argue for a link with the final section. Even if a link between the first three sections cannot be established it does not seriously weaken my interpretation: in that case I will simply claim that my interpretation of section (3) (the Raft Parable) is as justifiable as Horner's on the basis of the extant text and has the additional merit of fitting into a coherent overall theory of the nature of Buddhist ethics.

As regards section (1) it should be mentioned that the story of Ariṭṭha is also found in the *Vinaya* in two places with the inclusion of additional detail concerning the penalty inflicted for his refusal to renounce his wrong views. The fact that the story occurs there is not of great significance, and it is possible that the story was imported into the *Vinaya* from the *Majjhima*. At *Vin*.ii.25–7 Ariṭṭha is subjected to a formal act of suspension (*ukkhepaniyakamma*), while at *Vin*.iv.133–6 his misconduct is given as the origin of *Pācittiya* 68. Whichever of the three occurrences of the story is the original makes no difference to my argument since I am concerned primarily with the thematic issue. I will return to the question of composition later, but for now let us turn to a consideration of the text itself.

The Theme of the *Water Snake*

In the first part of the *Water Snake* the Buddha censures Ariṭṭha for stubbornly holding a wrong view of *dhamma*. The view could scarcely be more perverse: 'In so far as I understand *dhamma* taught by the Lord, it is that in following those things called stumbling blocks by the Lord, there is no stumbling-block at all.'[13] The stumbling-blocks in question are not spelt out in the text, but we may deduce from a remark of the Buddha's that Ariṭṭha was under the impression that he could pursue sensual pleasures without becoming attached to them.[14] Buddhaghosa sheds some further light on this by commenting that due to a lack of knowledge of the *Vinaya*, Ariṭṭha was ignorant of the specific stumbling blocks which had been declared for monks. Ariṭṭha had apparently persuaded himself that since laymen indulged in the 'five strands of sensual pleasure' yet still managed to count Stream-winners, Once-returners and Non-returners amongst their numbers then contact with women was also allowable for monks. Turning the teachings on their head he arrived at the conclusion that 'sexual intercourse was no sin'.[15] The brethren attempt to persuade Ariṭṭha to renounce this view but he clings to it tenaciously, and in the end is called to account by the Buddha. The Buddha rebukes him and according to the commentary and the *Vinaya* accounts expels him. At this point the Ariṭṭha episode ends and his name is not mentioned again in the *sutta*, although it appears subsequently several times in the commentary in connection with the other three sections of the Discourse. Ariṭṭha seems to have been the canonical archetype of pig-headedness: when discussing elsewhere the meaning of the term 'reluctant to renounce' (*duppaṭinissaggī*) in the context of false views, it is Ariṭṭha whom Buddhaghosa volunteers as an example (*DA*.iii.839).

The second section of the *sutta* is a stock passage on mastery of the *dhamma*, and it is here that the simile of the water-snake is introduced. This passage describes how certain 'foolish men' master *dhamma* – here meaning the scriptures – for the wrong reasons:

> Herein, monks, some foolish men master *dhamma*: the Discourses in prose, in prose and verse, the Expositions, the Verses, the Uplifting Verses, the 'As it was Saids', the Birth Stories, the Wonders, the Miscellanies. These having mastered that *dhamma* do not test the meaning of these things (*dhammā*) by intuitive reflection (*paññā*), and these things (*dhammā*) whose meaning is untested by intuitive reflection do not become clear; they master this *dhamma* simply for the advantage of reproaching others and for the advantage of gossiping, and they do not arrive at that goal for the sake of which they mastered *dhamma*. These things (*dhammā*) badly grasped by them conduce for a long time to their woe and sorrow. What is the reason for this? Monks, it is because of a wrong grasp of things (*M*.i.133).[16]

This is a clear warning against the misuse of scripture, a failing not unknown in many text-based traditions. It is interesting to note that the first discourse in the *Medium Discourses*, according to the commentary, was preached to curb the pride (*māna*) which had arisen in 500 Brahmins through their mastery of the Vedic and Buddhist scriptures (*MA*.i.16f). *Milinda's Questions (Miln*. 414) cautions that one who has mastered the scriptures should be humble, and the Buddha warns the Kāḷāmas not to be overly impressed by proficiency in the scriptures (*piṭaka-sampadānena*). The problem of religious arrogance born of scriptural learning which this portion of the Discourse addresses would certainly seem to have been a live issue.

It is worth noting that in this passage on scripture the Buddha does not contrast a wrong grasp of the *dhamma* with its transcendence, but with a right grasp of it (*suggahītattā*). He opposes the misuse of scripture to the correct use of it. Some 'young men of good family', in contrast to the 'foolish men' grasp *dhamma* aright, and as a result arrive at the goal of the religious life. In case there was any doubt Buddhaghosa confirms that the Buddha is here showing the advantage of a right grasp of his teaching.[17]

After warning against the misuse of scripture (and pointing out the benefits when it is used rightly), the Buddha compares the danger of grasping *dhamma* wrongly to the danger of grasping a water-snake at the wrong end. One who does so and is bitten suffers agony or death 'because of grasping the water-snake wrongly' (*dugahītattā . . . alagadassa*). This theme of the danger of grasping things wrongly is common to both these sections of the discourse. In the first, Ariṭṭha, motivated by lust, seizes hold of a skewed interpretation of the teachings and refuses to let go of it. Even when pressed repeatedly by his fellow monks his response is to dig his heels in and stubbornly and insistently hold onto and promulgate the heretical view. When censuring him the Buddha puts his finger on Ariṭṭha's error: 'But now, foolish man, *by your own wrong grasp* you slander me, injure yourself, and produce much evil.'[18] The third and following section in the Discourse is the Parable of the Raft, and I wish to argue that it, like the first two sections, is concerned essentially with illustrating the danger of a wrong grasp or misappropriation of good things rather than advocating their transcendence.

The Parable of the Raft

The parable describes how a traveller reaches a great waterway whose further bank is safe and secure but whose nearer bank is dangerous and frightening. To get to the other side the traveller makes a raft, probably a float or coracle of some kind (*kulla*),[19] by binding up loose grass, twigs, branches and foliage, and propels himself across using his hands and feet as paddles. The question the Buddha then raises is whether it would be appropriate for the man to continue on his journey carrying the raft with him. The reply is that it would not, and the Buddha then sums up saying: 'Monks, I have taught you *dhamma* in the Parable of the Raft, for crossing over with not for grasping hold of.' The word 'grasping' (*gahaṇa*) here echoes the 'wrong grasp' (*duggahīta*) of the teaching by Ariṭṭha, and also the 'wrong grasp of the scriptures' (*dugahīttatā dhammānam*) by the foolish men who master them for the wrong purpose. The Buddha is saying that he has taught *dhamma* in the Parable of the Raft so that people will realise that his teachings are to be used for the purpose he intended, namely reaching salvation, and not for anything else. It is a warning to the brethren not to pervert the teachings as a means to gratifying their personal desires, be it for carnal pleasure as in Ariṭṭha's case, or 'reproaching and gossiping' in the case of the foolish men.

Whether the *sutta* be a unitary composition or not, the title the *Discourse of the Parable of the Water Snake* is highly appropriate for the first three sections. Grasping hold of a snake only to have it twist round and sink its poisonous fangs into one's body is a vivid and powerful warning about the terrible danger of grasping things wrongly. This theme has nothing to do with transcendence: it is a warning not to grasp the teachings 'at the wrong end', so to speak, and suffer spiritual harm. As to the dangers involved, in the *sutta* the Buddha says simply that Ariṭṭha's 'wrong grasp' will 'be for a long time to his woe and sorrow', but further details are supplied by the commentary. Although described by the Buddha as a 'foolish man', Ariṭṭha seeks comfort in the fact that the Buddha also once rebuked Upasena Vaṅgantaputta as a 'foolish man' (*Vin*.i.59) but the latter went on to realise the six higher powers (*abhiññā*). However, the Buddha quickly scotches this lingering hope by likening Ariṭṭha's spiritual condition to the sterility of a detached, withered leaf. He points out that although a fire can be rekindled from a tiny spark the size of a firefly, Ariṭṭha lacks even the slightest glimmer of knowledge which could serve as a basis for spiritual development. Ariṭṭha is left crestfallen sitting in dejection and despair, 'scratching in the ground with his toe', and reflecting on his spiritual bankruptcy (*MA*.i.104).

I claimed above that the tradition has regarded this text as a unity and that it has not understood the Raft Parable in the manner proposed by Horner and others. The evidence for both these claims is to be found in the commentary. First, when commenting on the third section of the Discourse (the Raft Parable) Buddhaghosa specifically links the moral of the parable to the story of Ariṭṭha which occurs in the first section, mentioning Ariṭṭha by name as we shall see below. He also makes two further references to Ariṭṭha in relation to the fourth part of the *sutta* (*MA*.i.110, 113), but this does not directly concern the argument here. Second, the commentary makes no reference whatsoever in any shape or form to the interpretation of the parable suggested by Horner. There is no mention of transcendence, no word of 'going beyond good and evil' and no suggestion at all that the *dhamma* or any part of it is to be left behind at any stage of the Path. If the parable indeed had this extraordinary and momentous meaning surely it would not be passed over without a word?

So much for the general sense of the parable. We may enquire further, however, as to the precise meaning of the Buddha's concluding remark: 'You should understand, monks, from the Parable of the Raft that good things (*dhammā*) must be left behind, much more so evil things (*adhammā*).' This is a tentative translation because the meaning of this sentence is not immediately obvious, not least because of the multiplicity of meanings of the word '*dhamma*'. Since the word appears here in the plural form the statement cannot be easily understood as referring to the *Dhamma* itself in the sense of the totality of Buddhist teachings. Consequently, it is unlikely to imply that the wholesale transcendence of religious practice is envisaged at a certain stage of the Path. So following our alternative interpretation of the parable what, precisely, are the 'things' (*dhammā*) which are to be used but not grasped at?

One obvious possibility is that 'good things' is simply intended in the loose sense of 'good things in general'. The balancing of *dhammā* with *adhammā* tends to support this, since the latter has a fairly standard meaning, namely that of evil or wrongful things. Since a contrast is clearly intended the sense would be, 'Be careful not to become obsessed with good things, much less evil things.' We find the terms *dhammā* and *adhammā* paired off elsewhere, for instance in the *Incremental Discourses* in the context of 'crossing over'. There, it is the Ten Bad Paths of Action which constitute the near shore that are described as '*adhammā*', and the Ten Good Paths of Action which constitute the further shore that are described as '*dhammā*'. Crossing the stream signifies simply the passage from evil (*adhamma*) to righteousness (*dhamma*).

Buddhaghosa interprets the reference to going beyond 'good things' (*dhammā*) more specifically as a warning about the dangers of attachment to meditative experience. This is what he has to say.

> 'You must let go of even good things . . .' Here 'good things' (*dhammā*) means calming and insight meditation. The Lord (urges) the rejection of sensual delight in calming meditation and insight meditation. How does he do this with respect to calming meditation? (When he says) 'Thus, indeed, Udāyi, do I advocate the renunciation of the sphere of neither-ideation-nor-non-ideation. Do you, Udāyi, see any fetter, be it subtle or gross, whose renunciation I do not advocate?' (*M*.i.456). Here he (urges) the renunciation of sensual delight in calming meditation. (And when he says) 'And you, monks, should not cling to, treasure, or hanker after this view thus purified, thus cleansed'

> (*M*.i.260), here he (urges) the renunciation of sensual delight in insight meditation. But now in the present context, urging the rejection of both, he says 'You must let go of even good things, how much more so evil things.'
>
> This is the gist of it. 'Monks, I call for the rejection of sensual delight even in respect of such pure and excellent things (as calming and insight meditation). How much more so, then, in respect of this wickedness, vulgarity, vileness and lewdness, this act requiring ablution, wherein this foolish man Ariṭṭha, seeing no fault, says 'there is no stumbling-block in taking sensual delight in the five strands of sense-pleasure.' (The Lord is saying here) 'Do not, like Ariṭṭha, throw mud or rubbish on my teachings.' Thus he admonishes Ariṭṭha with this rebuke.'[20]

Whichever interpretation is preferred it seems clear that the Buddha is using the Raft Parable to remind the monks of two things: first, that the sole purpose of the collective body of knowledge and discipline which is the *dhamma* is to be a means for reaching salvation; and second, that the individual components of this, such as particular doctrines, practices, teachings or philosophical views (*dhammā*) must not be allowed to become the subject of an emotional attachment and assume a disproportionate status within the context of the whole. All the more so, he adds, must things which are unambiguously evil be rejected.

The Story of Sati

Further material relevant to the meaning of the Raft Parable can be found later in the *Medium Discourses* in the story of Sati the fisherman's son (*M*.i.256ff.). The structure of the story of Sati parallels the story of Ariṭṭha with slight but interesting differences. The pernicious view held by Sati concerns the continuation of consciousness from one life to the next. The Buddha rebukes Sati and sets out the correct view of consciousness. The text of the Raft Parable does not figure here but the Buddha concludes with an allusion to it:

> If you, monks, cling to, cherish, foster this view, thus purified, thus cleansed, then, monks, would you understand that the

Parable of the Raft is *dhamma* taught for crossing over, not for retaining?
No Lord
But if you monks do not (. . .)
Yes, Lord.[21]

Based on this passage the meaning of the Raft Parable is that one should not become slavishly attached to a view *even when that view is true*. One should understand the true nature of consciousness but not become fixated on it *qua* philosophical theory. It must be put to its proper use as part of the Path and within the context of the rest of Buddhist teachings. Applying Horner's interpretation of the Raft Parable here, however, would give a rather odd result, and require the conclusion that the correct view of the nature of consciousness had to be in some sense transcended. This makes very little sense. The Buddha does not say that the view is to be transcended, merely not clung to. The plain reading of the text is that the problem lies not in the view but in the development of an emotional attachment to the view. Buddhaghosa makes this absolutely clear:

> Here 'view' means right view through insight. It is perfectly pure by seeing the true nature (of things), and 'cleansed' by seeing (their) causal relations. 'If you cling' means if you dwell clinging with views tainted by craving. 'If you cherish' means 'if you dwell cherishing with views tainted by craving . . . 'For crossing over not for grasping hold of' means 'Understand that *dhamma* taught by me in the Parable of the Raft is for crossing over the four floods, not for grasping hold of with desire.'[22]

Both the text and the commentary here make quite clear that the Raft Parable is addressing the problem of attachment and fixation upon the *dhamma* or certain aspects of it, and not repudiating the *dhamma* with its ethical teachings in favour of a state 'beyond good and evil'. The structure of the Sati story resembles that of the *Water Snake* in that it starts with the exposition of a perverse view and ends with a reference to the Raft Parable as a corrective. The stories follow an almost identical sequence, apart from the different names and wrong views in each case. Admittedly, the intermediate section (2) is lacking, as is the full text of the Raft Parable, but the fact that we find this structural shell in two places in the

Medium Discourses strengthens the case for regarding the earlier sections of the *Water Snake* as at least a thematic if not a compositional unity. The Sati story does not seem to occur in the *Vinaya*, so it cannot have been borrowed from that source. If the Sati story was not borrowed, then perhaps neither was the Ariṭṭha story, and hence the *Majjhima* version of the Ariṭṭha story may well be the original.

In another context in the commentary on the *Medium Discourses* Buddhaghosa comments upon the composition of various discourses. From his remarks below it is clear that he regards the whole of the *Water Snake* as an integral unit.

> When using a parable the Lord sometimes sets out the parable first and then explains the meaning; at other times he explains the meaning and then gives the parable. Sometimes he teaches surrounding the parable with the meaning. For example . . . in the whole of *suttas* such as the *Discourse on the Parable of the Water Snake* where he says 'Herein, monks, some young men master *dhamma*: the Discourses' etc. down to 'Monks, it is like a man looking for a water-snake' he taught surrounding the parable with the meaning.[23]

Thus Buddhaghosa regards our second section as embodying the core parable of the Discourse and the other sections as containing the meaning. For him the central problem which the Discourse addresses is the danger of a wrong grasp, as symbolised by the water snake.[24]

It may be noted in passing that Nāgārjuna gives a warning similar to that of the *Water Snake* in chapter XXIV.11 of the *Middle Verses*; a wrong grasp of the doctrine of emptiness (*śūnyatā*), he cautions, is like picking up a snake at the wrong end. Here again it is the misuse of the teaching which is objected to rather than the body of the teaching itself.[25] As far as other Mahāyāna sources are concerned, the Raft Parable seems to be invoked mainly to support epistemological or ontological positions rather than ethical ones. The *Diamond Sūtra*, advocating the doctrine of *śūnyatā*, cautions that a *bodhisattva* should grasp neither at *dharma* nor *adharma*, apparently on the grounds that both are equally void of inherent existence.[26] The *Descent to Laṅkā*, on the other hand, makes use of the parable to support the philosophy of *cítta-mātra*.[27] Lamotte draws attention to the existence of the *Kolopama Sūtra* (*Fa Yu Ching*) which may shed further light on the origins of the parable. There is, of course, no reason why the parable could not be invoked in support of a range of quite different positions, so that the search for a consensus on its meaning may be futile. As Lamotte wisely says, 'We must examine the sense of *dharma* and *adharma* in each individual source.'[28]

To sum up: the theme of the *Discourse of the Parable of the Water Snake* and of the Raft Parable is not transcendence but a warning that even good things can be misused. The teachings are good but Ariṭṭha distorts them. The scriptures are good but some people twist them to their own ends. The raft is good but becomes a handicap if misused by being carried around. Calming and insight meditation are good but can be a hindrance if an attachment for them is allowed to develop. From a Buddhist perspective, those who do not follow the Way have little hope of salvation. The *Parable of the Water Snake* warns that even those who *do* follow the way can find themselves, if they are not careful, in a spiritual dead-end.

Above I have presented arguments of two kinds, circumstantial and textual, against Horner's interpretation of the Raft Parable. The view she proposed and which has been uncritically followed takes no account of the complexity or context of the passage upon which it is based. Even if my own account is totally wrong it at least reveals the need for a good deal of caution before leaping to any conclusions about the nature of Buddhist ethics on the basis of limited and problematic textual evidence. I must point out that the view of the nature of Buddhist ethics expressed in this book does not depend upon a particular interpretation of the Raft Parable: I have dwelt on it here only because so much has been made of it by others. The parable is a major plank in the transcendency thesis and it is supporters of Horner's view who must defend their interpretation of the text if they wish to base a theory of Buddhist ethics upon it.

This chapter has consisted of an exposition and critique of views which regard enlightenment as transcendent of ethical values. In the next chapter we seek to show how the passage from *saṃsāra* to nirvana is made through the Eightfold Path, and also develop a view of karma which allows ethics to play the soteriological role we have defined for it.

5
Ethics and Soteriology

The central claim of the transcendency thesis is that karma and nirvana are incompatible, antagonistic, and antithetical. The evidence adduced in support of this claim was reviewed in the last chapter and some fundamental problems were pointed out. The present chapter sets out to provide a more satisfactory account of the relationship between karma and nirvana which does no violence to the position of canonical Buddhism. We consider first of all (1) an alternative account of the Eightfold Path and its role as the medium between *saṃsāra* and nirvana. This is followed by (2) an attempt to define more precisely the meaning of the important ethical terms *kamma, kusala,* and *puñña* and the relationship between them.

1. THE NATURE OF THE EIGHTFOLD PATH

It is the purpose of the Eightfold Path to bring about the transition from *saṃsāra* to nirvana. Although there is clearly a sense in which the Path involves a 'journey', it may be more helpful to think of it as bringing about a transformation rather than effecting a movement or relocation. The Eightfold Path is only linear in a metaphorical sense: it does not list stages which are to be passed through and left behind so much as describe the dimensions of human good and the technique for their cultivation. The Eightfold Path is primarily something which is participated in, and by participating in the Eightfold Path one participates in those values, excellences or perfections which are constitutive of enlightenment, namely morality (*sīla*) and insightful knowledge (*paññā*). The following of the Eightfold Path is therefore best understood as the gradual cultivation of moral and intellectual virtue. Nirvana is the perfection of these virtues and not an ontological shift or soteriological quantum leap. The beginning and end of this development must take place in the same continuum otherwise the process could never begin at all. As the Eightfold Path is followed the practitioner participates more and more in the supramundane (*lokuttara*); both the final perfection of nirvana and the path which leads to it are *lokuttara*. 'Just as the Ganges and the Yamuna merge and flow along united,' says the Buddha, 'so too do *nibbāna* and the Path.'[1]

'Worldly' and 'Supramundane'

It is often assumed that for Buddhism ethics is a 'worldly' affair and must sooner or later be left behind. Apart from the Parable of the Raft, other scriptural sources have been interpreted as providing general support for the view that ethical considerations are only of preliminary or subsidiary importance. In the course of this discussion we will take another look at some of these passages. The *Discourse on the Great Forty* (*M*.iii.71–8), for example, is sometimes offered as evidence in support of the *kamma-nibbāna* dichotomy in view of the distinction it makes between worldly (*lokiya*) and supramundane (*lokuttara*) religious practice. The Buddha distinguishes here between wrong attitudes and two kinds of right attitudes towards the factors of the Eightfold Path.[2] The first kind of right attitude is described as *lokiya* and the second as *lokuttara*.[3] When discussing the first item of the Eightfold Path, Right View, the Buddha defines worldly Right View in terms of moral observances, and supramundane Right View by reference to *paññā*. It might be concluded from this that ethics is of a lower order of soteriological importance than insight (*paññā*) and therefore to be transcended.

This conclusion, however, misses the point of the distinction, and is not compatible with the rest of the discussion in the *Great Forty*. Instead, we urge that the identification of two kinds of right view should not be taken as the recognition, and perhaps the endorsement, of two distinct kinds of religious attitude or practice (i.e. kammatic and nibbānic). Nor is it intended to relegate morality to the lower, worldly, sphere. On the contrary, the point of the distinction is not to demean ethics but instead to emphasise the inclusive and comprehensive nature of the Eightfold Path. The first kind of right view is inferior not because it relates to *sīla*, but because it relates to *sīla* in isolation. Wrong view, according to the *sutta*, is the denial of religious values, specifically of the fact that religious and moral actions have consequences (*akiriyavāda*). The first kind of right view is the acceptance of religious values through acknowledging that religious and moral actions *do* have consequences, in other words the acceptance of the doctrine of karma (*kiriyavāda*). The superiority of the second kind of right view lies not in the fact that it has moved beyond ethics, but in the crucial supplementing of moral values by intellectual ones, and their joint implementation in the Eightfold Path. It is this that is said to be *lokuttara* and to lead to the end of rebirth. Things are *lokuttara*, says Buddhaghosa, by virtue of being associated with the Noble Path and its fruits (*MA*.i.196). Outside the context of the Eightfold Path ethics is a 'mundane' activity in that by itself it will not put an end to rebirth.

This is made clearer in the discussion of the three possible attitudes towards Right Speech, Action, and Livelihood. The first and worst attitude towards these things is to speak, act and live in ways that breach the precepts. The second or 'worldly' right attitude is to observe the precepts and live a moral life. The third or 'supramundane' right attitude is observing the precepts as part of the Eightfold Path – *not* passing beyond ethics to knowledge. It is in the Eightfold Path that the moral behaviour defined as Right Speech, Action and Livelihood become supramundane:

> What, monks, is Right Speech which is noble, pure, supramundane, a component of the Path? It is that abstinence, cessation, complete cessation and abstention from the four wrong forms of verbal conduct on the part of one who is cultivating the Noble Path, associated with the Noble Path, pure and noble in heart. This, monks, is Right Speech which is noble, pure, supramundane, a component of the Path.[4]

In this text the Buddha is not setting out two alternative paths for his followers, one *lokiya* (for laymen) and the other *lokuttara* (for monks), nor one for the slow and another for the quick. Instead he is making quite clear that there is only *one* path which deserves to be followed, namely the third and final option described in the text, whereby virtuous conduct now becomes a component of the Way to liberation. It will doubtless be the case that not everyone is capable of cultivating all aspects of the Path at once, but this is quite different from saying that there is a fork in the Way at which monks proceed in one direction in pursuit of knowledge and layfolk the other in pursuit of the moral life, or that ethics is a mundane activity. The three kinds of attitude described in the text are those of a) *akiriyavādins,* b) *kiriyavādins,* and c) followers of the Eightfold Path. They are held by (a) those who are without *sīla;* (b) those who possess *sīla* alone; and (c) those who possess both *sīla* and *paññā*.

The Eightfold Path is the cornerstone of Buddhism – not in the detail or order of its eight items but in its bilateral strategy for perfection. Only when seen in this light can we understand the Buddha's condemnation of religious teachings which do not contain the Eightfold Path (*D*.ii.151). He is not disparaging other traditions for the lack of a particular eight-limbed formula, but pointing out that those traditions which do not encourage the cultivation of both moral and intellectual excellence will not lead to salvation. The Eightfold Path is *lokuttara* since it leads to full perfection and the end of rebirth when this perfection is achieved. It is *lokuttara* because it crosses over (*uttarati*) from the world (*loka*).[5] Other belief-systems which fail to recognise the two overlapping spheres of human good do not achieve this crossing over. This deficiency is evident in the teachings of some of the Buddha's contemporaries who denied, amongst other things, the doctrine of karma, abolishing at a stroke any role for ethics in their soteriologies. Reference was also made in Chapter 2 to the Brahmanical understanding of the ways of knowledge (*jñāna*) and action (*karma-yoga*) as alternatives, and the Buddhist synthesis of them. By making the Eightfold Path the yardstick of salvation the Buddha is pointing out that such one-sided teachings are incomplete, unbalanced and cannot lead to full perfection – inevitably they conduce to repeated rebirth and are therefore *lokiya*.

The Path Goes All the Way

Nirvana and the Path lie in the same continuum. The follower of the Path does not need to make a final leap into the transcendent like an athlete doing the long-jump. As we saw in Chapter 2, the Path itself is a condensation of the stages described in the *Collection* which lead gradually up to Arahatship. Rhys Davids comments upon these stages as follows:

> Now it is perfectly true that of these thirteen consecutive propositions or groups of propositions, it is only the last No. 13, which is exclusively Buddhist. But the things omitted, the union of the whole of those included into one system, the order in

> which the ideas are arranged, the way in which they are treated as so many steps of a ladder whose chief value depends on the fact that it leads up to the culminating point of *Nirvāna* in Arhatship – all this is also distinctively Buddhist (*Dialogues*. 1:59).

This sentiment is echoed by Saddhatissa, who underlines the fact that this continuum of perfection is *internal* to the Eightfold Path:

> The ultimate ideal aim which may serve as the ultimate standard of right conduct, relates, according to Buddhist thought, to the supramundane or *lokuttara* state, and the connection between the moralities of everyday life and this *lokuttara* state is one which is entirely covered by the Buddha's teachings. It is, in fact, that which is known to Buddhists as *mārga, magga*, the Path, the Road, along which each person must travel for himself beginning with the practice of the common moralities up to the supramundane state beyond good and evil. From this point of view Buddhism can be said to provide the complete ethical study (1970: 18f.).

While agreeing with the Reverend Saddhatissa that the Eightfold Path is one of cumulative perfection culminating in nirvana we must differ from his opinion that its conclusion is 'beyond good and evil', unless it is to the state of final nirvana to which he is referring as, indeed, is suggested by a passage shortly afterwards:

> It must be emphasised at the outset that recognition of a state beyond good and evil in no way implies that a person who has performed a number of 'good' deeds may then relax morally and do anything he pleases; it merely hints at a state described by the Buddha when he was asked: 'Where do the four primary elements . . . entirely cease?' (1970: 19).

The Sequence of the Path

The fact that the Eightfold Path begins with *sīla* does not mean that morality is only a preliminary stage. The Eightfold Path begins with *sīla* but ends with *sīla* and *paññā*. *Sīla* is the starting point since human nature is so constituted that moral discipline (*sīla*) facilitates intellectual discipline (*paññā*). Until correct attitudes habits and dispositions have been inculcated it is easy to fall prey to speculative views and opinions of all kinds. This does not mean there is a direct line leading through *sīla* to *paññā*, or that morality is merely a means of limbering up for the intellectual athlete. No: morality is taken up first but constantly cultivated alongside insight until the two fuse in the transformation of the entire personality in the existential realisation of selflessness. We may say that *paññā* is the cognitive realisation of *anattā* while *sīla* is its affective realisation.

In the Canon this scheme of personal development is often expressed using a linear metaphor of a series of separate stages or hurdles, like rungs on a ladder. This metaphor can be misunderstood if it is not remembered that each of the stages is part of an overall pattern of cumulative development. Each stage develops out of and includes the previous ones. As an example of this we may consider the Buddha's description of the scheme of progress from morality to enlightenment in the *Incremental Discourses*. Here he describes how morality leads up to the highest goal:

> So, Ānanda, good moral conduct (*kusalāni-sīlāni*) has freedom from remorse as its aim and advantage; freedom from remorse has joy; joy has rapture; rapture has calm; calm has happiness; happiness has concentration; concentration has knowledge and vision of things as they really are; . . . disenchantment and dispassion; . . . release by knowledge and vision as their aim and advantage. So you see, Ānanda, good moral conduct leads gradually up to the summit.[6]

Clearly the meaning here is not that all of the stages are passed through once and forever left behind. *Sīla* is a central enduring feature of the conduct of the enlightened, as we shall see below. What the text describes is a series of spiritual breakthroughs and the order in which they occur for one following the Path. This is the sequence in which these developments will occur. The list is in experiential order and provides a guide to spiritual progress – it is *not* arranged according to priority of values. We may also note that the Buddha's statement here completely overturns the suggestion by King and Spiro that there is no means of transit between *sīla* and *nibbāna*.

A further illustration of the sequence of spiritual progress may be seen in the *Discourse on the Relay of Chariots* from the *Medium*

Discourses. The text describes the sequence from *sīla* to *nibbāna* using the analogy of a series of chariots by which King Pasenadi of Kosala might travel from Sāvatthī to his palace at Sāketa (*M*.i.148–50). The parable again emphasises the linear sequence of events since its purpose is to provide orientation in respect of subjective spiritual experience. It portrays the order in which personal development occurs, and in the context of the Eightfold Path the king's arrival at the palace is the product of *all* of the chariots in the relay and not just the last one.[7]

Ethics and the End of the Path

We can see that the Path and Nirvana lie in the same continuum if we shift our attention briefly from those who are still travelling to those who have arrived. The difference between the Buddha's perfection and that of someone still following the Path – profound though it may appear – is only one of degree. The attainment of nirvana-in-this-life marks the fulfilment of human potential, not its transcendence. If it *were* in some sense transcendent then the Buddha would have passed beyond the possibility of ethical predication and become a moral zero. Yet there is ample evidence that the Buddha continued to be characterised and to refer to himself in terms of the same ethical goodness being cultivated by his yet-unenlightened followers. It therefore makes little sense to describe him as having gone beyond 'good'. He had not transcended goodness but fulfilled it. What he had 'gone beyond' was the possibility of evil.

Of the Buddha's own moral perfection there can be no doubt: we have already seen that he is eulogised in this respect in the *Tracts*; and in the *Lion's Roar to Kassapa* the Buddha himself tells us that he is perfect in *sīla*:

> There are some *Samaṇas* and *Brāhmaṇas*, Kassapa, who lay emphasis on morality (*sīla*). They speak in many ways in praise of morality. But so far as regards the most noble and highest morality I know of no-one who is equal to myself, much less superior. For it is I who am the foremost in the highest morality (*adhisīla*).[8]

The Buddha speaks of his own moral perfection again in the *Incremental Discourses* and contrasts himself with five types of teachers who are deficient in various ways.

> But I, Moggallāna, am perfectly pure in morality and know that I am. I know that my morality (*sīla*) is perfectly pure, clean and stainless. My disciples do not supervise me in respect of morality and I do not expect them to.[9]

The Buddha's moral conduct, that is to say his interaction with other beings, is perfect. His behaviour is inspired by a disposition of benevolence to all beings, as was noted in Chapter 3. We have noted that the Buddha is described not merely as perfect in wisdom (*vijjā*) but as perfect in both wisdom and conduct (*vijjācaraṇasampanna*) (e.g. *Vin*. 3.1). These twin aspects of his perfection are brought out in the commentary to the *Path of Purification*:

> Here the Master's possession of vision shows the greatness of his understanding, and his possession of conduct the greatness of his compassion. It was through understanding that the Blessed One reached the kingdom of the Law, and through compassion that he became the bestower of the Law. It was through understanding that he felt revulsion for the round of rebirth, and through compassion that he bore it. It was through understanding that he fully understood others' suffering, and through compassion that he undertook to counteract it. It was through understanding that he was brought face to face with *nibbāna*, and through compassion that he attained it. It was through understanding that he himself crossed over, and through compassion that he brought others across. It was through understanding that he perfected the Enlightened One's state, and through compassion that he perfected the Enlightened One's task.[10]

So perfect is the Buddha's conduct that it is unnecessary for him to guard against misdeeds of body, speech and mind.

> Three things which a *Tathāgata* has not to guard against: a *Tathāgata* friends, is pure in conduct whether of act, or speech or thought. There is no misdeed of any kind concerning which he must take care lest another should come to know of it.[11]

Having achieved this state of spontaneous moral perfection himself, the Buddha encourages others to do the same, and expresses disapproval of all immoral conduct: 'I detest, O Brahman, evil conduct in body, word and thought, and the development of manifold bad and evil states.'[12]

The Buddha is said to be a 'Brahman' because he has rooted out all 'wrongful evil states'.[13] We are told by Buddhaghosa that the Buddha is unexcelled in ethics (*purisa-sīla samācāre*) (*DA*.iii.875), that he is the foremost in the promulgation of virtue (*kusala*) (*DA*.iii.847), that he always speaks the truth (*DA*.i.914), that nothing can make him depart from virtue (*kusala*) and that he recoils from vice (*akusala*) like a hen's wing from the fire (*DA*.ii.919).

Moral excellence is not peculiar to the Buddha alone and is possessed by all who attain perfection. The conduct of an *Arahat* images that of the Buddha to the extent of an inability to commit immoral actions.

> A monk who has destroyed the *āsavas* [i.e. an *Arahat*] is unable intentionally to kill a living creature, to take by theft that which has not been given, to have sexual intercourse, to tell a deliberate lie, or to take pleasure in things stored up, as he did before as a layman.[14]

There are more positive formulations describing the virtues *Arahats* continue to display:

> The *Arahats*, as long as they live, abandon the slaying of creatures and hold aloof from it, laying aside the rod and the sword they are modest and kind and dwell friendly and compassionate to all living beings.[15]

If the Buddha and the *Arahats* had truly transcended good and evil their conduct should not be susceptible to moral evaluation in terms of the moral criteria of the non-*Arahat*. Moreover, if the Arahat's perception of the world was ethically transparent why should what is conventionally described as 'immoral action' be impossible for him? And conversely, why should actions which display moral perfection be the norm in his case? The only satisfactory solution is that at the end of the Eightfold Path the *Arahat* still stands within the same ethical continuum in which he began to tread the path to enlightenment. The relationship of *kamma* to *nibbāna* is the relationship of ethics to soteriology, and far from being incompatible there is an integral and inalienable relationship between moral goodness and enlightenment. Since the Path is both the means and the end, there is no ontological gulf to be 'crossed over'.

2. *KAMMA, KUSALA,* AND *PUÑÑA*

In the discussion so far on the relationship between *kamma* and *nibbāna* I have tended to treat *kamma* as synonymous with 'moral action'. The notion of *kamma,* however, is more complex than this. As we have seen, textual sources constantly point out a key feature of kammic deeds, namely that they are inevitably followed by pleasant or unpleasant results. We must therefore analyse the concept of *kamma* further, and seek to understand the relationship between *kamma* as deeds and *kamma* as the consequence of deeds. We will seek to understand the nature of this relationship through an examination of the two key terms of moral (kammic) commendation – *kusala* and *puñña* – and show how they relate to each other and to *nibbāna*.

Kusala

Kusala denotes those things which are to be pursued if enlightenment is to be attained. Its contrary, *akusala,* characterises whatever is negative in this respect and is accordingly to be shunned. The Buddha unambiguously urges monks to abandon what is *akusala* and cultivate what is *kusala*:

> Monks, you should abandon what is evil (*akusala*). It can be done. I would not say you should do it if it could not be done . . . If abandoning evil conduced to woe and sorrow I would not say 'abandon evil'. But since it conduces to profit and happiness, I therefore say 'abandon evil'.
> Monks, you should cultivate what is good (*kusala*). It can be done, I would not tell you to do it if it could not be done . . . If cultivating the good conduced to woe and sorrow I would not say 'cultivate the good'. But since it conduces to profit and happiness, I therefore say 'cultivate the good'.[16]

The Buddha also states that the Cardinal Virtues (*kusalamūlāni*) eradicate their opposites and lead to *nibbāna*. In the person who cultivates the *kusalamūlāni*:

> The evil demeritorious states born of greed, hatred and delusion are abandoned, cut down at the root and made like a palm-tree stump, unable to grow again or arise in the future. In this world he lives undisturbed, free from woe, trouble and strife and attains *nibbāna* in this life.[17]

And again, the Buddha tells the monks not to suspend what is *kusala* but to increase it:

> Monks, I do not recommend a suspension of things which are *kusala,* much less a reduction. I recommend an increase in things which are *kusala* and not a suspension or a reduction.[18]

Note that the Buddha is addressing monks and not laymen, which indicates quite clearly that what is *kusala* is not to be eschewed by the *nibbāna*-seeker. And when discussing 'right effort' the Buddha says:

> A monk should exert and focus his mind, stir up zeal, strive, and produce eagerness to ensure the persistence, the non-decline, the increase, growth, development and fulfilment of *kusala* states.[19]

Kusala is not opposed to *nibbāna;* it is opposed to what is *akusala* or *kilesa*. The etymologies of *kusala* which Buddhaghosa provides indicate that *kusala* is opposed to what is contrary to *nibbāna,* i.e. evil and vice:

> Etymologically speaking, things are known as *kusala* because they shake, react against, disturb and destroy evil, wicked things. Or, *kusa* describes things which are latent in an evil way, and *kusa-la* (qualities) are so called because they cut off and sever those things which are *akusala*. Again, knowledge is known as *kusa* because it stops, reduces, or terminates evil things, and so the meaning is that good things (*kusala*) should be grasped and promoted, taken hold of by that *kusa*, or knowledge. Or just as the grass known as *kusa* can cut part of the hand with either edge, so these things cut off the vices in two ways, both in their latent and manifest forms. This is why they are known as *kusa* – because they cut like the *kusa* grass.[20]

Kusala describes those qualities or states which are intrinsically related to *nibbāna*. In the *Relay of Chariots,* as noted earlier, the Buddha describes how good moral conduct (*kusalāni sīlāni*) leads gradually to the highest state. Not only *sīla* is described as *kusala* but all qualities which are nibbanically orientated. In a well-researched article on the meaning of *kusala* and *puñña* Premasiri says of *kusala*:

> The *kusala* states are sometimes enumerated as the four bases of mindfulness (*cattāro satipaṭṭhānā*), the four modes of right endeavour (*cattāro sammappadhānā*), the four bases of psychic power (*cattāro iddhipādā*), the five faculties (*pañcindriyāni*), the five powers (*pañcabalāni*), the seven factors of enlightenment (*sattabojjhaṅgā*) and the eightfold path (*ariyo-aṭṭhaṅgiko-maggo*). In the same context it is said that when a monk, at the eradication of defilements enters and abides in the freedom of mind and freedom through wisdom in this very existence, having realised it by his own super knowledge, that state is the highest of *kusala* states (1976: 67f.).

Here the state of Arahatship is described as *kusala*. The Buddha too is described and refers to himself as one endowed with *kusala*. Ānanda says of him 'The *Tathāgata* . . . is one who has discarded all states that are *akusala* and is possessed of states that are *kusala*'.[21] The Buddha considered himself as one who had discarded numerous *akusala* qualities and cultivated *kusala* ones.[22] There is no sense in which *kusala* qualities are jettisoned prior to enlightenment – quite the contrary, for it is in *nibbāna* that they reach their full perfection. *Kusala* qualities are to be cultivated and perfected, not cultivated and abandoned. Premasiri summarises as follows:

> *Kusala* is generally referred to as a quality that should be cultivated. It is said that the cultivation of *kusala* conduces to happiness and welfare. The Buddha is referred to as one who has cultivated that which ought to be cultivated and eliminated that which ought to be eliminated, which may be understood amongst other things as a reference to his cultivation of *kusala* and elimination of *akusala* (1976: 71).

The Translation of *'Kusala'*

Kusala qualities partake of *nibbāna*, and their cultivation transforms an ordinary man (*puthujjana*) into an *Arahat*. Such qualities both reflect and promote the final good – they are virtues – and the most natural translation for *kusala* when used in a moral context is 'virtue' or 'goodness'. It is very common for *kusala* to be rendered as 'skilful', but it should be recognised that this translation carries with it a specific implication for the nature of Buddhist ethics, namely that it is utilitarian. Even then, it is a poor translation on aesthetic grounds, and we may note that utilitarian philosophers retain the traditional moral terminology of 'good', 'bad', 'right', and 'wrong'.

Like the English word 'good', the Pali *'kusala'* conveys approbation or commendation in both a moral and a non-moral or technical sense. We use the word 'good' in English when we speak of a 'good deed' or 'good man', implying moral approval; and we use the same word to denote technical approval, for instance when we speak of a 'good dentist' or a 'good plumber'. *Kusala* enjoys the same elasticity of meaning as the word 'good', in that it can denote either moral goodness or technical excellence according to context. The Pali Text Society dictionary recognises the distinct moral and technical senses of the term and gives appropriate English equivalents for both. As an adjective it defines *kusala* as 'clever, skilful, expert; good, right, meritorious', adding that it is 'Especially applicable in a moral sense'. The three synonyms before the semicolon denote the technical sense of *kusala* while the three which follow denote its moral sense.[23] Although I have no statistics to back this up there can be little doubt that in the *Nikāyas* the occurrences of *kusala* in a technical context are massively outnumbered by those in a moral context. So why, when translating the term into English, is the tail allowed to wag the dog and the moral sense suppressed in favour of the technical one?

The problem with using 'skilful' as a translation of *kusala* is that whereas 'good' and *'kusala'* extend in their respective languages to both moral and technical commendation, the English word 'skilful' does not. 'Skilful' denotes approval in the technical sense only and does not figure at all in the vocabulary of moral discourse in English. No-one would describe a simple act of generosity as a 'skilful deed',[24] and who has ever heard of a boy scout doing his 'skilful deed for the day'? Instead, one naturally speaks of 'good' or 'virtuous' deeds. While 'skilful' may be a perfectly correct translation of *kusala* when the term appears in a technical context (for instance, a skilful artisan), it is forced and awkward in a moral one. In English the natural way of describing the moral state of an *Arahat* is as 'endowed with virtue' (*sampannakusala*) and of the 'highest virtue' (*paramakusala*) (M.ii.25). Being 'endowed with skill', or of the 'highest skill', on the other hand, is an attribute of a master-craftsman, not a saint.

It is not difficult to see why the translation of *kusala* as 'skilful' has gained popularity. It is the natural outcome of the view that ethics in Buddhism is precisely what the use of the term 'skilful' would suggest, namely a technical or instrumental activity. If ethics is simply a means to the next higher stage and has no long-term or intrinsic relevance to the goal, then acts or individuals can be described as relatively skilled or less skilled depending on their success in the exploitation of the means. In this respect the nirvana-farer will cleverly aim to make use of the law of karma to advance his progress like a skilful sailor uses the wind to propel his ship. Conversely, evil deeds will be nothing more than a technical miscalculation. No doubt for some this is a satisfactory characterisation of Buddhist ethics, but it is one which cannot be allowed to hide in the closet behind the translation of *kusala* as 'skilful'. A defence of this translation will also require a defence of the view of Buddhist ethics on which it rests. If the Pali sources had wished to suggest commendation in the restricted technical sense that 'skilful' has in English they could have used words such as *dakkha* meaning 'dexterous, skilled, handy, able, clever'; *cheka*, meaning 'clever, skilful, shrewd; skilled in'; or *kalla* meaning 'clever, able, dexterous'.[25] There are references to dexterous potters (*dakkho kumbhakāro*),[26] able bath-attendants (*dakkho nahāpako*),[27] skilled surgeons (*bhisakko cheko*),[28] clever accountants (*gaṇako cheko*),[29] and dexterous disputants.[30] If the sources wished to stress that ethics was exclusively a technical or skilled activity after this fashion then the vocabulary was to hand, but *kusala* remains the preferred term. In a passage in *Milinda's Questions* where examples of moral and technical commendation are found together it is *kusala* that is reserved for moral approval while technical approval is denoted by *cheka* (*Miln*. 290–94).

Structured Virtues

It should be noted that progress depends upon a structured cultivation of the virtues in the manner set out in the Eightfold Path. A limited or random effort in the pursuit of *kusala* will not achieve the desired soteriological effect. Buddhaghosa sometimes speaks of two kinds of *kusala*, one leading to rebirth (*vaṭṭa-gāmī*) and the other leading to the end of rebirth (*vivaṭṭa-gāmī*) (e.g. *MA*.i.89ff.). As an instance of the former he mentions family affection, and of the latter the specific Buddhist practices such as the 'foundations of mindfulness' which lead to *nibbāna* (*DA*.iii.847). The distinction now as before is between virtuous action which is incorporated into a soteriological structure and that which is not. A little later he tells us that the monastic life is linked to the cultivation of '*lokuttara-puñña*' up to the destruction of the *āsavas*, and that this is described as '*kusala* which leads the end of rebirth' (*vivaṭṭa-gāmī*) (*DA*.iii.858). It would appear from this that *kusala* and *puñña* go hand in hand all the way up to enlightenment. The point, however, is that virtue is not a simple quantum, like a tank to be filled to the top. Only a specific blend or configuration of the virtues will achieve the desired result. Buddhaghosa makes this point in discussing the relationship of the five *indriyas*, showing how too much *paññā* can be a danger:

> However, what is particularly recommended is balancing faith with understanding (*paññā*), and concentration with energy . . . One strong in understanding and weak in faith errs on the side of cunning and is as hard to cure as a disease caused by medicine.[31]

He also points out how one overdeveloped in *paññā* can fall into error by thinking that virtue just means having good intentions; such a person never gets round to actually doing any good deeds, and as a result is reborn in hell.[32] The moral virtues and the intellectual virtues are each inadequate in isolation: Buddhist soteriological action requires a fusion of the two. The question of which specific virtues are to be cultivated can be found by reference to the Buddha's discourses or more conveniently in the Abhidhammic tabulations discussed in Chapter 3. By means of the right combination of virtuous qualities such as faith (*saddhā*), shame (*hiri*), remorse (*ottappa*), energy (*viriya*) and understanding (*paññā*), what is wrongful is renounced (*akusalaṃ pajahati*) and the good is cultivated (*kusalaṃ bhāveti*) (*A*.iv.353).

Puñña

The cultivation of virtue is accompanied by pleasant results, and in the commentaries *kusala* is often said to lead to pleasant consequences.[33] I suggest that it is the pleasant consequences of good deeds which are designated by the term '*puñña*' and not some separate category of moral action. As was the case with *kusala*, there is no reason for *puñña* to be avoided, as we see from the following: 'Monks, do not fear *puñña*, it is another name for happiness. That which is *puñña* is pleasant, enjoyable, lovely, delightful.'[34]

Premasiri is quite right to point out that *kusala* and *puñña* are related but not synonymous. He writes:

> There is reason to believe that in the Canonical period *kusala* signified something different from *puñña* although there are instances in which there is overlapping of the senses (1976: 67).

I suggest he is mistaken, however, in his interpretation that *kusala* and *puñña* refer to different classes of actions with different sets of consequences. He states:

> It becomes clear that acts of *puñña* were conceived in early Buddhism as deeds of positive merit, which bring about, as their consequences, enjoyment of a sensuous kind, but not generally of a spiritual kind. *Kusala* on the other hand emphasizes the non-sensuous, spiritual bliss, which results from it, and culminates in the eradication of the defilements of *rāga* (lust), *dosa* (hate) and *moha* (delusion). Hence the term that is invariably used in specifying the good actions which lead to the spiritual bliss of *nibbāna* is *kusala*, whereas the term more frequently used for specifying the good actions which lead to sensuous enjoyment and happiness in *saṃsāra* is *puñña* (1976: 69).

Premasiri does not, however, explain by virtue of what these two classes of actions are distinct and how they come to have such different consequences. Even the most simple 'deeds of positive merit' are *kusala*, and the designation of '*kusala*' is not restricted to lofty or spiritually sophisticated activity. To drive a wedge between *kusala* and *puñña* would require clear scriptural evidence denying that *kusala* could be predicated of *puñña* actions, and in the absence of such evidence it seems safe to assume that *kusala* and *puñña* do not denote qualitatively different types of acts. If they were opposed in some way and had such different soteriological implications there is little doubt that the Buddha would have taken care to point it out.

Two Aspects of the same Action

I suggest instead that *puñña* and *kusala* do not describe two kinds of actions but emphasise different aspects of one and the same action. Premasiri himself comes close to admitting this:

> That the use of *kusala* and *puñña* in the *Nikāyas* is sometimes overlapping is a fact that may be admitted. That a deed which was considered to be *puñña* was also considered to be *kusala* and *vice versa* is also admissible on the evidence of the Pali *Nikāyas*. For this reason there are instances in which *puñña* and *kusala* are used in the *Nikāyas* as if they were synonyms (1976: 72).

If the two terms overlap to this extent it is most unlikely that they refer to separate classes of actions. On the contrary, the reason for the overlap is that every virtuous action is *both kusala and puñña*. The meaning of *kusala* has already been made clear: *kusala* and *akusala* describe the moral status of actions and dispositions *vis-à-vis* the *summum bonum*. *Puñña*, on the other hand, describes the experiential consequences of moral activity suffered by the agent. *Puñña* refers to the felt consequences of an increase or decrease in virtue on the part of the moral actor. Since *nibbāna* is the end of suffering the participation in nibbānic goodness will be accompanied by a reduction in suffering (or an increase in happiness). Indeed, happiness and the accumulation of *puñña* are equated (*sukho puññassa uccayo*) (*Dh*.118), and Buddhaghosa tells us that one who is virtuous suffers no painful feelings (*DA*.iii.1050). The accumulation of vice, on the other hand, will indubitably lead to an increase in suffering.

The Position of the *Arahat*

What has complicated the picture is the apparently anomalous moral status of the *Arahat*. The *Arahat* is described in the Canon as being free from, or having passed beyond, *puñña* and *pāpa*,[35] and on the strength of this it is commonly asserted that he has 'gone beyond good and evil'. This rather bold claim must be treated with circumspection since, as we saw above, the *Arahat* certainly has not gone beyond *kusala*, and *kusala* is the term which *par excellence* denotes ethical goodness. So how is it that *kusala* can be predicated of the *Arahat* while *puñña* may not? How can he at one and the same time have perfected ethics and yet gone beyond it? The explanation for this may be as follows. An *Arahat* is perfect in virtue and for him the experiential consequences of virtue cannot fluctuate. As he has maximised his ethical potential there can be no increase or decrease in his virtue or in his happiness. He is completely good, and happiness, according to Buddhism, is tied to goodness.[36] Since his goodness can neither increase nor decrease neither can his happiness and hence neither can his *puñña*. *Puñña* is *kusala*-dependent: it is said that *puñña* increases as a result of undertaking virtuous (*kusala*) things.[37] However, when *kusala* is perfect and complete, *puñña*, as an experiential indicator or epiphenomenon of moral progress, is redundant. *Puñña* is a function of progress in *kusala*; since an *Arahat* no longer progresses in *kusala* it is meaningless to speak of him as producing *puñña*. He will, of course, continue to enjoy the secondary consequences of his virtue while he lives, but the experiential *quantum* of these consequences cannot be increased or decreased as they can for a non-*Arahat*. The *puñña–pāpa* continuum is therefore meaningful for the non-*Arahat* but meaningless for the *Arahat*. The *Arahat* has gone beyond the stage when it would be meaningful to speak of an increase or decrease in his happiness: he has gone beyond the possibility of *puñña* and *pāpa* (*puññañca papāñca bāhetvā*). The *Arahat* has participated to the fullness of his capacity in the supreme good; he has done what needed to be done and there is nothing further for him to achieve. His actions continue to display moral excellence since the sphere of *nibbāna* is also the sphere of *kusala*; the sphere of *puñña*, however, is now left behind.

Puñña and Rebirth

All *kusala/puñña* actions, i.e. all moral deeds, have consequences for the agent both in the present life and in future lives. Let us look briefly at what these consequences might be. We may take *sīla* as our example although the consequences of *dāna* are similar (*A*.iii.39). The five benefits of *sīla* which have already been listed in Chapter 2 are specified as follows:

1. A large fortune produced through diligence.
2. A good reputation.
3. Entering confident and unconfused into any assembly.
4. An unconfused death.
5. A happy rebirth in heaven.

We may note at once that all of these are secondary, contingent, consequences of moral actions. As I have said, the primary effect of *sīla* is deontic in that through *sīla* one participates in nibbānic values, in what is good and right. As regards the contingent non-moral consequences of ethical action listed above it will be noted that apart from the final one there is nothing particularly Buddhist about them. The same consequences might well have been expected by a contemporary of the Buddha in ancient Greece who cultivated the classical virtues of Prudence, Justice, Temperance and Fortitude. And leaving aside the possibility of future existences, the whole list of five could happily be accommodated within the framework of Christian ethics. This list of benefits demystifies *kamma* to quite an extent: all that is claimed in respect of the kammic consequences of moral virtue are the kind of auspicious results which might be expected in many cultures the world over.

Only the fifth benefit, the heavenly rebirth as one of a series of rebirths, has a Buddhist dimension to it, and the hedonic content of the new arising is spoken of in terms of *puñña* (e.g. S.i.18; *Dh*.18). It is noteworthy that at the moment of death there is said to occur a vision (*kammanimitta*) of the significant moral actions which will be determinative in respect of the forthcoming rebirth, and an intimation of the realm in which rebirth will occur (*gatinimitta*). It is in defining the conditions of rebirth that moral action determines most fundamentally the non-moral quality of our lives. *Puñña* defines the circumstances of this, from its location (heaven, hell, human or animal) down to matters of social status such as caste and wealth. In this way moral choices determine not only inward virtue (*kusala*), but also govern the external circumstances (*puñña*) of the world in which our future moral choices will be made. It follows that since the *Arahat* will not be reborn there is no sense in which the term *puñña* can apply to him.

Kant on Virtue and Happiness

The relationship between *kusala* and *puñña* constitutes the *summum bonum* of Buddhism in a manner similar to the way in which the conjunction of virtue and happiness is understood by Kant. Kant points out that the concept of the Highest Good (*summum bonum*) embraces two components in a synthetic relationship. First there is moral perfection or virtue as the supreme end (*bonum supremum*), or unconditional condition which is subject (instrumental) to no other. To this may be added the totality of non-moral goods (summed up as 'happiness') into a whole known as the *bonum consummatum* or complete good.[38] It is 'complete' in the sense of being complete in itself and not part of a yet larger whole of the same kind. Kant's view, stated in its simplest terms, is that it would be irrational if virtue were not conjoined with happiness, with the latter experienced in proportion to the former. In Buddhism the mechanism which ensures this conjunction is karma, while for Kant it was left in the hands of the supreme being. He writes:

> For to be in need of happiness and also worthy of it yet not to partake of it could not be in accordance with the complete volition of an omnipotent rational being, if we assume such only for the sake of argument. Inasmuch as virtue and happiness together constitute the highest good for one person, and happiness in exact proportion to morality (as the worth of a person and his worthiness to be happy) constitutes that of a possible world, the highest good means the whole, the perfect good, wherein virtue is always the supreme good, being the condition having no condition superior to it, while happiness, though something always pleasant to him who possesses it, is not of itself absolutely good in every respect but always presupposes conduct in accordance with the moral law and its condition.[39]

Applying Kant's distinction in the present context the *summum bonum* is *nibbāna*; the *bonum supremum* is virtue (*kusala*); and the *bonum consummatum* is the conjunction of virtue with happiness (*kusala* plus *puñña*).

Summary

Let us now summarise our views in respect of *kamma*. *Kamma* means action in the sense of 'religious' action, i.e. action which is soteriologically potent. Such action can either promote or hinder liberation. *Kamma* describes one's accumulated potential in this area with respect to the final goal. At one point King, taking a lead from Mrs Rhys Davids, comes close to recognising this when he writes: 'In this context to gain merit means to become increasingly more worthy, to gain more and more spiritual capacity which will enable one to achieve sainthood in the end' (1964: 55). He speaks of good *kamma* as 'the quantitative enlargement of the self', by which he means 'the long process of character-formation which, according to Buddhism, has preceded the appearance of the saint or Buddha, or for that matter, even the more-than-average good man' (1964: 60). 'This facet', he continues a few pages later, 'clearly modifies the crassness of the merit doctrine in the direction of a strengthening of the concept of cumulative worth, or intrinsic goodness, as its essential meaning' (1964: 63). Yet King cannot free himself from the notion that moral action is hostile to liberation and ultimately falls back upon the 'scaffold theory' of *kamma*.

Kamma in Buddhism is not simply a form of sympathetic magic by which the universe mechanically rewards moral action with material prizes. It is not an occult power but an aspect of Dependent-Origination; stated simply it is the principle that moral actions have consequences (*kamma-niyama*). *Kamma* is a value-free description of a class of actions which are of soteriological importance. All kammic actions stand in a relationship to the *summum bonum* and the moral status of this relationship is defined by the terms *kusala* and *akusala*. Kammic acts (these may be physical or mental) which are *kusala* are in harmony with nibbānic values. Kammic actions are cumulative and transformative and the primary effect of their performance is to either extend or reduce the scope of the actor's participation in nibbānic goods. The generation and experience of *kammic* acts and their primary consequences, which are internal to the agent, all take place within the five *khandhas*. As mentioned in Chapter Three, this may be described in terms of the eradication of *saṅkhāras*. There is in addition a set of non-moral secondary consequences entrained by moral acts which can be evaluated and quantified in hedonistic terms (*puñña/pāpa*). These consequences become manifest to some extent within the course of a lifetime but are experienced most dramatically in the circumstances of rebirth. When the individual *santāna* is completely purified in Arahatship, moral actions no longer act to eliminate vice; since there is no corresponding increase in happiness and no more rebirth it is said that the *Arahat* has gone beyond *puñña* and *pāpa*.

6

Ethics in the Mahāyāna

The nature of Mahāyāna ethics is complex and there is evidence of development in a number of directions, at times contradictory ones. This means that it can appear very different depending on the perspective adopted, a feature which makes it difficult to categorise. Hindery makes the following comment in his 1978 sketch of Mahāyāna ethics:

> There are enough references to precepts, virtues, and moral models to suggest that MB [= Mahāyāna Buddhism] involves a moral perspective not merely as a worldview, but directly as a system. In either case ongoing research may uncover the phenomenon that MB morality contains no precepts and values which cannot be found in alternate or even stronger forms in other major ethical traditions. On the other hand, it may more profoundly realise that a new moral gestalt or ethos ensouls this ethics with a unique and still unappreciated dynamic, one symbolised by *bodhisattvas*, who go on living for others and surrender not to death, and by savior Buddhas with extended hands (1978: 248).

In the Mahāyāna, ethics (*śīla*) is classified as one of the six Perfections (*pāramitās*) and in section (1) we examine the value-structure of the Mahāyāna in terms of these ideals. Following this we move on to consider developments in Mahāyāna *śīla* and we will approach these through a consideration of the Mahāyāna's own assessment of its superiority to the Hīnayāna in this respect. This task will occupy us in section (2) and will involve an examination of the innovative ethical categorisations introduced by the Mahāyāna which distinguish it from the Small Vehicle: here we consider both the normative ethics of the Large Vehicle and the apparently transmoral doctrine of Skilful Means (*upāya-kauśalya*). In section (3) we enquire further into the ethical implications of the doctrine of Skilful Means and distinguish two principal aspects of it. It will become clear that there was no Copernican revolution in

Buddhist ethics with the advent of the Mahāyāna and that its innovations in this field are best understood as a supplement to the morality of its predecessor rather than a rejection of it. It is fair, however, to speak of a 'paradigm shift' by which the Mahāyāna recalibrated the value-structure of the Small Vehicle.

1. THE PERFECTIONS

In Mahāyāna sources the path to enlightenment is set out in the form of a set of accomplishments or Perfections (*pāramitās*). The Perfections are most commonly enumerated as six, although the list is sometimes extended to ten. The list of ten is as follows:

1. Generosity (*dāna*).
2. Morality (*śīla*).
3. Patience (*kṣānti*).
4. Courage (*vīrya*).
5. Meditation (*samādhi*).
6. Insight (*prajñā*).
7. Skilful Means (*upāya-kauśalya*).
8. Vow (*praṇidhāna*).
9. Strength (*bala*).
10. Knowledge (*jñāna*).

The first six seem to have greater importance than the final four and are frequently discussed at length while the others are acknowledged but treated less exhaustively.[1] The six Perfections bear some resemblance to the five faculties (*indriyas*) of the Pali Canon namely Faith (*saddhā*), Energy (*viriya*), Mindfulness (*sati*), Meditation (*samādhi*) and Insight (*paññā*). It will be noted that *sīla* does not occur as one of the *indriyas* although it is found in the list of ten perfections (*pāramīs*) in the *Jātakas*; these are said to be the qualities that make a Buddha (*Buddha-kārakā-dhammā*).[2] The Mahāyāna scheme of the six Perfections may be related to the scheme of *Sīla*, *Samādhi* and *Paññā* in the Eightfold Path. This is explained in the commentary to the *Ornament of Mahāyāna Sūtras* where it is stated that the first three *pāramitās* correspond to 'Higher Morality' (*adhiśīla*), the fifth to 'Higher Meditation' (*adhicitta*), and the sixth to 'Higher Wisdom' (*adhiprajñā*), while the fourth (*vīrya*) is shared in common by all three divisions.[3] The equivalence between the six

Perfections and the three categories of the Eightfold Path may be seen in the following diagram:

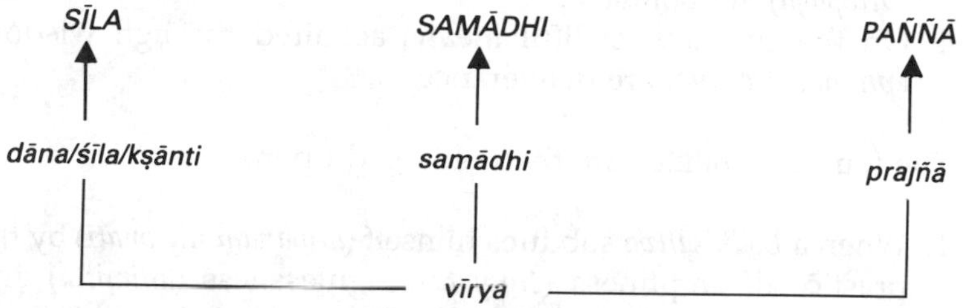

Ethics and Insight

As I have suggested is the case in the Small Vehicle, final perfection is also conceived of as bilateral by the Mahāyāna. Once again a distinction is made between the moral perfections and the perfection of insight or knowledge. We may note the change in terminology introduced by the Mahāyāna: whereas the Small Vehicle defines its basic values as insight (*paññā*) and morality (*sīla*) the Mahāyāna refers to these as insight (*prajñā*) and means (*upāya*), or insight (*prajñā*) and compassion (*karuṇā*). The terminological change reflects a new emphasis on the function of moral virtue as a dynamic other-regarding quality, rather than primarily concerned with personal development and self-control. As before, Mahāyāna sources are conscious of the importance of both of these components as constituents of the final good:

> For pure *Bodhisattvas*, their mother (*mātṛ*) is the perfection of wisdom (*prajñāpāramitā*), their father (*pitṛ*) is skillfulness in means (*upāyakauśalya*): the Leaders of the world (*nāyaka*) are born of such parents (*VNS*. VII.6.1.).[4]

So essential is this interdependence that in the absence of either element the result is bondage rather than liberation. This is stated in the *Teachings of Vimalakirti* (*VNS*. IV.16) where four possible combinations of the two components are set out:

1. Wisdom not acquired through skillful means (*upāyānupātta-prajñā*) is bondage (*bandhana*).

2. On the contrary, wisdom acquired through skillful means (*upāyopātta-prajñā*) is deliverance.
3. Skillful means not acquired through wisdom (*prajñānupāttopāya*) are bondage.
4. On the contrary, skillful means acquired through wisdom (*prajñopāttopāya*) are deliverance.

The four possibilities are then enlarged upon:

1. When a *Bodhisattva* subdues himself (*ātmanaṃ niyamati*) by the practice of emptiness (*śūnyatā*), signlessness (*ānimitta*) and wishlessness (*apraṇihita*), but abstains from adorning his body with the primary and secondary physical marks (*lakṣanānuvyañjana*), from adorning his Buddha-field (*buddha-kṣetra-alaṃkāra*) and from helping beings ripen (*sattva-paripācana*), this is wisdom not acquired through skillful means and it is bondage.
2. When a *Bodhisattva* subdues his mind (*svacittaṃ niyamati*) by the practice of emptiness, signlessness and wishlessness and, at the same time, adorns his body with the primary and secondary marks, he adorns his Buddha-field and helps beings ripen, this is wisdom acquired through skillful means and it is deliverance.
3. When a *Bodhisattva* settles (*avatiṣṭhati*) into false views (*dṛṣṭi*), the invasion of the passions (*kleśaparyutthāna*), the residual tendencies (*anuśaya*), affection (*anunaya*) and aversion (*pratigha*), but does not transfer to perfect enlightenment the good roots that he has cultivated, these are skillful means not acquired through wisdom and it is bondage.
4. When a *Bodhisattva* rejects (*jahāti*) false views, the invasion of the passions, residual tendencies, affection and aversion, and transfers to perfect enlightenment the good roots he has cultivated without producing pride (*garva*), these are skillful means acquired through wisdom and it is deliverance (*VNS.* IV.16f).

In (1) a *bodhisattva* turns his back on beings and seeks his own liberation in the manner of the *Śrāvakas*. Even though he knows the doctrine of *śūnyatā* he fails to understand the sameness (*samatā*) of all beings existentially as a result of affective inhibition. His development is unbalanced and his search for an individual enlightenment is doomed to failure. In (2) this error is not made and the knowledge the *bodhisattva* has gained is put at the service of all beings through his use of Skilful Means. In (3) a *bodhisattva* is caught up in the emotional confusion of *saṃsāra* and labours in vain because his actions are not guided by insight. In (4) a *bodhisattva* is not hampered in his activity by delusion and is able to direct his actions appropriately and efficiently towards supreme enlightenment. The two of the above four possibilities which constitute deliverance (numbers 2 and 4) show how *prajñā* and *upāya* are intertwined in the final good. If, however, there is any imbalance between the two and one is neglected the result is bondage and not liberation. sGam-po-pa explains why neither *prajñā* nor *upāya* are adequate by themselves:

> Why then, if this awareness (*prajñā*) is enough, should beneficial expediency (*upāya*) as expressed by liberality and the other perfections be necessary? The answer is that awareness (*prajñā*) alone is not enough . . . Any *bodhisattva* who resorts to the one without the other falls into a one-sided *Nirvāṇa*, into the desired peace and quietism of the *Śrāvakas*, and is, as it were, bound to this *Nirvāṇa*.

And *vice-versa*:

> If we resort to beneficial expediency (*upāya*) without discriminating awareness (*prajñā*), we do not go beyond the level and the path of unintelligent ordinary beings but remain bound by the chains of *saṃsāra* (*Jewel*, 1970: 203).

The simile is given of a man walking: *prajñā* is the eyes and *upāya* is the feet, and no progress is possible unless the two work in harmony. The same image is found in the *Perfection of Wisdom in 8000 Lines*:

> Just as, Kauśika, people born blind . . . cannot, without a leader, go along a path and get to a village, town or city; just so, Giving, Morality, Patience, Vigour and Trance cannot by themselves be called 'perfections', for without the perfection of wisdom they are as if born blind (tr. Conze, 1973: 136).

Different Emphasis

The *Perfection of Wisdom* literature naturally seeks to emphasise the importance of *prajñā,* but also points out the dangers of excess in this respect. According to the *Prajñā-pāramitā-upadeśa-sūtra*:

> If one practises only *prajñā* and not the other five *dharmas*, good qualities (*guṇa*) will be lacking . . . Whoever follows *prajñā* alone falls into false views (*mithyādṛṣṭi*) (quoted by Poussin, *Siddhi*, 623).

Without the first five perfections (*upāya*) there cannot be complete enlightenment but only the limited enlightenment of the *Śrāvakas*. The *Introduction to Madhyamaka* describes how morality is practised in three different ways by the followers of each of the three vehicles, and states that only when it is accompanied by great compassion (*mahākaruṇā*), Skilful Means (*upāyakauśalya*), and the non-abandonment of all beings does, it produce the perfect purity of the *bodhisattva*-stage. For followers of the *Śrāvaka*- and *Pratyekabuddha-yānas* however, morality is merely the cause of personal happiness and an auspicious rebirth, and does not benefit others (*M.Av.* 2.7). For the Mahāyāna, *śīla* is at one and the same time a source of purification and happiness for the practitioner and an example and benefit to others. This feature is brought out in the *Dharma-prabhāva* section of the *Bodhisattva Stage* (*Bodhisattvabhūmi*) which lists the consequences of each of the perfections. According to this (72) *śīla* has a fourfold advantage:

1. The *bodhisattva* abandons immorality (*dauhśīlyaṃ prajahati*).
2. He ripens other beings by his equanimity and power of attraction (*samānārthatāya ca saṃgraha-vastunā sattvāṃ paripācayati*).
3. He offers security to all beings by not obstructing them (*sarva-sattvānām ca sarva-prakārair aviheṭhanatāya abhayam anuprayacchati*).
4. He obtains a heavenly rebirth after death (*kāyasya bhedāt sugatau svargaloke deveṣūpapadyate*).

At the same time other sources confine themselves in a more Hīnayānic spirit to listing the purely personal advantages of *śīla*. The *Ornament of Mahāyāna Sūtras* (*MSA*. XVI.19) lists six qualities of *śīla*:

1. It has for its end a state of peace (*śamabhāvānta*).
2. It produces good rebirth and stability of mind (*sugati-sthiti-dāyaka*).
3. It is a foundation for all virtues (*sarvaguṇānām-pratiṣṭhā*).
4. It is calm (*śānta*) through pacifying the defilements (*kleśa-paridāha-śāntyā*).
5. It is without fear (*nirbhīta*).
6. It is associated with the production of merit (*puṇya-sambhāra-saṃyuta*).

The function, advantages and benefits of *śīla* described in Chapter 2 are found throughout Mahāyāna literature and the descriptions are not dissimilar to those found in sources from the Small Vehicle.[5] In its attitude to morality the Mahāyāna demonstrates both change and continuity with respect to the Small Vehicle. This will become apparent in the course of this chapter and particularly in the following section where we examine the Mahāyāna classifications of *śīla*.

2. THE CATEGORIES OF MAHĀYĀNA ETHICS

Our attention for the rest of this chapter will be directed to the ways in which the Mahāyāna classifies and understands its own morality and distinguishes it from that of the Small Vehicle. Signs of dissatisfaction with the rigidity of the latter are already in evidence among the Mahāsaṃghikas, who maintained the freedom of a Streamwinner (*sotāpanna*) to commit any offence save the five acts of immediate retribution (*ānantariya*) (Bareau, 1955: 67). The Gokulikas also felt that the *Vinaya* rules were inappropriate to the conduct of a *bodhisattva* (Dutt, 1970: 73). As pointed out by Dutt, the moral rules of the Mahāyāna are not conveniently grouped together in a *Vinaya* after the fashion of the Small Vehicle but are to be found in a variety of sources. 'Thus', he writes, 'we clearly see that the Mahāyānists depended upon the rules scattered in the Mahāyāna texts and did not possess a code of the *Vinaya* rules' (1930: 292). And the *Hōbōgirin* comments:

> The discipline of the *Bodhisattvas* never achieved the canonical uniformity which the Discipline of the Hearers had in the Small Vehicle: swayed by diverse tendencies it constantly oscillated between them.[6]

There are, however, certain texts which deal more specifically with moral conduct than others. Dutt continues:

> The only Mahāyānic works accessible to us that can be called a code of disciplinary rules are the Chinese *Brahmajāla Sūtra* and the two works of Śāntideva, viz *Sikṣāsamuccaya* and *Bodhicaryāvatāra*.

Dutt does not mention the *Bodhisattva Stage* which embodies a more systematic code of disciplinary rules than either of the two works of Śāntideva. Indeed, the *Chapter on Morality* (*śīla-paṭala*) of the *Bodhisattva Stage* is a more important *locus* for information on Mahāyāna *śīla* than either of the other two works. The text in fact describes itself as a *'bodhisattva-piṭaka'* (157.15) and provides a comprehensive (if in places somewhat radical) statement of Mahāyāna ethics. The text clearly regards itself as authoritative for Mahāyāna ethics and discipline and it would appear to be an early and influential source.[7]

Mahāyāna Superiority

The *Summary of the Mahāyāna* (*Mahāyānasaṃgraha*) provides a convenient summary of the superiority of Mahāyāna morality to that of the Hīnayāna. According to this the morality of the Mahāyāna can be summed up (*samāsatah*) as superior in four ways:

A. In its classifications (*prabheda-viśeṣa*).
B. In its common and separate rules (*sādhāraṇa-asādhāraṇa-śikṣāviśeṣa*).
C. In breadth (*vaipulya-viśeṣa*).
D. In depth (*gāmbhīrya-viśeṣa*).

This fourfold classification will provide a convenient basis for our discussion of Mahāyāna morality, and each point will be dealt with in turn. We will explore the content of each category through a variety of sources, although the content of point A (*prabheda-viśeṣa*) will be supplied entirely by reference to the *Bodhisattva Stage*. Each of the divisions will be considered in some detail with the exception of the third since this is merely a general statement of the overall superiority of Mahāyāna ethics. In brief, point A relates to an innovative threefold classification of *śīla*, and point B to the degree of latitude in the infringement of moral norms allowed to a *bodhisattva*. Point D embraces the fundamental and radical innovation of the notion of Skilful Means (*upāya-kauśalya*) as a category of transmoral action. A summary of the four points of superiority may be set out as follows.

A. Superiority in Classification
(*prabheda-viśeṣa*)

(a) Temperance (*saṃvara-śīla*)
(b) Cultivation of Virtue (*kuśala-dharma-saṃgrāhaka-śīla*)
(c) Altruism (*sattva-artha-kriyā-śīla*)

B. Superiority in Common and Separate Rules
(*Sādhāraṇa-asādhāraṇa-śikṣā-viśeṣa*)

(a) Serious Offences (*prakṛti-sāvadya*)
(b) Minor Offences (*pratikṣepaṇa-sāvadya*)

C. Superiority in Breadth
(*vaipulya-viśeṣa*)

(a) Multiple and Extensive Rules
(b) Gain of Immense Merit
(c) Disposition to procure welfare and happiness of all beings
(d) Establishment of Supreme and Perfect Enlightenment

D. Superiority in Depth
(*gāmbhīrya-viśeṣa*)

(a) The use of Skilful Means (*upāya-kauśalya*)

A. Superiority in Classification

This is the most important of the four 'superiorities' and will be dealt with at greater length since it is the foundation for the other three. According to the *Summary of the Mahāyāna*, as noted above, the morality of the Mahāyāna is distinguished by virtue of its comprehensive classifications and scope (*prabheda-viśeṣa*). The whole scheme of Mahāyāna ethics is encapsulated in this classification within which three facets or aspects may be distinguished:

(a) Morality as temperance or restraint (*saṃvara-śīla*).
(b) Morality as pursuit of the good (*kuśala-dharma-saṃgrāhaka-śīla*).
(c) Morality as altruism or supererogation (*sattva-artha-kriyā-śīla*).

We learn from the *Summary of the Mahāyāna* (*M. Saṃgr*. VI.2) that the first is the support (*niśraya*) for the other two. The second is the support for the qualities of a Buddha (*Buddhadharma-samudāgama*), and the third is the support for the maturation of beings (*sattva-paripācana*). The superiority of the Mahāyāna in this respect, as the commentary explains, lies in the fact that the *Śrāvakas* possess only the first of these three divisions. Accordingly, they are ignorant of the important third division and do not practise morality for the benefit of other beings. This threefold classification is widely accepted by Mahāyāna sources,[8] and a full and detailed exposition of it is given by the *Bodhisattva Stage*. First of all let us look at the explanation which the text gives of the threefold classification of Mahāyāna *śīla*; following this we may consider its significance as a *bodhisattva-piṭaka*.

(a) Morality as Temperance (*saṃvara-śīla*)
In the explanation of the first category (*saṃvara-śīla*) (141.1–144.1), it is said that a *bodhisattva* established therein abandons the world even if he possesses universal dominion (*cakravarti-rājyam*). He looks upon such dominion as if it were a piece of grass or ordure (*amedhya*). Moreover, his renunciation is undertaken out of purity of resolve (*āśayaviśuddhatā*) and not, as with some inferior persons (*nihīna-puruṣa*), out of the desire to earn their livelihood as renunciates. Nor is his motive the enjoyment of those pleasures which will accrue from the practice of *saṃvara-śīla*, and he looks upon all pleasures as they really are, namely as the entrance to an abyss of great and manifold terrors. Apart from the future pleasures which may arise from his good conduct, the *bodhisattva* takes no delight in present ones such as wealth and honour. He looks upon such things with true discrimination as if they were vomited-up food (*vāntāśanam iva*). Turning away from such worldly matters he delights in solitude.

The *bodhisattva* is strict in his observance of the training-precepts (*śikṣāpada*) and does not tolerate evil speech or the slightest evil thought. When his mind is distracted by behaviour of that sort he experiences intense remorse (*tīvra vipratisāra*) and sees the danger of it (*ādīnava-darsaṇa*). In future cases, when evil words and thoughts have barely had time to arise he recalls that vision and renounces those evil acts and thoughts. By constant exercise of renunciation (*pratisaṃharaṇa-abhyāsata*) he begins to take pleasure in not performing evil actions and in opposing them. By following all the *śikṣāpadas* of a *bodhisattva* he becomes restrained with the immeasurable and inconceivable (*acintya*) restraint of body and speech.

So much in relation to himself. In relation to others the *bodhisattva* established in *saṃvara-śīla* does not seek out their faults (*doṣa*) and inner weaknesses (*antara-skhalita*). He has no malicious or hostile thoughts in the presence of violent (*raudra*) beings. Instead, on the basis of great compassion, the *bodhisattva* experiences thoughts of sympathy and the desire to be of service. He has no thoughts of physical violence, angry scolding (*ākrośa-roṣa*) or rebuking (*paribhāṣana*). When a *bodhisattva* is established in *saṃvara-śīla* he becomes endowed with the fivefold faculty of non-heedlessness (*apramāda*) by which he makes amends for offences (*āpatti*) committed in the past and resolves not to repeat them. In summary it is said that he conceals his good points and reveals his sins; he is satisfied with little, patient in suffering, of unwearied nature, not arrogant (*anuddhata*), not fickle (*acapala*) and of calm deportment (*praśānteryā-pathá*).

(b) Morality as the Cultivation of Virtue (kusála-dharma-saṃgrāhaka-śīla)

This is defined as: 'Whatever virtue (*kuśala*) a *bodhisattva* accumulates (*ācinoti*) by body or speech towards the great awakening (*mahabodhāya*) after having taken up morality as temperance' (139.1–3). A *bodhisattva* who has established his morality through the practice of *saṃvara-śīla* bases himself upon it and makes efforts in learning, contemplation, in calming meditation (*śamatha*) and in insight-meditation (*vipaśyanā*). Apart from meditation there are numerous ways in which the *bodhisattva* accumulates what is good in this respect. He treats and serves his preceptor respectfully and attends the sick with compassion. As regards society at large he congratulates any well-said thing and pleases others when he speaks. He forgives others every transgression, always makes the proper resolutions (*samyak-praṇidhāna*) and pays respect to the three jewels. He is zealous and always resolved towards what is good (*kuśala-pakṣe*). He is vigilant (*apramāda*) in body and speech and guards the *sikṣāpadas* by mindfulness (*smṛti*), conscientiousness (*samprajanya*) and conduct. He guards the doors of the senses, knows moderation in eating, stays awake in the early and later parts of the night, serves virtuous persons (*satpuruṣa-sevī*) and relies on his spiritual friends (*kalyāṇa-mitra-samniśritaḥ*). He looks out for his own faults and rectifies them by confessing his transgressions (*atyaya*). In short, the effect of *kuśala-dharma-saṃgrāhaka-śīla* is the accumulation, preservation and increase of good qualities (*dharmas*) of the kind outlined above.

(c) Morality as Altruism (sattva-artha-kriyā-śīla)
This third and most important category goes by two names, being alternatively referred to as 'the morality which shows favour to beings' (*sattvānugrāhaka-śīla*). Both appellations convey quite clearly the function of this category, which is subdivided into eleven sections or varieties (*ākāra*) to be acquired one by one.

1. Taking part (*sahayī-bhāva*) in the various activities of beings. This covers a multitude of activities, such as accompanying people along the road (*adhva-gamanāgamana*), thinking and reflecting on what is to be done, and sharing in meritorious actions and misfortunes.
2. Taking care of the sick. As well as physical disabilities psychological disorders are also to be taken into account. The *bodhisattva* leads the blind and communicates to the deaf by sign-language (*hasta-saṃvācikayā*). He carries along those without limbs. For those less seriously afflicted he removes the torment of lustful desires (*kāma-cchanda*) and the other vices. He gives aid to travellers by offering them a seat and massaging their limbs (*aṅga-prapīdanena*).
3. Appropriate teachings (*nyāya-upadeśa*) in secular and sacred matters (*laukika-lokottareṣu artheṣu*). Here the *bodhisattva* instructs beings in a suitable way so that they will abandon evil conduct. He tries to instil faith and right views into those who have fallen by the wayside so that they may eventually transcend all suffering.
4. Being grateful for past services and undertaking appropriate service in return. This involves remembrance of those who have previously rendered service by treating such persons courteously. He offers help even when it is not requested, dispels the sorrow of evil and provides support.
5. Protecting beings from the diverse causes of fear. The *bodhi-*

sattva makes himself the protector (*ārakṣaka*) of beings against such manifold perils as wild animals, whirlpools, kings, thieves, opponents and demons.

6. Dispelling the grief in troubles (*vyāsana*) of a domestic nature involving possessions (*bhoga*) and relatives (*jñāti*).
7. Providing the means of subsistence (*upakaraṇa*) to those who are without them.
8. Attracting a following (*gaṇa-parikarṣana*) through the morality of attraction (*parigrāha-śīlena*). The *bodhisattva* gathers a flock around him and provides his followers with the equipment of the religious life namely a robe, an almsbowl, a bed and medicines for the sick. He also provides them with religious teachings.
9. The morality of being in sympathy or empathising with beings (*cittānuvartana-śīla*). Being in sympathy with beings the *bodhisattva* knows their thoughts and natures. This enables him to behave appropriately in the presence of difficult people. He greets and addresses others even if they do not speak to him. He does not become angry with others and has no desire to reproach them, although he may censure them out of his compassion for them. He does not mock or ridicule others. In general, he constantly considers the condition and state of mind of others through empathy with them.
10. The morality of commending good qualities. (*bhūta-guṇa-samharaṇa-śīla*). Here a *bodhisattva* gladdens others by discoursing with them on the virtues of morality (*śīla*), faith (*śraddhā*), renunciation (*tyāga*) and insight (*prajñā*). He also rebukes (*avasādayati*) beings who transgress but with a mind that is affectionate and unfailing in concern. He acts from sympathy (*anukampā*) and for the good (*hita*) of beings.
11. The use of magic powers (*ṛddhi-bala*) for the propagation of the faith (*buddhaśāsana-avatārāya*). The motives of the *bodhisattva* here are to shock (*uttrāsayitu-kāma*) and convert (*āvarjayitu-kāma*) beings. To do this he makes visible the evil destinies of beings of evil conduct, revealing the horrors of the many different hells. As a result of this the spectators desist from their evil ways. In addition he conjures up a great *bodhisattva* such as Vajrapāni or a huge and powerful demon (*yakṣa*) in order to discipline irreverent people in the assembly. He also brings them under control through a display of magic powers such as creating many forms of himself and passing

> through solid objects like walls and mountains. By performing miracles such as these he is able to win over, gratify and gladden his audience. The onlookers in turn develop those virtues which they previously lacked and enter into the fullness of morality (*śīlasaṃpadi*).

It is clear from the *Bodhisattva Stage* that in the Mahāyāna *śīla* has three functions or aspects: (a) temperance, continence, restraint and self-control (*saṃvara*); (b) a subjective personal moral perfection linked to intellectual cultivation in the quest for enlightenment; (c) an objective recipient-orientated dimension which focuses on the needs of others. It is principally the addition of the third factor which raises the Mahāyāna moral edifice over the head of its predecessor and allows it to claim superiority in scope (*prabheda-viśeṣa*).

A New Rule for Bodhisattvas

One result of this shift in the centre of gravity in Buddhist ethics was the drawing up of a new rule or code of conduct for *bodhisattvas*. The *Bodhisattva Stage* sets out a code of rules (*śikṣāpadas*) in the form of a *'bodhisattva-piṭaka'*. The text does not categorise these rules systematically although the first four are grouped together as 'Offences of Defeat' after the fashion of the Theravāda *Vinaya*. The commentarial tradition enumerates the list of offences as 45 or 46 (Tatz 1986:24). This includes some subdivision, and a complete itemisation yields a list of 52 rules which for convenience may be classified into four sections as follows:

A. *Offences of Defeat (pārājayika-sthāniyā-dharmā): Prohibited*

1. Self-vaunting (*ātmotkarṣanā*) and reviling others (*parapaṃsanā*) by one who is eager for gain and worldly honours (*lābha-satkāra*).
2. Not sharing possessions (*dharma*) and not distributing one's goods (*āmiṣa*) because of selfishness (*mātsarya*).
3. Reacting angrily and striking others.
4. Repudiating the *bodhisattva-piṭaka* (i.e. the present text) and establishing false doctrines.

B. *Prohibited*

1. Failure to perform some daily act of reverence towards the three jewels.

2. Toleration of the discontent (*asamtuṣṭi*) produced by the desire for wealth and honour (*lābha-satkāra*).
3. Disrespect towards a senior monk.
4. Refusing an invitation to a home or to a monastery.
5. Rejecting valuable offerings such as gold, silver and jewels.
6. Refusing to teach the *dharma* to those who request it.
7. Neglecting immoral beings.
8. Observing the minor rules of discipline (*pratikṣepaṇa-sāvadya*) of the *Śrāvakas* in the face of the conflicting needs of others. The three *pratikṣepaṇa-sāvadya* are:
   (a) desiring little (*alpārthatā*),
   (b) being free from responsibilities (*alpakṛtyatā*),
   (c) being free from cares (*alpotsuka-vihāratā*).

C. *The following are permitted*

1. Taking the life of someone about to commit an act entailing immediate retribution (*ānantarya-karma*) in order to prevent them suffering the evil consequences of that act.
2. (a) causing a cruel ruler to fall from his position of authority,
   (b) repossessing property taken from the *Saṅgha* or a *stūpa*,
   (c) causing monks who abuse their positions of authority to lose their rank.
3. Having sexual intercourse with an unmarried woman in order to prevent her producing thoughts of hostility if her advances are rejected.
4. Telling a lie in order to save the lives of beings or to save them from bondage and mutilation.
5. Separating beings from evil friends and bad company through slander.
6. Using harsh speech to discourage beings from evil.
7. Indulging in singing, dancing and idle chatter to convert beings who are attracted by these things.

D. *Prohibited*

1. Having recourse to the five false means of livelihood for a monk namely:
   (a) obtaining alms by hypocrisy (*kuhanā*),
   (b) boasting of religious qualities (*lapanā*),
   (c) hinting at something desired as a donation (*naimittikatā*),
   (d) getting something by means of threats (*naiṣpeṣikatā*),
   (e) getting a gift by referring to a similar gift received from others (*lābhena lābham-niścikīrsutā*).
2. Being excitable (*avyupaśānta*), laughing, sporting and making a

row (*samkilikilāyate*) in the company of others.
3. Teaching that a *bodhisattva* should not strive for nirvana and should not be frightened by the *kleśas* and *upakleśas*.
4. Paying no heed to well-founded words of rebuke (*apaśabda*).
5. Failing to serve the interests of other beings in order to avoid unpleasantness.
6. Returning abuse with abuse, anger with anger, blows with blows, or quarrels with quarrels.
7. Failing to make amends to others after transgressing against them.
8. Refusing an offer of appeasement by others.
9. Nursing a grudge (*krodhāśaya*) against others.
10. Gathering a following with the desire to be served and to obtain material benefit.
11. Sleeping too much.
12. Being excitable (*saṃrakta-citta*) and spending time in groups.
13. Failing to seek proper instruction in mental discipline.
14. Failing to counteract lustful desires (*kāma-cchanda*).
15. Being excessively devoted to trance.
16. Claiming that a *bodhisattva* should not listen to the teachings of the *Śrāvakayāna*.
17. Not exerting oneself in the *bodhisattva-piṭaka* and instead exerting oneself in the *Śrāvakayāna* or in the teachings of the heretics (*tīrthika-śāstra*).
18. Being content and pleased in following the teachings of the heretics.
19. Abusing the *bodhisattva-piṭaka*.
20. Exalting oneself and criticising others in public.
21. Failing to attend the settling of a discussion (*sāmkathya-viniścaya*) relating to the *dharma*.
22. Ridiculing or injuring a preacher of the *dharma* (*dharma-bhāṇaka*).
23. Failing to act as a companion to beings in their activities.
24. Failing to nurse a being who is sick.
25. Failing to teach right conduct to beings engaged in wrongful conduct.
26. Not being mindful of what is done for one (*akṛtajña*).
27. Failing to counteract the sorrow of beings due to domestic calamities (*jñāti-bhoga-vyasana*).
28. Failing to provide the necessities of life to those who request them.

29. Failing to teach and admonish an assembly after establishing one and failing to beg for the equipment of a monk (*pariṣkāra*).
30. Failing to consider the needs of others.
31. Failing to extol the virtues and good qualities of others and not applauding things which are well said.
32. Failing to censure, punish or expel those who have transgressed.
33. Failing to use magical powers to astonish and convert beings.

This marks the end of the list of *śikṣāpadas*. The breakdown of the list of 52 *śikṣāpadas*, in which only the first category is given a title, is as follows:

A	4 offences of defeat (*Pārājayika-sthānīyā-dharmā*)
B	8
C	7
D	33
	52

The *Chapter on Śīla* of the *Bodhisattva Stage* presents itself as the alternative code of conduct for a *bodhisattva* in contrast to the *Vinaya* and *Pātimokkha* of the *Śrāvakayāna*. The single most striking feature in the whole chapter is the group of seven injunctions (group C above) which explicitly authorises the breaking of the first seven of the Ten Good Paths of Action in certain circumstances.[9] The *bodhisattva* is said to commit these offences 'by way of Skilful Means' (*upāya-kauśalena*), and the whole notion of premeditated transgression by a *bodhisattva* is closely tied up with the notion of *upāya*. This interrelation will be considered more fully in section (d) below. The *Bodhisattva-piṭaka* does not seem to have been widely adopted as a normative code of religious conduct in Mahāyāna countries. In Tibet the Mulasārvastivāda *Vinaya* was followed and in China the *Brahmajālasutra*, enjoyed popularity. Both of these insist upon strict compliance with traditional disciplinary norms. In China the *'Bodhisattva-Prātimokṣa'* (*Yu Chia Chieh Pen*) enjoyed considerable prestige up to the time of the T'ang dynasty when it was eclipsed by the popularity of the *Brahmajāla Sūtra* (*Fan Wan Ching*) which acknowledges more explicitly the virtue of filial piety. It is interesting that apparently only the latest of the four Chinese translations (that of the T'ang dynasty) includes the category of permitted offences.[10]

B. Superiority in Common and Separate Rules

This second kind of superiority relates to the distinction between serious offences (*prakṛtisāvadya*) and minor offences (*pratikṣepaṇasāvadya*). According to this the morality of a *bodhisattva* is similar to that of a *Śrāvaka* in one respect but different in another. The similarity is that both are forbidden to commit serious offences, and the difference is that the *bodhisattva* is allowed to commit minor offences while the *Śrāvaka* is not (*M.Saṃgr*. VI.3). Without mentioning either of these technical terms, the *Sūtra on Skilful Means* (*Upayakauśalyasūtra*) summarises the general principle:

> The Buddha teaches Bodhisattvas precepts which need not be strictly and literally observed, but teaches Śrāvakas precepts which must be strictly and literally observed; he teaches Bodhisattvas precepts which are at once permissive and prohibitive, but teaches Śrāvakas precepts which are only prohibitive.[11]

Neither of the terms *prakṛtisāvadya* or *pratikṣepaṇasāvadya* seems to occur in Pali sources[12] although they are known to Vasubandhu (*Bhāṣya*. IV.29ac). Among Mahāyāna sources there is no clear agreement as to the degree of discretion allowed to a *bodhisattva* in the commission of minor transgressions, and we find various formulations of the principle allowing different degrees of laxity in different areas. The serious offences are instanced in *MSU*. VI.3 as 'murder (*prāṇātipāta*), theft (*adattādāna*), and illicit sexual relations (*kāmamithyācāra*), etc., which stem from passion (*rāga*)' (42b.7–16). Two examples of minor offences are also given namely cutting the grass (*tṛṇachedana*) and venturing out in the rainy season.[13] This distinction releases a *bodhisattva* from the straitjacket of the *Vinaya*. But in addition to being released from a restriction he is also charged with an additional obligation which the *Śrāvaka* does not bear. What is wrongful for the *Śrāvaka* may not be wrongful for a *bodhisattva*, but the *bodhisattva* now also has a *duty* to commit a minor offence if the interest of beings is at stake. An example is given in the commentary: if a *Śrāvaka* goes out in the rainy season he commits an offence, but if a *bodhisattva* does *not* go out he may be guilty of an offence if the interests of beings required him to go forth. A summary statement on what is permissible for a *bodhisattva* is given in the *Summary of the Mahāyāna*:

> In short (*samāsata*), *bodhisattvas* can perform and carry out any bodily vocal or mental act (*kāyavāgmanaskarma*) favourable for beings (*sattvopakāraka*) provided it is irreproachable (*niravadya*). This is how the superiority relating to communal and non-communal rules is to be understood (VI.3).

The key phrase in the above statement is 'provided it is irreproachable'. The commentaries illustrate what this means, first of all with a paraphrase:

> This (*niravadya*) means any act which assures the welfare (*hita*) and happiness (*sukha*) of beings without thereby arousing the passions such as greed etc. (*rāgādikleśa*), either in oneself or in another. All these acts a *bodhisattva* may perform (*MSU*. on VI.3).

And second with an example:

> It may come about that while being favourable to beings an act may not be irreproachable: for example, having illicit relations with a woman belonging to another. To exclude this kind of act the author says 'provided it is irreproachable' (*MSB*. on VI.3).

As far as the *Summary of the Mahāyāna* and its commentaries are concerned, then, serious offences relate most probably to the violation of the Ten Good Paths of Action or *pārājika*-type offences, and minor offences to breaches of the 'lesser and minor' precepts of the *Vinaya*.

The *Bodhisattva Stage* discusses the conduct of a *bodhisattva* with reference to the minor offences and also provides examples of serious offences. First of all it states that a *bodhisattva* must observe the regulations which are categorised as minor just as rigorously as the *Śrāvakas*, but then goes on to allow a certain amount of leeway, as in the *Summary of the Mahāyāna*. The relevant passage is quoted below:

> A *bodhisattva* practises the same discipline (*śiksā*) as the *Śrāvakas* without any difference at all with respect to the minor offences which have been established by the Lord in the *Prātimokṣa* [and]

> in the *Vinaya*, [but] on the basis of thinking of others (*para-cittānurakṣā*), for the production of faith in those without it and for the increase of faith in those who [already] believe. Why is that? Because even the *Śrāvakas*, who put their own interest first (*ātmārtha-parama*) are not without concern for the protection of others, and they train in the *śikṣās* for the production of faith in those without it and the increase of faith in those who believe. How much more so the *bodhisattvas* who are devoted to the interests of others! (*Bo. Bhū*. 164.19–165.1).

The text then goes on to mention the exceptions where a *bodhisattva* is concerned:

> But a *bodhisattva* does not practise the same *śikṣā* as the *Śrāvakas* in relation to the minor offences concerned with desiring little (*alpārthatā*), being free from responsibilities (*alpakṛtyatā*) and free from cares (*alpotsuka-vihāratā*), which have been laid down by the Lord for the *Śrāvakas*. Why is that? Because it is fitting (*śobhate*) for a *Śrāvaka*, who puts his own interest first and is not concerned for the interests of others, to desire little, be free from responsibilities and free from cares as far as the interest of other people is concerned. But it is not fitting for a *bodhisattva*, who places the interests of others above all else, to desire little, be free from responsibilities and free from cares as far as the interest of other people is concerned (*Bo. Bhū*. 165.2–9).

The passage goes on to illustrate this by saying that a *bodhisattva* should accumulate property and distribute it to others. He should collect hundreds and thousands of robes (*cīvaraka*), bowls and silken coverings and if he fails to do this and remains aloof like the *Śrāvakas*, then he offends against *śikṣāpada* of the *Bodhisattva-piṭaka* and is guilty of a serious offence (*kliṣṭa-āpatti*). As far as the serious offences are concerned, and of which more later, the following are listed as falling into this category:

1. Taking life.
2. Taking what is not given.
3. Improper sexual conduct.
4. Telling lies.
5. Separating friends.

6. Harsh speech.
7. Singing, dancing and idle talk.

The *Treasury* (*Kośa*. IV.35cd) concludes that the fifth of the Five Precepts (against intoxicants) is a minor offence, suggesting that the previous four precepts are serious offences. It also draws a distinction between things which are immoral (*dauhśīlya*) and things which although not immoral in themselves have nevertheless been prohibited by the Buddha (*Kośa*. IV.122bc). The example given of the latter is eating at the wrong time (*vikālabhojana*), from which it would seem that Vasubandhu regards the minor offences as breaches of monastic rules rather than gravely immoral acts.

Although there is no unanimity in our sources as to precisely which offences fall into each of the two categories there does seem to be some measure of broad agreement. The serious offences are transgressions of what we might call the 'core morality' of Buddhism as seen, for instance, in the Five Precepts, or at least the first four of them. The minor offences are transgressions of the 'lesser and minor' precepts which regulate monastic life, some of which are undertaken at certain times by layfolk. The prohibition on untimely meals always applies to monks, and occasionally to laymen who observe it as the sixth of the Eight or Ten Precepts. We might say that whereas the serious offences are judged to be universally morally wrong, the minor offences are transgressions of rules voluntarily assumed as part of a religious discipline.[14]

In claiming superiority in communal and non-communal rules, the Mahāyāna is pointing to its flexibility in respect of minor offences in contrast to what it must have regarded as excessive legalism on the part of the Small Vehicle. The call for a shift in priorities from a personal quest for salvation to concern for the needs of others meant that in certain circumstances conflict would arise between the monastic lifestyle and the need for action in the world. The Mahāyāna allowed monks a limited degree of flexibility in these situations subject to the twofold stipulation that (a) the act should benefit others; and (b) it should be performed from an irreproachable (*niravadya*) motive. Care is taken specifically to exclude from this provision acts of a grave or serious nature, and there is no suggestion that a breach of the fundamental moral precepts would be countenanced. The further development of the principle enunciated here is to be found in the notion of Skilful

Means, which can, perhaps, be regarded as the outcome of an attempt to extend the exemption granted in respect of minor offences to serious offences, and to this we shall turn in a moment.

C. Superiority in Breadth

The third kind of superiority claimed by the Mahāyāna is superiority in breadth or scope (*vaipulya-viśeṣa*). This is said to be fourfold:

1. Its multiple and extensive rules (*nānāpramāṇa-śikṣā-vaipulya*).
2. The gain of immense merit (*apramāṇa-puṇya-parigrāha-vaipulya*).
3. The resolve to procure the welfare and happiness of all beings (*sarva-sattva-hitasukha-kriyāśaya-parigrāha-vaipulya*).
4. The establishment of supreme and perfect enlightenment (*anuttara-samyaksaṃbodhi-niśraya-vaipulya*).

As stated earlier this is merely a summary classification. The first three items may be seen as corresponding to the three divisions of Mahāyāna ethics namely Temperance, the Cultivation of Virtue, and Altruism respectively, while the fourth describes their culmination in enlightenment. We may pass over this without further comment to the fourth and final distinguishing feature of Mahāyāna *śīla*.

D. Superiority in Depth (Skilful Means)

The final classification relates to the *bodhisattva*'s Skilful Means (*upāya-kauśalya*), possibly the single most important innovation in Mahāyāna ethics. The concept of Skilful Means has a long and distinguished history in Buddhism, but only in certain Mahāyāna texts is it pressed towards the radical ethical conclusions we consider below. Stated briefly in its starkest form, the doctrine authorises a *bodhisattva* to commit the Ten Bad Paths of Action (*daśa-akuśala-karmapatha*), to gain immense merit thereby, and rapidly to attain supreme and perfect enlightenment. Furthermore, a *bodhisattva* may perform acts of deception and inflict suffering on beings if it leads them into discipline (*vinaya*). Obviously, this makes the distinction between 'serious' and 'minor' offences redundant, since a *bodhisattva* is now authorised to commit even the most serious offences. It should be noted, however, that this authorisation is only granted under the rubric of this fourth section and is specifically linked to the development of Skilful Means; if this faculty is not developed then a follower of the Mahāyāna is authorised to infringe only the minor regulations of the disciplinary code and only then if the interests of others require it. The Buddha himself had authorised the modification of minor disciplinary regulations (*D*.ii.154).

When Can the Precepts be Broken?

Mahāyāna sources allow varying degrees of latitude to a *bodhisattva* when performing his saving work. Yet not infrequently, and paradoxically, these are often the same sources which elsewhere insist upon the strict observance of the precepts. Consider, for instance, *Entering the Path of Enlightenment*, IV.1:

> Thus a son of the Buddha firmly takes up the thought of enlightenment; henceforth he should strive unfailingly not to violate the precepts.[15]

And compare this with V.84 of the same text:

> Having so understood, a *bodhisattva* should always be diligent in the interests of others. Even what is forbidden is allowable for one who seeks the welfare of others with compassion.[16]

What is a *bodhisattva* to make of this conflicting advice? Prajñākaramati's comment on the latter verse is as follows:

> Thus, having realised the highest truth, he should always be zealous in procuring the welfare and happiness of beings. And if someone should object, 'How can he avoid committing an offence (*āpatti*) while engaged in what is forbidden? [the reply is that] the Lord has taught that what is forbidden may be performed by one who perceives with the eye of knowledge a special benefit for beings therein. And the teachings of the Lord bring about salvation. But the foregoing [exemption] does not apply to everyone: only to [cases of] the exercise of compassion in its highest degree by one who is of a compassionate nature, who is without a selfish motive, solely concerned with the interests of others and totally dedicated to this [ideal]. In this way there is no offence for one who is skilled in means

(*upāya-kuśala*) and who works for the interests of others with insight (*prajñā*) and compassion (*karuṇā*)'.[17]

This is a key statement of the principle sanctioning a breach of the moral code in certain well-defined circumstances. However, matters are not always so clear cut in other sources, and the Mahāyāna does seem to have engaged in a good deal of heart-searching over the status of its moral precepts. As on important issues in most traditions we find both 'progressive' and 'conservative' points of view. For the moment I wish to consider further the way in which the progressive or 'permissive' attitude is revealed in Mahāyāna sources. I will then consider the evidence for the opposite 'hard line' position.

Permissive Attitudes

Other more loosely formulated expressions of the permissive principle stated by Prajñākaramati above occur throughout the Mahāyāna. 'If he sees greater advantage for beings', says the *Compendium of Conduct* (*Śikṣā* 93.12), 'let him transgress the rule'.[18] According to the *Sūtra on Skilful Means*, quoting the Buddha:

> If a *bodhisattva* should produce a root of good in a single being and be guilty of a transgression which would send him to hell for 100,000 *kalpas*, then he should commit that offence and bear the pain of hell and not forsake the good of that single being (*Śikṣā*. 93.20–22).

In the *Sūtra on Skilful Means* the Buddha says that he himself in a previous life killed an evil trader to save the lives of five hundred people, and in the *Yogācārya-bhūmi-śāstra* it is said that *bodhisattvas* should do the same if lives are threatened by a vicious robber.[19] Elsewhere, *bodhisattvas* are encouraged to engage in sexual activity: 'They purposely become courtesans in order to attract men, and after baiting them with the hook of lust establish them in the Buddha-knoweldge.'[20]

In the *Trance of Heroic Progress* the *bodhisattva* Māragocarānulipta creates magical duplicates of himself to satisfy two-hundred goddesses in the retinue of Māra since he perceives they are ripe for salvation (*MCB*. 13: 200). A little later the Buddha explains that it is through the *bodhisattva's* magical power that he is able to do this, while all the time remaining in the state of trance (*MCB*, 13: 222).

The Requirement of Insight or Compassion

The *Compendium of Conduct* links the transgression of moral norms to the possession of perfect insight (*prajñā*):

> Even if, Kaśyapa, a being should be involved in these ten paths of evil action, yet if he accepts the Tathāgata's teaching on causation, if he recognises that there is no such thing as a self or a being or an animating principle (*jīva*) or a person (*pudgala*); and if he recognises that all *dharmas* are unmade, unproduced, of the nature of illusion (*māyā*) and non-defilement and pure by nature, and if he accepts that all *dharmas* are fundamentally pure, then I predict no evil destiny for that being (*Sikṣā*. 96.7–12).

The *Sūtra on Skilful Means* takes a similar view:

> Though a Bodhisattva may have defilements and amuse himself with the five sensuous pleasures, still, because he has the wisdom seed of emptiness, signlessness, nonaction and nonself within him, he will not fall to the miserable planes of existence[21]

Here it is knowledge which absolves one from blame, yet at other times the scales tip towards compassion, and acts which are motivated by attachment to others are said to be blameless. *Rāga* is elevated to a virtue and *dveṣa* is the only vice, as we see in the *Upāliparipṛcchā*:

> If, Upāli, a *bodhisattva*, a great being, who is established in the Mahāyāna, should commit offences due to attachment (*rāga*) as numerous as the sands of the Ganges, and if he should commit just one offence out of aversion (*dveṣa*) by the standard of the *bodhisattva*-vehicle . . . that offence of aversion outweights all the others. Why is that? It is because aversion, Upāli, leads to the abandonment of beings [whereas] *rāga* leads to their attraction (*saṃgrahāya*). Therefore there is neither danger nor fear for the *bodhisattva* in that vice (*kleśa*) which leads to the attraction of beings . . . So I say to you, Upāli, that any offence due to

> attachment (*rāga*) is no offence at all. As the excellence of one who wins over beings has already been referred to, the present instruction refers to one whose intentions are compassionate (*Śikṣā*. 92.4–10).

The same passage is also quoted in the *Bodhisattva-Prātimokṣa-Sūtra* (Dutt, 1930: 283f.) which indicates the popularity of the principle it enshrines. It may be compared with a passage from *The Definite Vinaya:*

> The World Honoured One answered Upāli, 'If, while practicing the Mahāyāna, a *Bodhisattva* continues to break precepts out of desire for kalpas as numerous as the sands of the Ganges, his offense is still minor. If a *Bodhisattva* breaks precepts out of hatred, even just once, his offense is very serious. Why? Because a *Bodhisattva* who breaks precepts out of desire [still] holds sentient beings in his embrace, whereas a *Bodhisattva* who breaks precepts out of hatred forsakes sentient beings altogether' (Chang, 1983: 270).

The *Compendium of Conduct* expresses the principle more concisely in a slightly later passage: 'And so in cases where there is advantage for beings, an offence arising from attachment (*rāga*) is declared to be no offence.'[22] Here the emphasis is upon a close emotional relationship with others in contrast to a doctrine of absolution through *prajñā*.

It will be seen from these examples that the freedom allowed to a *bodhisattva* is enormous and a wide spectrum of activities are permitted to him, even to the extent of taking life. We have seen that the *Bodhisattva Stage* authorises the latter (C.1) and the *bodhisattva* even derives great merit from the deed (*bahu ca puṇyaṃ prasūyate*). When actions of these kinds are performed there are usually two provisos which must be satisfied: (a) that the prohibited action will conduce to the greater good of those beings directly affected by it; and (b) that the action is performed on the basis of perfect knowledge (*prajñā*) or perfect compassion (*karuṇā*). In the case of perfect knowledge the rationale seems to be that from the point of view of ultimate truth there is no such thing as a rule or a being; and in the second case from the standpoint of relative truth the interests of others are all-important and must be furthered whatever the cost to oneself.

Conservative Views

Yet despite this apparent relaxation of the rules there is a countervailing insistence in Mahāyāna literature upon the strict observance of the precepts. Sometimes, as noted above, both attitudes are found within the same text and a *bodhisattva* is encouraged both to be vigilant in preserving the precepts at all costs and yet to break them whenever he sees an advantage in doing so. The *Sūtra on Skilful Means*, although in general promoting the use of *upāya*, speaks in praise of the precepts in a brief reference to the Perfection of Morality:

> [The *Bodhisattva-Mahāsattva*] himself keeps the precepts and makes offerings to those who keep the precepts; he persuades those who have broken the precepts to observe the precepts, and then bestows offerings upon them. This is the *pāramitā* of discipline (Chang, 1983: 430).

The need for vigilance in the precepts is explained in *Entering the Path of Enlightenment*: it is not that the *bodhisattva* himself will perish but that his lack of exertion in keeping to the rules will cause him to fail the others whom he has vowed to save: 'And this is why any failing by the *bodhisattva* is extremely serious: by his failing he places the welfare of all beings in jeopardy.'[23]

The fact of his own transgression is only of incidental importance: the really serious matter is the repercussion of his failing upon others. The duty of a *bodhisattva* is to *all* beings, so the seriousness of his failing is multiplied accordingly. This is emphasised in verse 10: 'One is doomed by destroying even the welfare of a single being: what, then, [of doing the same] to all those beings who dwell in the immensity of space?'[24] Such is the reasoning which leads a *bodhisattva* to avoid scrupulously even the most minor transgressions – namely that there is no such thing as a minor transgression when the context of his field of activity is seen as infinite. To avoid potentially catastrophic consequences a *bodhisattva* must be ever vigilant in the perfection of morality. Moreover, a *bodhisattva* cannot himself attain enlightenment by merely developing *bodhicitta*, but must also practise the *bodhisattva*-saṃvaras and *śikṣās* laid down by the Buddha (*BCA*. 91ff.). Nor should a *bodhisattva* dissuade others from the observance of the *Prātimokṣa* claiming that simply to read the Mahāyāna *sūtras* is sufficient (*Śikṣā*. 38.5–8; *BCA*. 146f.).

The *Brahmajāla Sūtra* insists upon the scrupulous observance of all its injunctions. If any of the *Prātimokṣas* are transgressed the consequences are severe: all good qualities are lost along with the ten stages of perfection (*bhūmi*), and rebirth will occur in one of the three inferior realms where the offender will not hear of the Three Jewels for two or three eons. The *Prātimokṣas* are not to be transgressed even to the extent of a grain of dust (*BJS*. 39). Other statements of the hard-line position occur in various Mahāyāna sources. The *Precious Garland* advises: 'For your own sake always speak the truth, even if it should cause your death or ruin your kingdom; do not speak in any other way' (v.274). This sentiment is echoed by sGam-po-pa who counsels us 'to keep to the truth and never willingly tell a lie not even for the sake of our life' (*Jewel*, 1970: 145).

In some respects the Rule of the Mahāyāna was even more severe than that of the Hīnayāna, for instance in respect of diet. The *Descent to Laṅkā* argues strongly in favour of vegetarianism regarding it as a way of life more suitable for a *bodhisattva* (*Laṅk*. 244ff.).[25]

In other aspects the discipline of the monks of the Mahāyāna was no less rigorous than that of their Hīnayāna brethren. A comment of I. Tsing's, who was greatly interested in matters of *Vinaya*, reveals how seriously conformity to monastic discipline was taken in China:

> The homeless mendicants should strictly confine themselves to the rules of the *Vinaya*. If they are not guilty of transgressing them they are acting in conformity with the *sūtra*. If there be any transgression of the precepts their obedience is at fault. As priests, they should not even destroy one stalk of grass, though the temple be covered with it. They should not even steal a grain of rice, though they be starving in a lonely field (*Record*, 195).

According to I. Tsing the Mahāyāna had no *Vinaya* of its own and shared that of the Hīnayāna. It seems there was considerable interest in the study of the *Vinaya* in China, perhaps even too much if we are to give credence to his lament:

> In China the schools of the *Vinayadharas* are also prejudiced, and

lecturers and commentators have produced too many remarks on the subject . . . Consequently one's aspiration (after the knowledge of the *Vinaya*) is baffled at the beginning, and one's attention flags after attending to but one lecture. Even men of the highest talent can only succeed in the study after becoming grey-haired, while men of medium or little ability cannot accomplish their work even when their hair has turned perfectly white (ibid: 15f.).

3. TWO KINDS OF SKILFUL MEANS

So far we have seen that the Mahāyāna on the one hand accords the precepts only a token and provisional status, but on the other displays an almost obsessive rule-worship which equals or exceeds the legalism it condemns in the Hīnayāna. What is to be made of its puzzling and paradoxical statements and injunctions? The sanctioning of the most serious transgressions is closely bound up with the complex notion of skilful means (*upāya-kauśalya*), and to help unravel this it may be helpful to distinguish two principal senses of the term. First of all, as we saw when discussing the Perfections, *upāya* stands for the cultivation of moral qualities as encompassed in the first five Perfections. In this sense *upāȳa* and *prajña* go together very much like *śīla* and *paññā*, and *upāya* and *śīla* cover roughly the same ground. *Upāya* here refers to normative ethics, and we may refer to this as $upāya_1$.

The second sense of *upāya*, which we may call *upāya*-$_2$, would seem to be not so much the concern of the common man as an attribute of those who are already perfect in ethics and insight; it is the *upāya* of *bodhisattvas* of the seventh stage (*upāya-kauśalya-bhūmi*) and beyond, whose powers and perfections are supernatural. Upāya$_2$ is depicted as an activity of the Buddhas and Great *Bodhisattvas* (*Bodhisattva-Mahāsattvas*) and it is only they who have the knowledge and power to use it. It is by virtue of $upāya_2$ that *bodhisattvas* transgress the precepts from motives of compassion and are said to do no wrong. The two aspects of *upāya* distinguished above govern firstly a *bodhisattva's* own personal development and perfection and secondly his relationship to others as a harbinger of salvation. The *Bodhisattva Stage* distinguishes two aspects of *upāya* along similar lines;[26] these are internal (*adhyātma*) and external (*bahirdhā*), and each has six divisions as follows:

Internal

1. Directed towards the acquisition of all Buddha-*dharmas*.
2. Compassionate concern for all beings.
3. Perfect knowledge of all conditioned things.
4. Desire for that knowledge which is unexcelled enlightenment.
5. An undefiled passage through *saṃsāra*.
6. Zeal in the desire for the Buddha-knowledge.

External

1. From the small good roots of beings a *bodhisattva* produces great results.
2. He causes immense good roots with little effort.
3. He removes obstacles which keep beings away from the Buddha's teachings.
4. He makes those who are only halfway cross over.
5. He ripens those who have already crossed.
6. He delivers those who are already ripened.

According to this scheme a *bodhisattva* first of all perfects himself and then radiates his perfection towards others. Part of his perfection is from the start a concern for others, yet he is able to display this more fully and effectively once he has achieved perfection himself. According to the *Ornament of Mahāyāna Sutras* the value of the Perfections is twofold: firstly to purify the performer and secondly to ripen other beings by attracting them to the faith (*MSA*. XVI.13). After a *bodhisattva* has perfected his moral conduct he continues to practise it not out of a desire for merit but to instruct other beings. The *Large Treatise on the Perfection of Wisdom* puts it as follows:

> But he does not aspire for any fruit from his morality, which he could enjoy in *Saṃsāra*, and it is only for the purpose of protecting and maturing beings that he courses in the perfection of morality (tr. Conze, 1975: 535).

Upāya$_1$

While a *bodhisattva* is engaged in the process of self-cultivation through the *pāramitās* he is concerned only with *upāya*$_1$, and only after he has achieved the perfection of insight and means does the possibility of *upāya*$_2$ arise. *Upāya*$_1$ is concerned with normative ethics but *upāya*$_2$ is not. As far as *upāya*$_1$ is concerned, we have seen that the Mahāyāna allows *bodhisattvas*-in-training a slight degree of latitude in respect of minor offences. This does not amount to a slackening in discipline and there is evidence that the Mahāyāna became stricter in its discipline than the Hīnayāna. *Upāya*$_1$ does not enjoin laxity in moral practice but rather the greater recognition of the needs and interests of others. One's moral practice is now for the benefit of oneself and others by means of example. Through its emphasis on *karuṇā* the Mahayana gave full recognition to the value of ethical perfection, making it explicit that ethics and insight were of equal importance for a *bodhisattva*. *Upāya*$_1$, then constitutes the endorsement by the Mahāyāna of the binary nature of final perfection which it felt the Hīnayāna had failed to recognise or emphasise sufficiently.

Upāya$_2$

Turning to upāya$_2$, we submit that this is the provenance of the Buddhas and Great *Bodhisattvas* and does not concern normative ethical conduct. The great *bodhisattvas* are embodiments of supreme value, and in their compassion-inspired antinomian conduct we see a symbolic as opposed to normative statement of the importance attached by the Mahāyāna to concern for others. In the doctrine of *upāya*$_2$ this is elevated to the status of a supreme principle which overrides all other considerations. In order to indicate that *upāya*$_2$ is not a doctrine for universal consumption or application, its practice is linked to the advanced stage of the seventh *bhūmi*. By the seventh *bhūmi*, *bodhisattvas* are perfect in the two divisions of the first six Perfections, namely ethics and insight. In a sense the final four Perfections are a recapitulation of the first six, since once again we see the *bodhisattva* demonstrating ethical perfection (*upāya*) in conjunction with perfect knowledge (*jñāna*). We may go so far as to aggregate stages seven (*upāya*), eight (*praṇidhāna*) and nine (*bala*) to the sphere of ethics and contrast these with the tenth stage of knowledge (*jñāna*). Thus the binary division within the first six perfections is reflected within the extra tier consisting of the latter four. This extra tier was added on, perhaps, specifically to distinguish the 'super-perfections' of the *Bodhisattva-Mahāsattvas*.

After reaching the dual perfection implicit in the first six Perfections the *bodhisattva* has reached the upper limits of human perfectibility. In *Pāramitās* seven to ten he stands upon the threshold of the transcendent, and at this point the Great *Bodhisattvas* symbolise the supreme ideals of Insight (*prajñā*) and Compassion (*karuṇā*). We see both these values epitomised in the two great *bodhisattvas* of the Mahāyāna tradition: Mañjuśrī as perfect insight and Avalokiteśvara as perfect compassion. These two great *bodhisattvas* may be regarded as hypostacies of the Buddha himself.[27] Most commonly in the Mahāyāna Insight and Compassion are invoked together, but at other times henotheistically with the result that either one or the other is lauded as the supreme good. In this respect Dayal detects a shift with the passage of time:

> In the early Mahāyāna, Wisdom and Mercy are regarded as equally important . . . In fact, Wisdom is considered to be somewhat more important than Mercy . . . The glorification of Wisdom reaches its climax in the Madhyamika school of philosophy . . . But the later Mahāyāna emphasises Mercy more than Wisdom . . . As the ideal gains ground, the *bodhisattva* Avalokiteśvara increases in importance till he becomes the supreme and unique *bodhisattva*. The Mahāyāna slowly passes from the ascendency of Mañjuśrī to the reign of Avalokiteśvara . . . *Karunā* (mercy, pity, love, compassion) and its personified symbol, Avalokiteśvara, are all-in-all. This is the last word and the consummation of the Mahāyāna (1932: 44ff.).

In the doctrine of *upāya*$_2$ we see the scales tip decisively in favour of *karuṇā* at the expense of *prajñā*. Indeed, *prajñā* is pressed into the service of *karuṇā* through the identification of its content with *śūnyatā*, the emptiness of all phenomena. Given the universal absence of inherent existence postulated by the emptiness teachings of the Madhyamika, there is nothing to impede the activity of *karuṇā*, which is now allowed to exert itself without restriction. *Upāya*$_2$ then, is the outcome of the blending of *karuṇā*, with a particular interpretation of the content of *prajñā*

Ethics and Metaphysics

The doctrine of *upāya*$_2$ is a fusion of ethics and metaphysics. Those who sought to promote compassion as the supreme quality of a *bodhisattva* were able to exploit the doctrine of emptiness in an ingenious (if dubious) way to help overcome the more restrictive normative aspects of Buddhist ethical teachings. The justification for the employment of *upāya* thus proceeds along the lines that the precepts cannot be broken since there is no such thing (ultimately) as a precept. This is the tack taken by Vimalakīrti in his encounter with Upāli (*VNS*. III.31-7) and it is a paradox which the Perfection of Wisdom literature and the Mahāyāna *sūtras* delight in exploiting (although only a minority seek to derive antinomian conclusions from it). The doctrine of *upāya*$_2$ represents the far point of the pendulum swing in the tradition's exploration of the relationship between moral and intellectual good. Despite the greatly enhanced status of ethics in the Mahāyāna compassion is still not content, and struggles to be entirely free of the remaining moral prohibitions which deny it full expression. The Small Vehicle was accused of having subordinated ethics to knowledge, to have undervalued concern for others in the quest for an intellectual goal. Ironically the Large Vehicle, or at least that strand within it which promotes the doctrine of *upāya*$_2$, now falls into the other extreme of subordinating knowledge to ethics. The philosophical teachings are used to remove any obstacles to the uninhibited outpouring of compassion. Perhaps this might be seen as a new twist to an old problem. Where the end encompasses two values there will always be an attempt to play one off against the other. Opponents of the Buddha attempted to attack Buddhist ethics with Buddhist philosophy by questioning how ethics could exist at all in the absence of a moral subject, as was entailed by the no-self teachings.[28] Turning this around, the *upāya*$_2$ doctrine now asks how, in the light of universal (as opposed to individual) emptiness, can there be anything to *impede* the outpouring of moral concern?

The elevation of love or compassion to the status of a supreme end is also found outside of Buddhism, and I will return to a discussion of the features of such systems in Chapter 7. For the present I will only say that there is something suspicious about the justification which some texts offer for the use of *upāya*$_2$. This concerns the attempt to argue to an ethical conclusion from metaphysical premises, or from a fact to a value. The argument put forward is of a reductionist kind and assumes a lowest common denominator for all levels of reality, namely emptiness. Since precepts are empty of inherent existence like everything else, the argument runs, they must also be devoid of moral force, and therefore cannot act as a brake or check on the compassionate *bodhisattva*. However, ethics cannot be overridden in such a simple way. Although facts are not irrelevant to values they have no priority, and ethical issues must be addressed with ethical arguments: they cannot be brushed aside by reference to facts of a scientific, ontological or metaphysical nature. Furthermore, although I cannot go into the question in detail here, it is doubtful that the doctrine of emptiness strips away the force of ethical precepts in the manner supposed. The doctrine teaches that phenomena are devoid of inherent existence, not that they are unreal or non-existent. The precepts and the moral life are not in any sense abolished by the doctrine of emptiness, at least as far as mainstream Madhyamaka is concerned. According to Candrakīrti, the belief that the doctrine of emptiness entails the denial of the precepts is an extreme and erroneous view.[29]

Whatever its philosophical merits, we may enquire whether the *upāya*$_2$ inspired behaviour of the moral heroes of the Mahāyāna is to be taken as a model for imitation in everyday life. As I have interpreted the doctrine above it does not have direct normative implications of this kind for the following reasons.[30] In Mahāyāna literature *upāya*$_2$ is the province of the Buddhas and Great *Bodhisattvas*. Their actions are located predominantly in the domain of myth and symbol (Pye, 1978: ch.4), which alerts us to the fact that such activity requires interpretation rather than simple imitation. At the end of the *Sūtra on Skilful Means* the Buddha gives this warning:

> Good man, now I have finished explaining and revealing my ingenuity [*upāya*]. You should keep this a secret and not speak of it to lowly, inferior people who have few good roots. Why? Because even Śrāvakas and Pratyekabuddhas cannot comprehend this sutra, much less can lowly, inferior, ordinary persons believe or understand it. Ordinary people cannot learn ingenuity, and so the Sutra of Ingenuity is of no use to them; not a single ordinary person can accept or practice it. Only Bodhisattvas can learn and teach the doctrine of Ingenuity (Chang, 1983: 464).

There seems to be little sign that *upāya*$_2$ was adopted as a basic principle of ethics in Mahāyāna countries, and there is clear evidence that in Japan at least it was not (Pye, 1978: ch. 8). If certain deeds in history were justified by appeal to the principle these remain exceptions to the rule. The Mahāyāna, for the most part, continued to be rigorous in its observance of the basic precepts. Some easing in respect of *Vinaya* restrictions was achieved by introducing the distinction between serious (*prakṛiti-sāvadya*) and minor (*pratikṣepaṇa-sāvadya*) offences, and allowing the latter to be overridden where circumstances warranted. The basic principles of ethics, as represented for instance by the Ten Paths of Action, appear to have been adhered to rather than sacrificed to the situational demands of *upāya*. We may also note that the section of thc *Bodhisattva-piṭaka*, which explicitly authorises breaking the precepts (section C), or dispensations like it, do not appear to have been incorporated into the disciplinary codes of Mahāyāna countries. Whilc thc influcncc of such texts was no doubt felt it is the older and more rigorous attitudes to monastic practice which seem to have prevailed.

Summary

We may summarise the Mahāyāna ethical developments as follows:

1. The Mahāyāna was critical of the failure of the Small Vehicle to recognise the importance of ethics in soteriology.
2. It redressed this deficiency by emphasising that ethical perfection involving concern for others (*karuṇā/upāya*) was of equal importance to insight (*prajñā*).
3. The Mahāyāna formulated an expanded tripartite conception of ethics embracing: (a) temperance (*saṃvara*); (b) the cultivation of virtue (*kuśala-dharma-saṃgrāhaka-śīla*); and (c) altruism (*sattva-artha-kriyā-śīla*).
4. It allowed a degree of flexibility such that minor variations in monastic practice were permissible in circumstances where the needs of others demanded it.
5. The continued ascendency of ethics and its relation to metaphysics was explored symbolically in the figures of the Great *Bodhisattvas* and their antinomian conduct (*upāya*$_2$). The 'Skilful Means' of the Great *Bodhisattvas* symbolises the triumph of compassion (in the form of Situation Ethics) over knowledge, and marks the furthest point reached in the Mahāyāna's reaction against the values of the Small Vehicle.

The purpose of this chapter was to explore the theme of change and continuity in the soteriological role of ethics in the Great Vehicle. We have now completed our investigation into Buddhist sources and in the following chapters we assess our findings in the light of Western theories of ethics in an attempt to characterise the overall structure of the Buddhist ethical system.

7

Buddhism and Utilitarianism

I teach only suffering and the end of suffering.

The Buddha

The ultimate end . . . is an existence exempt as far as possible from pain . . . secured to all mankind . . . and . . . to the whole sentient creation.

J. S. Mill

Woe to those who creep through the serpent-windings of Utilitarianism.

Immanuel Kant

I now wish to place the scheme of Buddhist ethics described thus far in the context of Western ethical theory and see if a useful analogue may be found to further our understanding of the Buddhist ethical system. There is a need for caution in the field of religious ethics in imposing the classifications of one system on another, as David Snellgrove has pointed out (1956). Michael Pye also warns that 'there is admittedly a problem about the correlation of *Mahāyānist* ethics and western approaches to ethics' (1978: 14). However, while there is undoubtedly a need for caution we must at some point make a tentative venture into the field. Future research will be considerably assisted if we are able to elucidate a general pattern, scheme or framework within which Buddhist ethics may be located. In this chapter and the next we consider two Western models which bear at least a *prima facie* relationship to Buddhism, namely Utilitarianism and Aristotelianism. In this chapter I discuss the resemblances between Buddhism and Utilitarianism, and in the next chapter the resemblances between Buddhism and Aristotelian ethics. The present chapter is arranged as follows: first (1) I will summarise the main features of utilitarian ethical theory and then (2) assess its similarities with Buddhist ethics. Finally (3) I will consider a specific Western ethical model – Situation Ethics – a utilitarian hybrid based on agapistic principles which may be thought to resemble certain features of Mahāyāna ethics, and in particular the doctrine of Skilful Means.

1. UTILITARIAN THEORIES OF ETHICS

Stated in its simplest form a Utilitarian theory of ethics is one in which 'the good is defined independently from the right, and then the right is defined as that which maximises the good' (Rawls, 1980: 24). The content of the good is derived from intuition or common sense and is regarded as a utility to be increased. This utility may be variously defined, e.g. as pleasure (most commonly), wealth, or as various other forms of satisfaction left undefined ('preference utilitarianism'). The right act, then, is that act which of all available alternatives will maximise the good as previously specified, that is to say, the act which will produce the greatest happiness (or other good) for those affected by its consequences. There are many varieties of utilitarian ethical theory, but I will concentrate here on the classical formulation of the doctrine as developed by Bentham and Mill. After describing the main features of the paradigm we will be in a position to assess the correspondence between it and Buddhist ethics. All variations of the classical doctrine are in any event marked by their common acceptance of the 'Principle of Utility'.

Bentham

Let us begin by considering the definition of this principle given by Bentham in *An Introduction to the Principles of Morals and Legislation*:

> The principle of utility is the foundation of the present work: it will be proper therefore at the outset to give an explicit and determinative account of what is meant by it. By the principle of utility is meant that principle which approves or disapproves of every action whatsoever, according to the tendency which it appears to have to augment or diminish the happiness of the party whose interest is in question: or, what is the same thing in other words, to promote or oppose that happiness. I say of every

action whatsoever; and therefore not only of every action of a private individual, but of every measure of government (1970, 11f.).

As a social reformer it was with 'measures of government' that Bentham was primarily concerned, and his version of utilitarianism played an important role in the political culture of Britain in the first half of the nineteenth century.[1] As MacIntyre points out, the philosophy can be applied most successfully to institutions such as prisons and hospitals where it is possible to have a rough idea of how many people's lot will be bettered or worsened by particular measures (1967: 237). At the same time, Bentham believed that public policy could only be shaped and implemented effectively if it took account of the facts of human nature as testified to by the psychological constitution of individual human beings. The most important feature of this constitution he took to be the fact that men are motivated to do whatever they do by their desires, and that these desires are for the experience and increase of pleasure and the avoidance of pain. He begins his *magnum opus* with the following magisterial statement:

> Nature has placed mankind under the governance of two sovereign masters, *pain* and *pleasure*. It is for them alone to point out what we ought to do, as well as to determine what we shall do. On the one hand the standard of right and wrong, on the other the chain of causes and effects, are fastened to their throne. They govern us in all we do, in all we say, in all we think: every effort we can make to throw off our subjection, will serve but to demonstrate and confirm it (1970: 11).

The consequences of actions are therefore valued to the extent that they consist of sensations of pleasure, or conversely, inhibit the experience of pain. Such is the utility to be promoted, and Bentham made this clear in his exemplification of a utility:

> By utility is meant that property in any object, whereby it tends to produce benefit, advantage, pleasure, good, or happiness, (all this in the present case comes to the same thing) or (what comes again to the same thing) to prevent the happening of mischief, pain, evil, or unhappiness to the party whose interest is considered' (1970: 12).

As stated above, then, 'ought' and 'right' are defined in terms of maximising the 'good' (1970: 13, S.10). If one asks 'Why should I seek to maximise the good?' the answer is that human nature is so constituted that this is inevitably what people do anyway: utilitarianism simply acknowledges this as the basic factor in human motivation. It is the simplification or reduction of the complexities of ethics to an apparently simple factual basis which gives utilitarianism its appeal. Complex and nebulous matters of value upon which it is notoriously difficult to reach agreement can now be translated into simple matters of fact, which greatly assists decision-making. Judging the rightness of competing courses of action therefore becomes an exercise in calculation, a cost-benefit analysis on the balance-sheet of pleasure and pain. Pleasures and pains may come from a variety of sources, and Bentham lists fourteen sources of pleasure and twelve sources of pain.[2] Alongside this check-list must be considered such factors as the intensity and length of the sensation which is experienced or anticipated. To assist in this computation Bentham elaborated a 'felicific calculus' (1970: ch.4) according to which pleasures and pains may be measured and quantified by reference to: intensity, duration, certainty or uncertainty, propinquity and remoteness, fecundity, purity and extent (the last applies when more than one individual will be affected by the consequences).

The principle of utility, Bentham argued, provides a secure foundation for morals and legislation: it demystifies moral judgements and provides an empirical standard for objective scrutiny in matters of right and wrong. It is, moreover, of universal application, since human nature is similarly constituted the world over. Although morality and law vary between cultures they should in principle conform to one standard alone, namely that of utility. If they do not they stand in need of correction. The principle of utility is inviolate. 'Systems which attempt to question it,' writes Bentham, 'deal in sound instead of sense, in caprice instead of reason, in darkness instead of light' (ibid: 11).

Utilitarians are concerned only with consequences (hence utilitarianism is a 'consequentialist' theory of ethics); and the felicific calculus is simply a device for quantifying consequences of actions in terms of pleasure. For Bentham pleasure was an homogenous category which allowed for no differentiation or grading in respect of different kinds of pleasure. Opponents were quick to point out that on this basis the pleasure of the opera is no better than the pleasure of an animal in the farmyard – hence Carlyle's curt dismissal of utilitarianism as 'pig philosophy'. Bentham himself was unmoved by this: 'Prejudice apart', he wrote, 'the game of push-pin is of equal value with the arts and sciences of music and poetry. If the game of pushpin furnish more pleasure, it is more valuable than either.'[3] Bentham's psychology, derived from Hartley, was of the crude mechanical and associationist kind and drew much criticism. The task of refining the psychological foundation of utilitarianism and fending off its critics passed along with Bentham's mantle to J.S. Mill.

Mill

Mill attempted to overcome the defects inherent in Bentham's unitary notion of 'pleasure' by making a distinction between 'higher' and 'lower' forms of pleasure (1957: 8f.). The higher forms, such as the study of philosophy, are to be preferred to the lower forms such as the pleasures of 'wine, women and song'. Mill sought to introduce the notion of a continuum of pleasures with the higher outweighing the lower: 'It is better to be a human being dissatisfied than a pig satisfied; better to be Socrates dissatisfied than a fool satisfied' (1957: 9).[4] As is often pointed out, however, once Mill introduces this distinction he has begun to introduce non-utilitarian values. What can be greater than pleasure for a utilitarian other than more pleasure? If appeal must be made to other values, such as aesthetic quality, to account for human motivation, then the ideal of a single standard to which human drives are reducible is an illusion. Mill suggests that factors such as pride, liberty, power, excitement and dignity may make a human being unwilling to settle for pleasure alone – all of which *ex hypothesi* should not be more desirable alternatives. As Alan Ryan notes: 'To say that Socrates prefers his way of life, even if he is constantly dissatisfied, is to say that he thinks it better, not that he thinks it more pleasant' (1974: 111). If something may be better irrespective of hedonistic associations it must be acknowledged that pleasure and pain are not the final arbiters of human values. Yet such a claim is precisely the attraction of utilitarianism, that it simplifies conflicting moral systems by converting their divergent values into a single universal currency. If it cannot do this then it fails to be comprehensive and must give up its claim to be grounded in a universal feature of human nature. To escape from this dilemma Mill falls back on the notion of certain qualities or actions, such as those which are dignified, noble or courageous, as being indirect means for maximising general, as opposed to individual, welfare. Actions which are normally praised on non-utilitarian grounds, such as self-sacrifice, are explained as being useful in general to society at large. In this way Mill is able to claim that utilitarianism is altruistic: one's own good counts for no more than anyone else's, and so the aim of utilitarian ethics is the good of all and not merely the happiness of the agent.

In *Utilitarianism* Mill is at pains to stress the unselfish character of his ethical system. First of all he restates Bentham's principle of utility as the 'Greatest Happiness Principle' as follows:

> According to the Greatest Happiness Principle . . . the ultimate end, with reference to and for the sake of which all other things are desirable (whether we are considering our own good or that of other people), is an existence exempt as far as possible from pain, and as rich as possible in enjoyments, both in point of quantity and quality (1957: 11).

Notice that Mill, perhaps more conscious of the definitional problems associated with pleasure than Bentham, has subtly reversed the priority in the latter's statement of the principle by placing the exemption from pain before the increase in enjoyments. He goes on in the above passage to derive the principles of ethics from the Greatest Happiness Principle in the way Bentham had done:

> This, being, according to the utilitarian opinion, the end of human action, is necessarily also the standard of morality; which may accordingly be defined, the rules and precepts for human conduct, by the observance of which an existence such as has been described might be, to the greatest extent possible, secured to all mankind; and not to them only, but, so far as the nature of things admits, to the whole sentient creation (ibid.).

Notice also that Mill refers to 'rules and precepts' whereas Bentham spoke only of actions. We might also note the characteristic Buddhist sentiment in the final clause with the reference to 'the whole sentient creation'. A knowledge of Indian religious ideas may have come to Mill through his father, James, who amongst his other talents was an historian of India.[5]

At several points in *Utilitarianism* Mill castigates those who would use utilitarian principles to pursue their own self-interest: 'As little is there an inherent necessity that any human being should be a selfish egotist, devoid of every feeling or care but those which centre in his own miserable individuality' (1957: 13). 'The utilitarian morality', he writes, 'does recognise in human beings the power of sacrificing their own greatest good for the good of others' (1957: 15). It does not only recognise this power but seeks to encourage it:

> The happiness which forms the Utilitarian standard of what is right in conduct, is not the agent's own happiness, but that of all concerned. As between his own happiness and that of others, utilitarianism requires him to be strictly impartial as a disinterested and benevolent spectator. In the golden rule of Jesus of Nazareth, we read the complete spirit of the ethics of utility (1957: 16).

In expecting impartiality between the satisfaction of one's own needs and those of others Mill is denying the first principle of utilitarianism, namely the self-interest axiom. If men are so constituted that they seek first their own pleasure, how can they also be disposed to sacrifice their own satisfaction to that of others? If it is suggested that one should serve the interests of others in the expectation of receiving reciprocal benefit then the result is a contract theory of morality adrift from the psychological moorings of utilitarianism. I will return to the problems of utilitarianism later with specific reference to Buddhism. For the present I wish to focus upon the distinctions between the forms of the doctrine put forward by Bentham and Mill which in the course of time have developed into Act Utilitarianism (AU) and Rule Utilitarianism (RU) respectively. I will briefly outline these two forms of the theory together with a third member of the utilitarian family, Negative Utilitarianism (NU), since it is these three forms of the theory which bear the most resemblance to Buddhism. After this I shall consider to what extent Buddhism may be related to these systems.

Act Utilitarianism

AU is the form of utilitarianism advocated by Bentham. According to this principle, what is right can be decided by a direct appeal to the principle of utility. AU does not seek to lay down general guidelines for similar situations – each situation must be treated as unique and be given an independent evaluation of its consequences. Both direct and indirect consequences must be taken into account, the latter including an assessment of the likely influences of the act upon others. Modern advocates of the theory include J. J. C. Smart and (in a modified form) Joseph Fletcher. Smart summaries AU as follows:

> Roughly speaking, act-utilitarianism is the view that the rightness or wrongness of an action depends only on the total goodness or badness of its consequences i.e. on the effect of the action on the welfare of all human beings (or perhaps all sentient beings) (Smart and Williams, 1973: 4).

Hodgson offers the following definition of the AU principle:

> An act is right if and only if it would have best consequences, that is, consequences at least as good as those of any alternative act open to the agent (1967: 1).

And David Lyons characterises AU in the following way:

> Roughly speaking . . . Act-Utilitarianism is the theory that one should always perform acts the effects of which would be at least as good as those of any alternative. These are right actions; all others are wrong. It is one's duty, or over-all obligation, to perform right acts only; and thus if one act has the best consequences, that act is *the* thing to be done (1970: 9).

Rule Utilitarianism

The beginnings of RU may be found in the work of Mill. As we have seen, he speaks of the utility of rules rather than acts, and emphasises the importance of rules in regulating conduct rather than focusing upon independent decisions in individual situations. In order to know what to do we should appeal to a rule rather than continually recalculate the consequences of certain types of actions. The rules themselves, however, will be arrived at on the basis of utilitarian considerations: specific rules must be chosen because they are conducive to the general greater good than other rules, and for no other reason. When they cease to be more effective they must be modified or replaced. The principle of utility is thus still the ultimate standard but is now appealed to at the level of rules rather than at the level of individual acts. RU is defined by Smart, Hodgson and Lyons as follows:

> *Smart*: 'Rule-utilitarianism is the view that the rightness or wrongness of an action is to be judged by the goodness and badness of the consequences of a rule that everyone should perform the action in like circumstances' (1973: 9).
>
> *Hodgson*: 'According to the ethical systems which come under the name rule-utilitarianism, an act is right if it is in accordance with a rule the following of which has, or would have, good (or the best) consequences' (1967: 5).
>
> *Lyons*: 'By rule-utilitarianism I shall mean that kind of theory according to which the rightness or wrongness of particular acts can (or must) be determined by reference to a set of rules having some utilitarian defence, justification, or derivation' (1970: 11).

Let us now characterise a final form of utilitarianism relevant to our enquiry, NU.

Negative Utilitarianism

Earlier we noticed a subtle shift in Mill's statement of the principle of utility away from that of Bentham by placing exemption from pain before the increase of pleasure in his definition of the 'Greatest Happiness Principle'. All forms of utilitarianism recognise that pleasure and pain are correlatives. Bentham's 'two sovereign masters' are pain and pleasure (in that order) and his statement of the principle of utility embraces the prevention of 'mischief, pain, evil, and unhappiness' (1970: 12). Mill states that every supporter of the principle of utility 'from Epicurus to Bentham' has understood it to apply to 'pleasure itself, together with exemption from pain' (1957: 5). He defines the 'ultimate end' as 'an existence exempt as far as possible from pain, and as rich as possible in enjoyments' (1957: 11).

Smart, taking his cue from Popper, describes the doctrine of NU as holding 'that we should concern ourselves with the minimum of suffering rather than with the maximisation of happiness' (1973: 29). Popper himself enumerates NU as the second of the three most important principles of humanitarianism and equalitarian ethics (1962: i.235 n.6). It is:

> The recognition that all moral urgency has its basis in the urgency of suffering or pain. I suggest, for this reason, to replace the utilitarian formula 'Aim at the greatest amount of happiness for the greatest number', or briefly, 'maximise happiness', by the formula 'The least amount of avoidable suffering for all', or briefly, 'minimise suffering'.

Smart points out that Popper's utilitarianism here is inconsistent with his other two principles, namely toleration and the opposition of tyranny, which he appears to hold on non-utilitarian or deontic grounds. And as noted above, the general formulation of the principle of utility already enshrines the ideal of decreasing suffering as well as augmenting pleasure. In seeking to 'replace' the standard formula with his new one Popper merely narrows down the original by ruling out the injunction to maximise happiness. It is also unclear what is meant by 'suffering'. If it means 'pain', which seems to be Popper's intention, then he can be understood as calling for a new emphasis in our ethical priorities. This would involve tackling the basic and obvious instances of human suffering before turning our attention to improving the lot of those who are not in such manifest dire straits. If it is to include mental pain, dissatisfaction and discontent the matter becomes more complex. Would there be a duty, for instance, to minimise the suffering of someone who was merely envious of the good fortune of others? Actual physical suffering does seem to have a prior claim on our moral sensibilities, as may be seen from the response to disaster appeals. 'In my opinion', says Popper, '. . . human suffering makes a direct moral appeal, namely, the appeal for help, while there is no similar call to increase the happiness of a man who is doing well anyway' (1962: i.284 n.2).

It is also easier to agree on what is a case of physical suffering than it is to agree on which particular aspect of happiness should be maximised. It is this clear and simple awareness of the good to be brought about that gives NU its appeal. Drawing an analogy between ethics and natural science Popper argues that it is simpler to formulate objectives negatively:

> It adds to clarity in the field of ethics if we formulate our demand negatively, i.e. if we demand the elimination of suffering rather than the promotion of happiness. Similarly, it is helpful to formulate the task of scientific method as the elimination of false theories (from the various theories tentatively proffered) rather than the attainment of established truths (1962: i.285 n.2).

As H.B. Acton points out, however, while the moral claim of suffering may be more *urgent*, it is not necessarily more *important* than our obligation to those who are not in immediate distress (1963: 94). A further qualification is that Popper's call for the 'elimination' of suffering must be seen more narrowly as a call for the *minimisation* of suffering since it would otherwise lead to undesirable consequences. For instance, as Ninian Smart has argued, it would be the duty of a powerful ruler on NU grounds to destroy the human race if this could be done painlessly thus eradicating suffering once and for all (1958: 542f.). Again, in the absence of a theory of rebirth, suicide would be a commendable choice. Indeed, according to MacIntyre, one of the earliest exponents of NU, Hegesias, had to be prevented from teaching at Alexandria due to the number of suicides among his audience (1967: 101f.). Overall, however, in restating the principle of utility Popper is first and foremost, I think, encouraging us to concentrate our minds on the clear and indisputable facts of suffering and tackle the most urgent and practical problems first. This emphasis on the immediacy of suffering is reminiscent of Buddhism, which takes suffering as the starting point of its analysis of the human predicament in the first of its Four Noble Truths. We now turn to a consideration of the ethical form of the Buddha's teaching in the light of the utilitarian theories outlined above.

2. BUDDHISM AND UTILITARIANISM

There is an obvious similarity between the objectives of NU and Buddhist soteriology in that both aim at the reduction of suffering. Because of its belief in rebirth, however, Buddhism does not regard death as bringing suffering to a final end. Since suffering is said to be inherent in existence, only the stopping of rebirth will provide a permanent solution which guarantees the end of suffering. Again, within Buddhism itself there is a difference of aim: for the Small Vehicle the end of suffering is largely conceived of as a personal aim, whereas for the Large Vehicle it is seen as a universal one. A *bodhisattva* does not regard his task as complete until all beings have passed beyond the reach of suffering. Nevertheless, in spite of these qualifications, we may accept that both Buddhism and NU are committed to the reduction of suffering as an immediate goal.

The notion of suffering in Buddhism includes mental and physical suffering, which are encapsulated in the term *dukkha*. The goal of diminishing *dukkha* is common to all forms of Buddhism, and the Buddha himself made 'suffering and the end of suffering' the primary focus of his teaching. Pleasure and pain may both be thought of simply as degrees of *dukkha*. According to the *Precious Garland* they are correlative: 'Just as a lessening of pain is fancied to be real pleasure, So a suppression of pleasure is also fancied to be pain' (v. 362, tr. Hopkins, 1975).

As pointed out by King and Spiro, the whole of the Buddhist universe can be conceived of as strung out across a hedonistic continuum ranging from the lowest hell through the heavens to nirvana, at which point suffering ceases forever. Karma is the mechanism which regulates movement within this continuum, and may be defined as the principle that a moral antecedent will have a hedonistic consequence. That is to say, that a moral or immoral act (or volition) will have a result which can be entirely quantified in terms of pleasure and pain experienced by the actor. On this view karma is primarily a means for the reduction of suffering. It may be pointed out in passing that it is unlikely that karma could do away with human suffering altogether since not all suffering is due to karma; the Buddha recognised that flesh is also heir to adventitious sufferings, for instance in the case of certain illnesses (A.v.110). On the other hand, the karmically-generated blissful state of the gods is free of what most people would regard as 'suffering'.

On the understanding of karma outlined above there is a similarity between Buddhist ethics and consequentialist theories such as utilitarianism which grade moral action in terms of the non-moral utility subsequently produced. A further similarity might be seen between the Buddhist precepts (listed in Chapter 2) and the forms of RU. On this basis it might be said that the precepts are respected because of their overall or average utility in maximising desirable consequences (i.e. diminishing *dukkha*). At first blush, therefore, we may be tempted to categorise Buddhism as a system of NRU. In other words Buddhist ethics would be utilitarian; ethical decisions would be taken by reference to rules or precepts rather than determined on the spot in each case; and the primary aim (the utility) would be the reduction of suffering rather than the maximisation of happiness. The final escape from suffering would then be an intellectual achievement not involving ethics at all. While there is undoubtedly an interesting parallel between Buddhism and Utilitarianism when expressed in this fashion I believe that on closer examination the similarities turn out to be more apparent than real.

Formal Considerations

The first reason why Buddhist ethics cannot be utilitarian is a formal one. Unlike utilitarian theories Buddhism does not define the right independently from the good. There exists a clear conceptual relationship between the two, and they cannot be defined independently. Nirvana is the good, and rightness is predicated of acts and intentions to the extent which they participate in nirvanic goodness. The right and the good in Buddhism are inseparably intertwined. If an action does not display nirvanic qualities then it cannot be right in terms of Buddhist ethics whatever other characteristics (such as consequences) it might have. We have already seen this demonstrated in the relationship between *kusala* and nirvana. An action is judged to be *kusala* to the extent that it is harmonious with nirvanic values, and not to the extent that its *consequences* display or promote certain qualities. In Buddhism there is no *ex post facto* conferral of rightness upon actions as there is in utilitarianism. An action is right or wrong from the moment of its inception – its nature is fixed by reference to nirvanic values and it cannot subsequently change its status. Wrong (*akusala*) acts cannot turn out 'in the event' to have been right by virtue of their proximate or remote effects; nor can right (*kusala*) acts turn out to have been wrong in view of their consequences. For a utilitarian theory of ethics, however, both of these are real possibilities since rightness and goodness are separately defined.

Motive

A second reason concerns ethical motivation. In Buddhist ethics it is the motivation which precedes an act that determines its rightness. An act is right if it is virtuous, i.e. performed on the basis of Liberality (*arāga*), Benevolence (*adosa*) and Understanding (*amoha*). It is the preceding motivation (*cetanā*) which determines the moral quality of the act and not its consequences. In Buddhism acts have bad consequences because they are bad acts – they are not bad acts because they have bad consequences, as a utilitarian would maintain.[6] Moreover, for utilitarians motive is irrelevant whereas for Buddhists it is crucial. For utilitarians a good motive may be defined as one which produces an increase in the specified utility. Even a criminal motive may be a good motive for a utilitarian if it produces greater happiness than the alternatives. In utilitarian systems motive cannot be evaluated apart from consequences. There cannot, therefore, be any such thing as a good or bad motive until its consequences have been quantified. One of the peculiar features of utilitarianism is that it has no preference between acts which are conventionally regarded as good and evil so long as they achieve the same end. Utilitarians do, however, evaluate agents and motives analogically, and Smart explains how these descriptions are to be understood:

> A good agent is one who acts more nearly in a generally optimific way than does the average one. A bad agent is one who acts in a less optimific way than the average. A good motive is one which generally results in beneficent actions, and a bad motive is one which generally ends in maleficent actions (1973: 48).

Mill specifically rejects the view that the rightness of an action depends upon the motive from which it is done.[7] He distinguishes, as does the law, between motive and intent. Motive is 'That which moves or prompts a person to a particular course of action, or is seen by him as the ultimate purpose or end he seeks to achieve by that action.' It is to be distinguished from intent, which is 'the more immediate foreseen end to which he directs his acts.'[8] Yet for Mill neither intent nor motive have intrinsic moral worth, which contrasts sharply with the Buddha's insistence upon the morally determinative status of *cetanā*. A utilitarian may accept that certain motives, such as benevolence and generosity, do tend to further the production of happiness in society. This, however, is merely a fortuitous conjunction, and there is no necessary connection between the two. For utilitarians there are no intrinsically good motives, while for Buddhism action inspired by the three Cardinal Virtues is intrinsically good. In terms of Buddhist psychology, as we saw when discussing the *Abhidharma* in Chapter 3, the locus of good and evil is to be found in the human psyche – not in the consequences of actions in the world at large.

Kusala v *Puñña*

Let us bear in mind here the discussion of *kusala* and *puñña* as twin attributes of karmic actions in Chapter 5. The claim that Buddhism is consequentialist stems from the failure to distinguish between these two aspects of karma. While karmic actions do invariably have hedonistic consequences this is not where their moral value resides. Such a view puts the cart before the horse by reasoning that since the consequences were pleasant, the act which preceded them must have been good. In fact the logic of moral validation in Buddhism works the other way round. To illustrate how consequences, or *puñña,* may be related to but not identical with moral value (*kusala*) we may draw an analogy between *puñña* and praise and blame. Imagine that someone performs a virtuous (*kusala*) action and as a result of this is praised by and earns the respect of many people. What was it that made the act virtuous: the praise which followed it or some quality of the act itself? For a utilitarian it is the praise and the satisfaction taken in it by the agent, but for a deontologist (and for Buddhism) it is the intrinsic (*kusala*) worth of the act itself. Approbation is pleasant – this is *puñña* or the secondary consequence of the action; but approbation is not the criterion of moral goodness – this is to be established on independent grounds. Praise and blame and good and bad karma follow along as a consequence of moral and immoral actions but they do not act retrospectively to legitimate or condemn the moral quality of the action which engendered them.

A number of other problems surround the treatment of karma within a utilitarian framework. The existence of these problems does not show conclusively that Buddhist ethics is not utilitarian, but only that such an interpretation leads to conflict and incoherency when viewed alongside other fundamental Buddhist principles and doctrines. The utilitarian reading depends upon a particular view of karma, that is, as the principle that a moral cause will produce only a non-moral effect, such that moral goodness has no intrinsic soteriological value. On this reading karma partakes of the nature of *saṃsāra* and is therefore, as King and Spiro point out, hostile to nirvana. As well as the many problems and contradictions raised by this view which we have explored so far – such as how the transition from *saṃsāra* to nirvana can ever be made – some further difficulties which flow from this view of karma are considered below.

Internal and External Consequences

Karma is only one consequence of ethical action. We may refer to it as an internal consequence since it affects only the individual who performs the action. Human actions, and particularly moral actions, however, are not performed in a vacuum: there are also consequences in the world at large which we may refer to as external consequences, for example when a recipient benefits from a gift. Assuming that Buddhism is utilitarian, which sets of consequences are to count in our calculations? For the moment let us assume that it is the first set only. On this understanding Buddhism becomes a form of ethical egoism, and moral action becomes a means to further the private interests of the individual. This leads to the paradox that other-directed dispositions such as compassion (*karuṇā*) benevolence (*mettā*) and sympathetic joy (*muditā*) are cultivated for selfish purposes. Despite the counter-intuitive nature of this claim, the absence of textual evidence in support of it, and the abundance of textual evidence against it, it has been seriously advanced by Buddhist scholars, as noted in Chapter 1, and indeed is the logical outcome of the understanding of karma advocated by King and Spiro. However, the practice of Buddhist virtues such as the Divine Abidings would present a formidable psychological double-bind since one could only wish others well to the extent that one's own interests were thereby furthered. This odd conclusion is an indication that something is wrong with premises of the argument, and I have indicated in Chapter 4 where the problems with this view lie.

Let us consider now that both sets of circumstances are to count: the internal set being karmically guaranteed and the external set to be assessed as best one is able before the action is performed. In these circumstances one acts wherever possible in a manner which will benefit both oneself and others. On the application of utilitarian principles difficulties will arise here both in respect of quantification and in terms of conflict between the two sets of consequences. Quantification is difficult since, failing the power of the divine eye (*dibba-cakkhu*), the workings of karma remain obscure and difficult to fathom. It is, accordingly, very difficult to know what the karmic consequences of any action will be. Let us assume, however, a situation in which telling a deliberate lie will result in a good deal of 'external' happiness and involve only a minor amount of karmic suffering for the actor and perhaps very little or none at all if he has a good stock of merit. Since greater overall happiness would be produced by telling the lie it would, for a Buddhist Act Utilitarian, be the right course of action. But does Buddhism advocate overturning the precepts in such a fashion? There is little, if anything, in Theravāda sources to indicate that it would. The only consequentialist patterns of justification we have noted so far are Mahāyāna developments, and even there are ringed with caveats and provisos. Only the doctrine of *upāya*$_2$ could conceivably justify the programmed subordination of the precepts, and this doctrine is, to say the least, by no means clear cut.

A final problem concerns the position of the *Arahat*. Once the *Arahat* has transcended karma, what is it that is now to determine his moral conduct? If moral acts no longer have consequences for him then consequences cannot be the criterion of rightness. So why should he continue to follow rules which are fashioned on the basis of a utility in which he no longer has any interest? It is difficult to see from where, in terms of RU, the rules now derive their legitimacy. It is even more puzzling why the enlightened continue to respect them so scrupulously and are said to be incapable of breaking them.

Consequences and Rightness

It was noted in Chapter 2 that a heavenly rebirth is often cited as one of the benefits of a moral life. This state of existence is the highest which karma can bestow. On a utilitarian view, then, this is the highest good achievable through ethics and acts which produce it are by definition right. However, such a view is contradicted in the Canon when the Buddha invokes a criterion whereby even acts which produce divine bliss can be judged wrong. A passage in the *Questions of Sakka* (D.ii.85) tells how the gods (*deva*) defeated the demons (*asura*) and as a result experienced joy (*veda*) and happiness (*somanassa*). However, when making a moral assessment of this behaviour, the Buddha focuses not on the joyful experiences produced but on the nature of the acts which gave rise to them. In this case the pleasant consequences are not in fact commended since they were produced through violent means. It is said that such violent acts are not conducive to dispassion (*nibbidā*) and knowledge (*abhiññā*) and do not lead to nirvana. The happiness of the gods is then contrasted with the joy and satisfaction of hearing the *Dhamma*, which does produce the spiritual transformation required. This episode suggests that pleasant and unpleasant consequences do not lie at the root of Buddhist moral evaluation.

Obligation and Value

In the above discussion I have argued that Buddhism cannot be characterised adequately either in terms of utilitarian theories of obligation or in terms of utilitarian theories of value. Thus neither the maximising obligation nor the notion of a utility maximised are the central concerns of Buddhist ethics. In reaching this conclusion we have considered three forms of utilitarianism: AU, RU, and NU. Of these three AU is the purest form of the utilitarian principle and there are good arguments that the order two (and further variants) can be collapsed into it.[9] RU is basically a time-saving form of AU and NU is effectively included in the principle of utility by both Bentham and Mill. However, no form of utilitarianism can adequately characterise Buddhist ethics since it is not based fundamentally on a maximising principle.

In respect of value theory Buddhism has little in common with utilitarianism since it is not basically concerned with the generation and experience of states of affairs. Indeed, the constant regeneration of experience is precisely what Buddhism seeks to avoid. Even pleasurable states are, in Bradley's words, 'merely a perishing series of moments'; they are transient, superficial and ultimately valueless. For utilitarianism when one series of pleasurable states terminates another should be generated as quickly as possible; for Buddhism this grasping at what is impermanent is the root cause of suffering. Bernard Williams makes the point that its commitment to the pursuit of states of affairs is one of the basic weaknesses of consequentialism. It tends to ignore other values in its search for an anaesthetic against the painful experiences of life. If the goal of human life was merely the experience of pleasurable states who would not plug into the philosophers' experience machine at once?[10] Williams criticises utilitarianism for its failure to take seriously the value of human integrity and to overlook this in its headstrong pursuit of goods (Smart and Williams, 1973: 82; 99–103). Utilitarianism regards moral sentiment as merely a quotient in a calculus, and this leads to emotional alienation and a loss of personal integrity. Williams writes:

> Because our moral relation to the world is partly given by such feelings, and by a sense of what we can or cannot 'live with', to come to regard those feelings from a purely utilitarian point of view, that is to say, as happenings outside one's moral self, is to lose a sense of one's moral identity; to lose, in the most literal way, one's integrity (Smart and Williams, 1973: 103f.).

To conceive of moral value in terms of states of affairs is to trivialise it and ultimately deny it. It is to make it superficial, but in Buddhism moral value is not like this – it is dynamic, transformative, and a fundamental part of our psychological make-up. Moral development is a cumulative process involving the cultivation and expansion of moral sentiment: it cannot be reckoned up and cashed in as *karma-vipāka*. E.H. Johnston recognised this many years ago:

> *Karman* is thus a more vital conception in earlier Buddhism than it was reduced to later; it is not merely *vipāka*, the recompense in a future existence of the good and evil deeds committed in past existences, as held by the Vaibhāsikas, but it is the creator of the individual's moral character from the religious standpoint (1937: 37).

It is hardly conceivable that Buddhism should find intrinsic value in *karma-vipāka*: as a transient series of states it is the epitome of impermanence (*anicca*). Nor does it need a Buddhist to realise the ultimate disvalue of such pleasurable sensations. Bradley writes:

> Pleasure and pain are feeling, and they are nothing but feelings . . .This means that they exist in me only as long as I feel them, and only as I feel them, that beyond this they have no

> reference to anything else, no validity, and no meaning whatever. They are 'subjective' because they neither have, nor pretend to, reality beyond this or that subject. They are as they are felt to be, but they tell us nothing. In one word, they have no content: they are as states of us, but they have nothing for us (1927: 94).

The kind of states described above are superficial and ephemeral whereas the moral life in Buddhism finds teleological fulfilment in nirvana. For Buddhists the virtues are of value because they have a *telos* whereas the transient pleasures or satisfactions sought by Utilitarianism do not. Bradley again:

> The practical end, if it is to be a practical goal and standard, must present itself to us as some definite unity, some concrete whole that we can realise in our acts, and carry out in our life. And pleasure (as pain) we find to be nothing but a name which stands for a series of this, that, and the other feelings, which are not except in the moment or moments that they are felt, which have as a series neither limitation of number, beginning nor end, nor in themselves any reference at all, any of them, beyond themselves . . . And it is clear at once that this is not what is required for a practical end (1927: 95).

To sum up: despite a *prima facie* resemblance, the characterisation of Buddhist ethics as utilitarian is unsatisfactory for the reasons outlined above. Buddhist ethics can only be characterised as utilitarian if it is accepted that ethics has no ultimate value, no intrinsic relation to enlightenment, and serves only as temporary insulation from suffering within which intellectual goods can be pursued. I have admitted that Buddhism can be depicted along these lines by the selective use of (mainly Theravādin) sources. However, I do not believe that such an account could explain the partnership of ethics and insight emphasised throughout the mainstream tradition. We have rejected this depiction in favour of the view that Buddhist ethics can only be correctly understood when seen as inextricably linked to the *summum bonum*. Before taking leave of Utilitarianism there is one aspect of Mahāyāna ethics to which we must return – the doctrine of *upāya*.

3. SKILFUL MEANS AND SITUATION ETHICS

In many ways the Mahāyāna concept of Skilful Means (*upāya-kauśalya*) seems susceptible to analysis along AU lines since rules are frequently disregarded if the subsequent benefit for beings is thought to warrant it. In particular, with its increasing emphasis upon *karuṇā* the Mahāyāna ethos comes to resemble the Christian ethic of agapism. This is founded upon the injunction to love god and one's neighbour (*Matt*.22: 37–40) which is given precedence over all other obligations. Agapism may take many forms, but it is commonly coupled with a maximising obligation along utilitarian lines to promote the well-being of one's fellow man. Such, in essence, is the system of Situation Ethics espoused by Joseph Fletcher – a form of act-agapism in which each ethical decision must be assessed afresh in the situation in which it arises with the goal of maximising the well-being of one's neighbour. Let us set out Fletcher's system in more detail and then consider the similarities and differences between it and the *upāya* doctrine.

Situation Ethics

Fletcher accepts that Situation Ethics is 'a radical departure from the conventional wisdom and prevailing climate of opinion' (1966: 13) but sees it as a rediscovery of the essential Christian values which have been overlaid by centuries of casuistry. Situation Ethics claims that in practice, in any situation demanding ethical choice, the right decision cannot always be ordained beforehand in a code of laws or deduced from those laws; nor can it be reached by coming to the situation empty-handed with no principles at all. The correct orientation for ethical decision, argues Fletcher, should be taken with reference to the single principle of love. He writes:

> *Christian* situation ethics has only one norm or principle or law (call it what you will) that is binding and unexceptionable, always good and right regardless of the circumstances. That is 'love' – the *agape* of the summary commandment to love God and the neighbor (1966: 30).

This is the 'First Proposition' of Situation Ethics: 'Only one thing is intrinsically good; namely, love: nothing else at all' (1966: 57). This is not to say that the traditional moral guidelines are never satisfactory – in fact it might turn out that they are followed most of the time – but only that if there is conflict between them and the demands of love in the situation the latter must prevail. Traditional moral principles therefore become rules of thumb for ethical decision-making. Fletcher is opposed to any kind of ethical system-building but we must be clear about exactly what he objects to in this practice. Although he fastens mainly on to the impracticality of *applying* pre-cast rules equitably he also denies, as a utilitarian, the intrinsic *validity* of the rules themselves. He writes: 'The situationist never says, "Almsgiving is a good thing. Period!" but only "Almsgiving is a good thing *if*"' (1966: 26). Thus when Situation Ethics ignores a rule against stealing it does not only *allow* stealing but also regards it as correct, right and desirable.

Fletcher distinguishes between what he calls an ontological, intrinsic ethic (the view that what is good is enshrined in the rules) and an existential, extrinsic one (the view that what is right depends on the situation). Situation Ethics clearly belongs in the second category. 'We are to tell the truth', writes Fletcher, 'for loves sake, not for its own sake. If love vetoes the truth, so be it. Right and wrong, good and bad, are things that happen to what we say and do, whether they are veracious or not, depending how much love is served in the situation' (1966: 65).

Love

It is clear that love occupies the central place in Situation Ethics and it is important to qualify this rather nebulous term. It is used in Situation Ethics as the equivalent of *agape*, which in turn is defined as 'goodwill at work in partnership with reason'. It is to be distinguished sharply from romantic love (*eros*) and love in friendship (*philia*) which have narrower objectives. While these two are emotional, *agape* is a disposition of the will and an attitude of mind (1966: 79). *Agape* is non-reciprocal. It is one-way but not unidirectional and its target is not restricted to one group. It even extends to enemies. In short, it is an altruistic other-directed disposition which seeks no reciprocation.

The most obvious point of contact between Situation Ethics and AU is in their rejection of action-guiding principles and norms. Each and every ethical decision is to be reviewed afresh in the light of its projected consequences. In view of this an opponent might claim that Situation Ethics demands 'more critical intelligence, more factual information, and more self-starting commitment to righteousness than most people can bring to bear' (1966: 81). To this the reply is that we must rely on our own faculties more than before and make greater efforts to find out the facts before acting. As Fletcher puts it: 'Situation ethics puts a high premium on our knowing what's what when we act' (1966: 84).

Knowledge

Knowledge is the essential counterpart of love. As Paul Ramsey puts it, love must 'figure the angles' and prudence must be relied on to find 'absolute love's relative course'. Each decision-making situation is unique, and the solution needs to be found from within the context of that situation once it has been examined and correctly understood. For the act to be right, one's assessment of the circumstances and the consequences of the action must be correct: if the desired goal is achieved (the maximum distribution of love) the act was right; if it is not achieved, the act was wrong. 'Our situation ethics', writes Fletcher, 'frankly joins forces with Mill' (1966: 115). The Principle of Utility is now modified from 'the greatest good of the greatest number', to 'the greatest *agape* of the greatest number'. Love's aims are the increase of love itself in the world, and courses of action are selected on the basis of an 'agapeic calculus' modelled on Bentham's felicific calculus.

To conclude this summary we may recapitulate the main points. Situation Ethics takes as its central principal that only one thing, love or *agape*, is intrinsically good. Love is to be linked with reason to determine the right course of action in any situation. The right act is defined as that which furthers the increase of love beyond any of the alternatives, even at the expense of infringing moral norms. According to Fletcher Situation Ethics is founded upon six Propositions, as follows:

1. Only one 'thing' is intrinsically good; namely love: nothing else at all.
2. The ruling norm of Christian decision is love: nothing else.
3. Love and justice are the same, for justice is love distributed, nothing else.

4. Love wills the neighbour's good whether we like him or not.
5. Only the end justifies the means; nothing else.
6. Love's decisions are made situationally, not prescriptively.

Formal Similarities

It was suggested in Chapter 6 that *upāya* has two forms, a normative and a non-normative one. The normative one is that which is taken by Buddhists as a model for imitation and implementation, and which involves the personal cultivation of the first six Perfections. The non-normative version of the doctrine is the *upāya* displayed by the Great *Bodhisattvas* which involves them in forms of antinomian conduct and which, I have suggested, is best interpreted as the symbolic affirmation of the importance of *karuṇā*. However, I think it is fair to say that a case could be made out according to which the *upāya*$_2$ doctrine, if taken as referring to normative ethics, could be regarded as structurally similar to Situation Ethics. Like the latter it would be 'a radical departure from the conventional wisdom and prevailing climate of opinion', but would doubtless regard itself as a rediscovery of the basic ideal of compassion displayed by the Buddha but overlaid by centuries of religious conservatism. An *upāya*-inspired ethic would break free of the code of laws passed on through tradition and approach the situation of ethical decision-making not empty-handed but armed with a revised scale of values in which compassion (*karuṇā*) is predominant.

Fletcher makes love the supreme principle of Christian ethics, and there is undoubtedly a tendency for Mahāyāna ethics to be dominated increasingly by the single value of *karuṇā*. On the meaning of *karuṇā* Dayal has this to say:

> It should be rendered into English by such words as 'love', 'pity', 'mercy', 'compassion', and all their synonyms, or approximate synonyms put together. No one word can convey an adequate idea of what *karuṇā* means. It is mentioned in an enormous number of passages in all the principal treatises. It is perhaps the word that occurs most frequently in Mahāyāna literature (1932: 178).

Āryaśūra and Śāntideva eulogise *karuṇā* and exalt it above all other virtues. Śāntideva quotes the *Dharmasaṅgīti-sūtra* to the effect that a *bodhisattva* needs only *karuṇā* to gain all the attributes of Buddhahood:

> The *Bodhisattva* Avalokiteśvara, the Great Being, said this to the Lord. 'A *bodhisattva*, Lord, should not practise too many things. One virtue (*dharma*) alone, Lord, should be faithfully served and fully perfected by him, in which all the virtues of a Buddha are encompassed. And what is that? – it is Great Compassion (*mahākaruṇā*). It is through Great Compassion, O Lord, that all the Buddha-qualities are encompassed for *bodhisattvas* (*Śikṣā*. 151: 14–18).

As more and more emphasis is placed upon the welfare of others as the sole end, the means employed to achieve it are questioned less and less. The *bodhisattva* who is motivated by *karuṇā* will seek the well-being of his fellow creatures and choose that course of action which has best consequences irrespective of moral norms which might prohibit it. It is, of course, assumed that the act *will* promote the well-being of others, and this is where *prajñā* plays its part in 'figuring the angles'. As noted in the discussion of *upāya* in Chapter 6, knowledge now becomes a secondary good at the service of compassion. In Situation Ethics love finds its metaphysical justification in the nature of god, but no such equivalent resource is claimed in the case of *karuṇā*: the concept of the 'embryonic Buddha-nature' (*tathāgatagārbha*) is perhaps the closest the Mahāyāna comes to such a metaphysical ground.

Although I have suggested in Chapter 6 that *upāya*$_2$ was not widely followed as a normative doctrine, it nevertheless has the potential to be developed in this way. Since there is a scriptural basis for the doctrine it would not be surprising to find traces of its influence, perhaps as justification for exceptional deeds. I do not know if the doctrine of *upāya* is invoked specifically in this connection, but the benefits arising from the death of gLang-dar-ma are apparently regarded by some Tibetans as sufficient justification for his assassination.[11] On the contemporary scene one might expect to find the doctrine invoked to legitimise the use of violence against the Chinese occupation of Tibet. I note that Geshe Kelsang Gyatso describes Mahāyāna ethics in terms reminiscent of Situation Ethics (1980: 132–4; 146–50).

Granted the formal similarity between Situation Ethics and *upāya*$_2$, to establish whether or not the Situation Ethics principle of *upāya* was ever invoked for normative justification, and in what circumstances, would, as noted above, require a study of historical sources which is beyond our present scope. It is perhaps worth noting that Situation Ethics has not in general found favour with mainstream Christianity, and has been criticised as a distortion of Christian ethics in giving undue emphasis to only one aspect of its teachings. In practical terms sweeping aside the traditional precepts is not without its dangers, and may expose many people to both responsibility and temptation they are ill-equipped to bear. It may turn out that *upāya*$_2$, like Situation Ethics itself, was not an idea which found favour with the majority of Buddhists, and (if indeed it was ever seriously promoted as a normative doctrine) may well have been regarded as an eccentric development best kept at arm's length.

We are now in a position to summarise the different attitudes adopted by the Mahāyāna with respect to the precepts:

1. Absolutism: all of the precepts are absolute moral rules and are not to be infringed under any circumstances.
2. Qualified Absolutism: the core precepts are absolute moral rules but the 'lesser and minor' precepts are *prima facie* obligations which may be varied in the light of competing moral claims. This is the distinction between serious and minor offences.
3. Situational: the *upāya*$_2$ of the Great *Bodhisattvas* is to be taken as a model for imitation and a paradigm for ethical choice. We may characterise this alternatively as Agapistic Act-Utilitarianism (AAU).

One final point concerning the equivalence of Situation Ethics and *upāya* needs to be made. For Fletcher a loving motivation and a successful outcome provide absolute justification – it is by reference to these two criteria that we determine the rightness of actions. Likewise, in certain Mahāyāna passages, a breach of the precepts on the basis of *upāya* results in good karmic consequences. At other times, however, motivation on the basis of *karuṇā* and beneficial consequences for one's fellow man do not provide absolute justification since the *bodhisattva* is left to suffer the negative karmic consequences of his actions (e.g. *Śikṣā*. 93.20–22). This indicates that certain breaches of the precepts were still felt to be objectively wrong. If so, the implication is that there is a further criterion of rightness beyond compassionate motivation. The texts which adopt this position therefore underline the importance of altruism and supererogation while still reserving a deontological basis for moral validation. Such an attitude may represent either an independent position or an earlier stage in the development of the full-blown doctrine. A systematic chronological survey of the sources would be required to determine the various stages in the evolution of the Situation Ethics of *upāya*$_2$.

8

Buddhism and Aristotle

For often we think about things in India

Aristotle, MM: 1899.21

For Aristotle only the wise are virtuous and only the virtuous wise

Anthony Kenny, Aristotle's Theory of the Will, p. 80

In spite of their different social and cultural contexts there are many formal parallels between the ideal of human perfection conceived by the Buddha and that envisaged by Aristotle. Both regard human nature as a complex of intellectual and emotional factors and consider that the final good for man lies in the full development of his potential in these two dimensions. For both, again, this is a gradual, cumulative process. The state of perfection finally reached – nirvana for Buddhism and *eudaemonia* for Aristotle – is characterised by happiness and is the final goal of human endeavour.

The Virtues

This state of perfection is the *telos* of human aspiration, and while there are inevitable cultural differences in its characterisation in India and Greece there is a broad measure of agreement in respect of its formal content. Essentially it consists in man fulfilling his function through the development of his potentiality in accordance with a specific conception of a goal or end. The similarity is an abstract conceptual one; the form in which this perfection manifests itself will be influenced by judgements as to which particular qualities constitute the ideal. As well as a shared concept of an ideal end they also have in common a programme for its realisation involving the furtherance of human potential through the medium of certain practices known as virtues. In connection with Aristotle, MacIntyre writes: 'The virtues are precisely those qualities the possession of which will enable an individual to achieve *eudaemonia* and the lack of which will frustrate his movement towards that *telos*' (1981: 139).

But the virtues are not simply instrumental means to an end which transcends them. What is distinctive about the virtues is that they participate in and *constitute* the end. As MacIntyre says:

> But the exercise of the virtues is not in this sense *a* means to the end of the good for man. For what constitutes the good for man is a complete human life lived at its best, and the exercise of the virtues is a necessary and central part of such a life, not a mere preparatory exercise to secure such a life. We thus cannot characterise the good for man adequately without already having made reference to the virtues (1981: 140).

The virtues are the means to the gradual realisation of the end through the incarnation of the end in the present. Living in accordance with the end is, to borrow a phrase from Cooper, 'a progressive articulation of the end itself'. It is a project which is progressively realised through time in the transformation of personality. Whereas Aristotle allows for only one lifetime, in Buddhism this slow maturation takes place over the course of many lives – there is no 'sudden enlightenment' without prior cultivation, and liberation does not supervene, to quote Aristotle, 'like an adventitious charm'. I have argued that in Buddhism morality is not merely a means to an end. The Buddha displayed this clearly in the exercise of the moral virtues both before and after his enlightenment – they were a necessary and central part of his life. It is because of this internal relationship between virtue and the *summum bonum* that the Aristotelian and, as I will argue, Buddhist ethical schemes, are teleological rather than consequentialist.

Sources and Similarities

The main body of Aristotelian ethical theory is to be found in three treatises: the *Nicomachean Ethics* (*NE*); the *Eudemian Ethics* (*EE*); and the *Magna Moralia* (*MM*). The order of composition seems to have been in the reverse of the order in which I have listed them, with the *NE* constituting Aristotle's mature reflections on ethics. The *MM* is probably a summary or report, not in his own hand, of Aristotle's earliest lectures on ethics, while the *EE* is a genuine work of Aristotle preceding the composition of the *NE*. There are three chapters common to both the *EE* and the *NE* and it seems likely that these chapters (V–VII of the *NE* and IV–VI of the *EE*) were originally written for the *EE*.[1]

The points of contact between Buddhist and Aristotelian ethics which I wish to develop are as follows:

(1) The Goal: I will argue that *eudaemonia* and nirvana are functionally and conceptually related in that both constitute that final goal, end and *summum bonum* of human endeavour. It is not suggested that they are experientially identical or have the same metaphysical or soteriological consequences (e.g. the end of rebirth). For Aristotle the goal of human perfection has no transcendental implications: it is a perfection to be manifested in this world alone and specifically in the social context of the *polis*. After the death of Plato in 347 BC Aristotle moved rapidly away from the notion of a transcendent reality enshrined in the doctrine of the Forms, and his concern with ethics is empirical and pragmatic. Ethics, for Aristotle, is a subdivision of the architectonic science of politics, and his quest overall is for meaning and fulfilment in the concrete social and political situation in which the individual finds himself. We shall find, therefore, no point of contact between Aristotelian ethics and the transcendent dimension of nirvana.

(2) Psychology: The goal or terminus of human perfection described as *eudaemonia* or nirvana is conceived of as embracing a bilateral perfection. The parameters of the goal are determined by the facts of human nature and its potential for development. I will briefly set out Aristotle's psychology – his doctrine of the soul – and compare this with Buddhist psychology. I will conclude that both espouse a binary theory of human nature and human good. Having considered the nature of the goal and the relevant facts about human nature we will also comment upon the method by which this nature is to be transformed so as to approach its *telos*. The transformation is made through the medium of the virtues, and I will consider the nature of the relationship between the virtues and the goal.

After dealing with points (1) and (2) above I will focus in (3) on a single point of contact between the two systems, namely their conception of moral choice and its operation. The faculty of moral choice for Aristotle is *prohairesis* and for Buddhism it is *cetanā*: for both it is the pivot around which virtue and vice revolve. I hope to demonstrate the conceptual similarities in respect of the operation of this faculty in each case and thereby establish a specific point of contact between Aristotelian and Buddhist ethics. The exploration of further points of contact will be a task for future research. Finally, in (4), I will conclude the chapter with a few general remarks about the role of desire and the effective faculties in Buddhist soteriology. In sum, in this chapter I will outline similarities in respect of the goal or end, the starting point, and the means of passing from the latter to the former. I am not suggesting that we will find anything approaching complete agreement between the Buddha and Aristotle on these points, although there are many similarities and interesting points of contact. It does appear, however, that Aristotelianism provides a useful Western analogue which will be of use in elucidating the foundations and conceptual structure of Buddhist ethics.

1. *EUDAEMONIA* AND NIRVANA

Aristotle's starting point is the goal-directed nature of human activity. All deliberate human action, be observes (*NE*, I.1), aims at some goal or end. Some of these goals are ends in themselves while others are means to still higher ends. Men are not always clear about what their higher ends are and sometimes act in a confused and contradictory manner. The mature and responsible man, however, (to whom Aristotle addresses his lectures: *NE*, I.3 1095a.1), will seek to clarify his values and arrive at some conception of where his happiness, fulfilment, wellbeing, and flourishing lie. It is this final long-term end of flourishing which is constitutive of Aristotle's notion of *eudaemonia*, and it is this end which gives meaning and direction to individual lives.[2]

A Second-Order End

Conceptually, *eudaemonia* can be characterised as a second-order end – a kind of umbrella covering a range or cluster of primary or first-order ends. These first-order ends will be selected on the basis of their conformity with the second-order end and will be pursued to the extent that they form a harmonious combination with other first-order ends. *Eudaemonia* as a second-order end, therefore, provides an orderly framework for the pursuit and attainment of subordinate or first-order objectives. In other words, one will select and participate in objectives according to and to the extent that such objectives are conducive to one's overall long-term flourishing or *eudaemonia*. Aristotle puts it as follows:

> If, then, there is some end of the things we do which we desire for its own sake (everything else being desired for the sake of this), and if we do not choose everything for the sake of something else (for at that rate the process would go on to infinity, so that our desire would be empty and vain), clearly this must be the good and the chief good. Will not the knowledge of it, then, have a great influence on life? Shall we not, like archers who have a mark to aim at be more likely to hit upon what is right? (*NE*, I.2, 1094a18–25)

Aristotle goes on to characterise further this good achievable by action: it must be final (*teleion*), self-sufficient (*autarkes*), that is to say which 'when isolated makes life desirable and lacking in nothing' (*NE*, I.2, 1097 b14–15); again it must be 'most desirable of all things, without being counted as one good thing among others' (*NE*, I.2, 1097 b16–17). In short, as Cooper puts it, the final human good will have the following three characteristics: (a) it is desired for its own sake; (b) everything else that is desired is desired for the sake of it; (c) it is never chosen for the sake of anything else (1975: 92).

A Dominant End

Eudaemonia, as a second-order end, must not be confused with the notion of a dominant end. Let us take power as an example of the latter. A man who identifies his final good as the wielding of power may aim to become wealthy, cultivate the friendship of influential people, take up a career in politics and marry into the aristocracy. All of these things will be for him subordinate ends since they are chosen to increase his power (the dominant end). This does not, of course, prevent him enjoying them in themselves, and not until these things frustrate the dominant end will they be perceived as disvalues. Yet it is clear that they may do exactly that: things which are generally recognised as basic human goods, such as friendship and affection, may all too easily stand in the way of power. The person who desires power may find it can only be purchased at the expense of subverting truth, honour and friendship. And if power is truly a dominant end for him he will not hesitate to sacrifice these things. Such a conception is essentially utilitarian. Since a dominant end may conflict with and exclude other goods such a notion cannot adequately characterise *eudaemonia* since this is inclusive of other goods rather than opposed to them.

To lack even a dominant end is the mark of a confused person: faced with a plurality of competing appetites and goals among his first-order ends he will be without a criterion for choice and be pulled in different directions. Thus, says Aristotle:

> Everyone who is able to live according to his own choosing sets up some goal (*tina skopon*) for the good life – honour, or reputation, or riches, or intellectual cultivation – by looking to which he will perform all his actions (since not to organise one's life with a view to some end is a sign of great stupidity) (*EE*. I.2, 1214b 4–14, tr. Cooper).

To have one's actions geared towards a dominant end, then, would be a step in the right direction. But geared towards *which* end? Aristotle mentions four possibilities above: honour, reputation, wealth, and intellectual cultivation. Must one be selected at the expense of the others, and if so, on what basis is the evaluation to be made? Again, could any of these things alone constitute the complete good for man which Aristotle conceives *eudaemonia* to be? It seems not, since any of these concrete goods could be supplemented by the addition of another. Would it not be letter, for example, for a millionaire to be wise as well as rich? *Eudaemonia*, then, cannot be defined as a single dominant end after the fashion of utilitarianism. This is how Aristotle puts it:

> The self-sufficient we now define as that which when isolated makes life desirable and lacking in nothing; and such we think *eudaemonia* to be; and further we think it most desirable of all things, without being counted as one good thing among others – if it were so counted it would clearly be made more desirable by the addition of even the least of goods; for that which is added becomes an excess of goods, and of goods the greater is always more desirable. *Eudaemonia*, then, is something final and self-sufficient, and is the end of action (*NE*, I.7, 1097b 13–22).

'Aristotle explicitly recognizes', says Cooper with reference to this passage, 'that flourishing must be conceived of as including a number of good things rather than as dominated by a single end' (1975: 99).

Let me summarise Aristotle's line of thought so far. Human action is goal directed; men pursue many and varied goals, but let us imagine there is one goal which constitutes the final good for man. What will this goal be like? It will not involve the random pursuit of multiple goods (a plurality of first-order ends), nor even one particular good amongst others (a dominant end). Rather it will include a number of good things (yet to be defined) in harmonious combination: this is how we are to understand *eudaemonia* or human flourishing.

Nirvana

I believe that the formal characterisation of *eudaemonia* provided by Aristotle can be applied to nirvana.[3] Whatever else nirvana is, it is indisputably the *summum bonum* of Buddhism and may be characterised, like *eudaemonia*, in the way described above: (a) it is desired for its own sake; (b) everything else that is desired is desired for the sake of it; (c) it is never chosen for the sake of anything else. This formal equivalence of *eudaemonia* and nirvana seems unexceptionable, and in fact involves little more than the conceptual unpacking of the notion of an inclusive final goal. So far I have discussed only the formal structure of *eudaemonia* as a second-order end and said nothing about its content, since this information must await a consideration of Aristotle's anthropology in the following section. However, since an account of the Buddhist conception of the final goal as consisting of *sīla* and *paññā* has already been provided we may take this opportunity to illustrate why nirvana can only be understood as a second-order end and not in terms of the dominant-end model.

Paññā as a Dominant End

I suggested in Chapter 1 that the major problem for Buddhist ethics is to understand the nature of the relationship between *sīla*, *paññā*, and nirvana. A widely held view of Buddhist soteriology makes dominant a single end, namely knowledge or insight (*paññā*). This is an idea which I have challenged in this book on the grounds that it does not adequately embrace the fullness of human perfection which constitutes nirvana. The soteriological goal of

Buddhism has suffered from a predominantly intellectualist interpretation by scholars, which has led to it being identified with a particular kind of cognitive experience.[4] This is an impoverishment of its true meaning. It is the failure to acknowledge the ethical dimension of nirvana that lends plausibility to the utilitarian characterisation of Buddhist ethics we examined in the last chapter. In the discussion of utilitarianism there we considered whether Buddhism was utilitarian with specific reference to the relationship between moral action (*kamma*) and its non-moral hedonistic consequences (*kamma-vipāka*). This is the most obvious sense in which Buddhism might be thought of as espousing a maximising policy, namely with respect to the production of merit (*puññā*). Merit itself, however, according to the intellectualist thesis, is subordinate to the ultimate goal of knowledge. Since the dominant soteriological end is *paññā*, ethical (and all other) goods may be pursued only to the extent that they are conducive to the promotion of the dominant end, namely knowledge. This immediately raises the question of the status of the other objectives commended in Buddhist literature. Taking the Six Perfections as an example, what is now the status of the first five, namely Generosity, Morality, Forbearance, Courage and Meditation? Of course, there would be nothing illogical in the suggestion that although the sixth, Knowledge (*prajñā*), is the supreme goal (the dominant end), the other five are acknowledged and pursued as well (first-order ends). Yet if so these other ends must do nothing to frustrate the pursuit of knowledge. On this reading morality (and any other first-order end) would be secondary and subsidiary, and could make no claim upon the agent which conflicted with *prajñā*. A dominant end functions to regulate choice and in any conflict between, for example, morality and knowledge, it would always be morality which was sacrificed. It would follow that there could be no objection to breaches of the precepts which were instrumental to the acquisition of knowledge. Let us take the simple example of stealing a religious text in order to study it. We will assume that no-one else requires it so that the aggregate of knowledge is not reduced overall. If knowledge is a dominant end then the theft of the text for study is good and right. It might be argued that the act is still wrong because the evil karmic consequences flowing from it might in some way frustrate the future acquisition of knowledge. However, this complication could be eliminated by postulating the case of an individual with a stock of good karma sufficient to smother any negative results of the theft. The pursuit of knowledge by such a person would be furthered by the theft and therefore stealing the text would be right. No doubt more extreme examples could be formulated involving cruelty and torture as means to knowledge: all would be legitimate means if knowledge is truly a dominant Buddhist end.

Again, on this reading, it is difficult to see why morality should be important at all beyond a certain limited point. Its function here would be twofold: one cosmological and the other psychological. The first function would be to provide a suitable form of rebirth, let us say as a human being; and the second would provide the necessary peace of mind for intellectual pursuits. Once these goals had been achieved there could be no incentive whatsoever to cultivate non-intellectual goods. If *prajñā* were a dominant end, once the minimum moral investment for a suitable rebirth had been made, morality should be sacrificed to knowledge at every opportunity. No amount of moral good could outweigh even the slightest amount of intellectual good. Intellectual pursuits should always be given priority and since intellectual realisation is purely an individual matter one's own interests must always come first. Indeed, it may be truer to say that it was the overvaluation of intellectual goods rather than simple self-interest which led the followers of the Small Vehicle to pursue a private salvation.

The view described above which makes knowledge a dominant end for Buddhism fails to do justice to the rich and complex pattern of other worthwhile ends commended in the texts. The Buddha recognised a plurality of human goods and does not appear to have regarded these as subordinate to intellectual cultivation. In other words, ethical goodness does not appear to be a first-order end which may be sacrificed to a dominant end. The first five Perfections are not subordinate to the sixth: rather all are coordinate parts of the second-order end which is nirvana. There is nothing to suggest that the Buddha commended virtues such as generosity and compassion only with the proviso that they be abandoned in favour of intellectual advancement however small. Indeed, as noted in Chapter 2, there is the suggestion in the Canon that if a choice is to be made it is *sīla* that should be cultivated in preference to *paññā* (*A*.ii.7f.). We may conclude, then, that the intellectualist thesis of *paññā* as a dominant end cannot account for the value which Buddhism sources place upon morality and other non-intellectual human goods such as love and friendship.[5]

The Classification of Aristotelian Ethics

To conclude this section we might enquire how the Aristotelian ethical system is to be classified. It is not utilitarian since it recognises a plurality of goods which cannot be traded off against a single utility. '*Eudaemonia*', says Aristotle, 'is composed of certain good things . . . it is nothing else beside these, it *is* these' (*MM*.1184a 26–29). By partaking of these good things one partakes of the end, and one may be said to flourish to the extent that one participates in the basic goods constitutive of *eudaemonia*. Morality is not a means to the end of happiness; rather happiness supervenes on excellent activity 'like the bloom on the cheek of youth'. Here lies the difference between Aristotle and utilitarianism, that Aristotle does not separate the right from the good whereas utilitarianism does. Cooper writes concerning Aristotle:

> For although he does hold that virtuous action is a means to *eudaemonia*, or human good, *eudaemonia* is itself not specified independently of virtuous action; on the contrary, *eudaemonia* is conceived of as identical with a lifetime of morally virtuous action (1975: 88).

Nor must we fall into the other extreme and classify Aristotle among the deontologists:

> It does not follow, of course, that Aristotle must be classed as a deontologist: for although he agrees with Kant in rejecting maximisation schemes of all kinds in favor of a definitely structured life, he does not think of moral constraints themselves as imposed on persons without regard for (and even despite) their own good, as Kant . . . tends to do. In Aristotle's theory, human good *consists* (partly) in virtuous action (1975: 88).

So how, then, should we classify Aristotle's ethics? I suggest that it is best described as teleological, if we understand this term as excluding consequentialist theories. For Aristotle, unlike consequentialism, the end or *telos* is intrinsically related to the means through which it is pursued. By teleological, then, we should understand the continual expansion of individual capacity towards the goal of complete perfection, rather than the generation of a single transient utility. Buddhism too, is best understood as a teleological system which provides the framework for personal cultivation and accomplishment this time through a series of lives structured in accordance with a specific conception of human nature and its *telos*. I will turn now to a consideration of other points of contact between the two systems.

2. ARISTOTLE'S PSYCHOLOGY

In the preceding section it was argued that *eudaemonia* and nirvana are not to be conceived of as identical with a single human good and must embrace a plurality of first-order ends. I will now outline, by reference to Aristotle's doctrine of human nature, his conception of the basis upon which the choice of these ends will be determined. The purpose of Aristotle's ethical enquiry is to determine the good for man (*to anthropinon agathon*), i.e. in what his flourishing consists. And in order to determine the good for man, says Aristotle, we must know something of the nature of man (*NE*.I.13). Since man is a composite being (*sunthetos ousia*) his good will lie in the perfection of those elements of his nature which admit of perfectibility. Since matter is ethically neutral, human virtue is the virtue 'not of the body but of the soul' (*NE*.I.13). *Eudaemonia* is therefore defined as excellent activity of the soul (*NE*.I.7), and an analysis of the powers of the soul will indicate the spheres in which this excellence or virtue may be achieved.

The Soul or Psyche

To understand how Aristotle arrives at his binary conception of human perfection we must consider his theory of the bipartite division of the soul and show how this is related to the final goal of human flourishing. Greek notions of the soul (*psyche*) are no less complex and varied than their Indian counterparts. However, at the risk of oversimplification, we may say that a simple conception of the psyche would be as something which plants and animals possess but inanimate objects, such as rocks, do not.[6] Man, as the highest of the animate creatures, also possesses the faculty of reason or intellectual power known as *nous*. Aristotle's views on the soul changed during the course of his life, but his mature position is that of the *De Anima*.[7] For Aristotle the soul is the form of an animate body, it is the organisational principle which gives form to substances. Substances are compounds of form and matter, and the soul or psyche is the form of living organisms, such as the human body. Matter is the potential and soul is the form (*eidos*), essence (*ousia*), definition (*logos*), or actuality (*energeia* or *entelecheia*) of this potential. Just as matter and form are inextricably related, so are the soul and the body. Man is composite (*sunthetos*) but body and soul are aspects of the same substance. Body and soul are related non-dualistically: the soul does not stand over against the body as a separate thinking thing, and psychological phenomena are essentially psycho-physical. Aristotle explains the relationship between soul and matter by the use of a metaphor familiar to Buddhism in another context. 'There is no need to enquire', he says in the *De Anima*, 'whether the soul and the body are one any more than there is to enquire whether the wax and the shape given to it by the stamp are one, or generally the matter of anything and that of which it is the matter' (*B*.1.412b 6–8). However, Aristotle does suggest in the *De Anima* that the reasoning faculty of the soul (*nous*) may have an independent existence from the soul–body aggregate and be separable from it.[8] He does not, however, specify what kind of individuality would belong to a mind thus separated.[9]

In *De Anima* II, Aristotle acknowledges different degrees of sophistication of the psyche according to a hierarchy of faculties or powers. The five powers in ascending order are nutrition, appetite, sensation, locomotion, and thought. The lower the form of life the fewer of these powers it possesses: plants, for example, possess only the first while only man possesses them all. The second power, that of appetite (*orexis*), is the genus of which desire or lust (*epithumia*), passion or anger (*thumos*), and wish or volition (*boulesis*) are the species.[10] The third, sensation, includes the five senses, the input from which is processed by a 'common sense', which is a faculty of *nous*. The power of thought in general has two applications, one theoretical and the other practical.

The Two 'Parts' of the Soul

This rather complicated scheme of the powers of the soul collapses into a neat binary division according to which the soul has a rational part and a non-rational part (*D.An.*, III). We may most easily think of this in terms of the distinction between the cognitive and affective or in the simplest terms the head and the heart. This

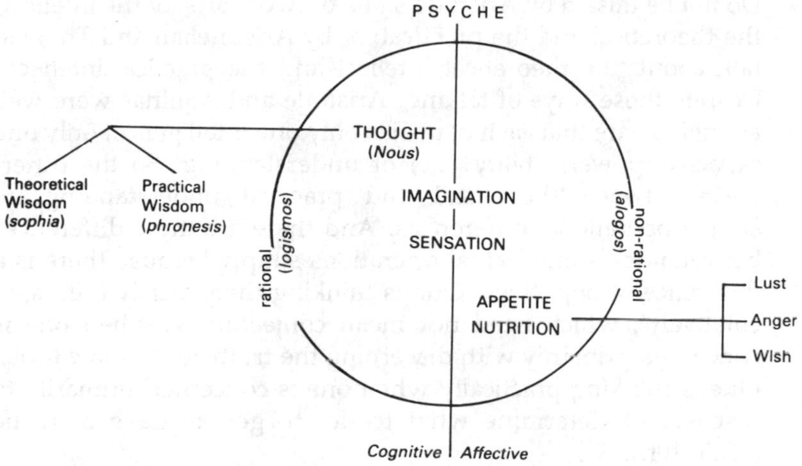

Figure 1. The powers of the Aristotelian psyche

distinction is not entirely clear-cut and some powers of the soul may straddle both sides: this is true of the power of sensation, and Aristotle also speaks of an 'imaginative' part of the soul as belonging to both sides. Before going any further let us illustrate the main terms and distinctions introduced so far in the form of a diagram (Figure 1). Intellectual perfection, the excellence of *nous*, has two aspects: theoretical wisdom (*sophia*) and practical wisdom (*phronesis*). *Sophia* is that power of *nous* responsible for the 'perception of self-evident truths, such as the geometrical axioms'.[11] It is 'concerned only with permanent truths, which man is powerless to change.'[12] The best English equivalent for *nous* in this sense is 'intuition'[13] or 'insight'. There is a close similarity between *sophia* and *paññā*, the latter being essentially concerned with the realisation of the universal truths of impermanence (*anicca*), suffering (*dukkha*), and no-self (*anattā*).

The second aspect of intellectual virtue lies in practical wisdom (*phronesis*). Practical wisdom is the perfection of the rational part of the mind in its capacity to select right means to good ends. The distinction between *sophia* and *phronesis* is an abstract one and they are best conceived of as different modes or operations of *nous*. As Finnis points out, these two functions should not be compartmentalised:

> Do not be misled by Aristotle's talk of two 'parts' of the intellect, the theoretical and the practical; or by Aristotelian and Thomist talk about 'the theoretical intellect and the practical intellect'. Despite these ways of talking, Aristotle and Aquinas were well enough aware that each of us has only one intelligence, only one capacity (power, ability . . .) of understanding. So the differences between 'theoretical' and 'practical' understanding are simply operational differences. And there are these differences between one's intellectual operations simply because there is a difference of objectives. One is thinking theoretically (i.e. 'speculatively', which need not mean conjecturally) when one is concerned primarily with discerning the truth about some topic. One is thinking practically when one is concerned primarily to discover or determine what to do, to get, to have or to be (1983: 10f.).

Phronesis is a productive agent in human flourishing and is crucially involved in the cultivation of moral virtue: it proceeds by deliberation and terminates in choice. It is concerned with a particular thing to be done and the selection of means to ends. It channels the non-rational drives of the soul towards correct moral choice, and it is this pragmatic function which distinguishes it from *sophia* or intuition. Aristotle distinguishes between them in the following manner: the intuitive mode of *nous* 'is of the limiting premisses (*horoi*) for which no reason can be given, while practical reason is concerned with the ultimate particular, which is the object not of scientific knowledge but of perception' (*NE*.VI.8 1142 a25–7). The objects of *sophia* are theology (or metaphysics), mathematics, and physics (*NE*.VI.8, 1142 a17–18), while the object of *phronesis* is 'not knowledge but action' (*NE*.I.3, 1095 a5–6). They deal respectively in what is necessary and what is contingent. Both, however, aim at truth: the contemplative intellect aims at truth, while the practical intellect aims at 'truth in agreement with right desire'. It must be assumed, although Aristotle does not say this in so many words, that *phronesis* also includes an intuitive appreciation of the goodness of ends.[14] Knowing an end as good, practical wisdom calculates the means of attaining it and this process of calculation issues in the choice (*prohairesis*) of a course of action.

Sophia and *phronesis*, then, are intellectual virtues, and as such may be distinguished from the moral virtues. Allan summarises as follows:

> *Sophia* and *phronesis* are virtues of the mind; they are produced by teaching; and they consist in knowledge of true rules – accompanied, in the case of *phronesis*, by skill in applying such rules intuitively to given situations . . . From these *intellectual* virtues, we have to distinguish the virtues of *character* (justice, bravery, temperance, etc.) which, according to Aristotle's view, are essentially correct emotional dispositions, produced by training or habituation begun in early youth. These virtues, each in its proper sphere, consist not in knowledge of true principles, but in habits of liking and aversion (1970: 126f.).

These 'habits of liking and aversion' (which are reminiscent of *rāga* and *dosa*) are the twin poles of the emotional magnet, and the nature of the field generated between them determines our non-cognitive potential. The structured disposition which this potential acquires is character, and virtues and vices are dimensions of character. Aristotle gives the following definition of ethical virtue. It is:

> A state of character (*hexis*) concerned with choice (*prohairesis*) lying in a mean, i.e. the mean relative to us, this being determined by a rational principle, and by that principle by which the man of practical wisdom (*phronimos*) would determine it (*NE*.II.6, 1106b36–1107a2).

Virtue is a state of character, a settled disposition to choose rightly. Aristotle's further insight was that the right choice normally lies in a mean between extremes: bravery, for instance, is the mean between rashness and cowardice. There is no need for us to consider Aristotle's doctrine of the mean here and we may take him simply to be recommending the 'middle way' as a general principle of conduct and action. If a disposition is in accord with reason and conduces to human flourishing it is a virtue: if it is not in accord with reason and is detrimental to human flourishing it is a vice. The 'character' of an individual may include both virtues and vices at the same time, but moral virtue is manifested by making the appropriate ethical response in different situations: this response will be in accordance with reason and in harmony with the good for man. Vice is the failure or inability to respond in this way.

This is a good point at which to update our earlier diagram to take into account the subsequent discussion and illustrate

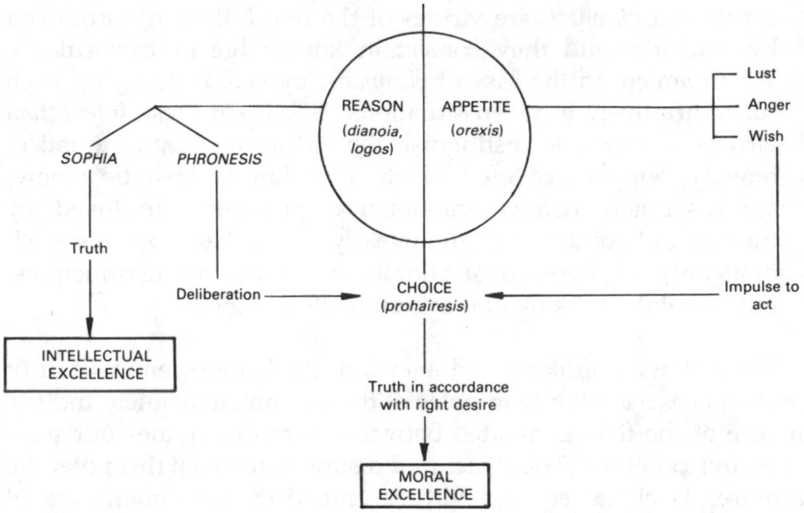

Figure 2. The powers of the Aristotelian psyche and their functions

Aristotle's conception of the operation of moral choice in terms of the powers of the psyche. Figure 2 illustrates the interaction of the two parts of the soul in the sequence leading to choice (*prohairesis*). On the one hand, the non-rational appetitive aspect (*orexis*) provides the stimulus to action from within the emotional spectrum of lust, anger and wish. On the other hand, the rational part of the soul, through the faculty of Practical Wisdom (*phronesis*) evaluates the ends to be attained by action and deliberates as to the means. The whole process terminates in choice (*prohairesis*), and choices made in accordance with the true goal or end (*telos*) of man will be conducive to human flourishing (*eudaemonia*).

Summary and Reflections

The rather abstract concept of *eudaemonia* with which we began this discussion has now received some colour. We are now in a position to understand the definition in the *Eudemian Ethics* that 'flourishing is the activity of a complete life in accordance with complete excellence' (*EE*.II.1.1219a38–9). 'Complete excellence' means all the excellences of the psyche, or at least those which are distinctly human (powers of the nutritive faculty such as breathing are therefore excluded). Since the psyche is binary there are two categories of excellence, namely those pertaining to the mind (*dianoetike*), i.e. *sophia* and *phronesis*; and those pertaining to character (*ethike*), such as the moral virtues of courage, temperance and generosity, etc. It should be remembered that Aristotle's discussion of the psyche and his categorisation of its powers is simply heuristic: in reality its nature does not permit of a clinical dissection and it has no 'parts'. Thus, as Allan points out, the separation of the virtues of character from *phronesis*, which is a virtue of the mind, is a logical, not a real one (1970: 127). In fact, *phronesis* cannot be attained without moral virtue, and moral virtue without *phronesis* is blind. Practical Wisdom (*phronesis*) and moral virtue are inseparable in action and are almost inseparable conceptually. Aristotle sometimes contrasts them by saying that virtue makes the end right and *phronesis* adopts the right means. In practice, however, as Ackrill notes, the two cannot be disentangled:

> Since the pursuit of an objective involves thinking of it, while carrying out things necessary to be done depends on having a desire to do them, thought and desire seem to be involved with one another at each stage of effective deliberation and action. Both have to be faultless if a man is to be either *phronimos* or morally good; and if they are, he is both *phronimos* and good (1973: 29).

The above is a brief sketch of the relation between Aristotelian psychology and Aristotelian ethics. I believe there are interesting parallels in the relation between ethics and psychology in Buddhism. For Buddhism, as for Aristotle, human nature is a compound of mental and physical elements. On the one hand, there is physical form (*rūpa*), and on the other the four psychic (*nāma*) faculties of feeling (*vedanā*), cognition (*saññā*), mental formations (*saṅkhāra*), and consciousness (*viññāna*).[15] In terms of the psyche the basic human predicament is likewise emotional and/or intellectual deficiency epitomised by craving (*taṇhā*) and ignorance (*avijjā*). This deficiency leads to the formation of complexes (*saṅkhāras*) which bring about rebirth until they are dissolved. For both Buddhism and Aristotle human perfection lies in the balanced operation of the cognitive and affective aspects of the psyche, in other words in the correct operation and harmonious interpenetration of reason and emotion. In the final analysis, and for

Aristotle just as much as Buddhism, it is not possible to completely disengage the moral from the intellectual. The cognitive faculties are crucially involved in moral virtue: as seen in Chapter 2, *sīla* and *paññā* are 'washed around together'.

The end must lie within the parameters of human perfectibility, and to establish where these lie requires the co-operation of psychology. Psychology can illumine our understanding of human potential by establishing the facts about human nature. Since the final good must embrace all human potential for excellence, psychology can help us to adumbrate the form this good will take. Thus from the knowledge that the psyche is bipartite we can determine that neither part of the soul can be excluded arbitrarily from *eudaemonia*. But this is as far as anthropology, or any other factual enquiry, can take us. It may help to describe the form of the good but it cannot determine its content. To derive judgements of value from a factual description of the soul would be a form of the Naturalist Fallacy. It would make ethics depend upon theoretical rather than practical wisdom whereas the concern of ethics is not primarily theoretical understanding but practical choice and action. A purely descriptive, non-evaluative analysis of man cannot deal in the currency of human good; by itself it provides only a thin one-dimensional picture of human nature. A rounded conception of human nature and human good will require contributions from both disciplines. As Finnis puts it, 'Ethics is not deduced or inferred from metaphysics or anthropology. But a mistaken metaphysics or anthropology will block one's reflective understanding of the way in which one participates in the human goods' (1983: 22). Let us now consider in more detail a specific point of contact between Aristotelian and Buddhist ethics which will help to illustrate the interaction of these two faculties.

3. THE PSYCHOLOGY OF MORAL CHOICE: *CETANĀ*, *PROHAIRESIS*, AND WILL

In the preceding section we saw that Aristotle distinguishes between the cognitive and affective aspects of the psyche and subdivides the cognitive functions into theoretical and calculative applications. The binary model of reason and emotion is a useful conceptual too, and can be used to further our understanding of Buddhist ethics by depicting the faculties of the Buddhist psyche (*citta*) in terms of the Aristotelian framework discussed so far. In both cases the excellence of reason is to be found in intuitive insight and the excellence of the emotions in moral perfection. Buddhism has no single term which is the equivalent of *phronesis* and it does not explain how correct moral decisions are arrived at in terms of its psychology with the precision we find in Aristotle and Aristotelian exegesis. Nevertheless, the material exists out of which such an explanation can be fabricated. This is essentially a task for further research but I will make a start in this section by attempting to elucidate the meaning of the key ethical term *cetanā* in the light of Aristotle's understanding of the faculty of moral choice, or *prohairesis*.

Moral Choice in Buddhism

Figure 3 illustrates the distinctions made in Buddhist psychology, as discussed in Chapter 3, between the cognitive faculties and processes (*saññā*) and the affective ones (*vedanā*). We saw there that patterned dispositions or complexes (*saṅkhāra*) are formed from the interrelationship of the cognitive and affective powers of the psyche. The rational powers of the mind may be thought of as having two applications: one concerns the intuition or understanding of principles or propositions (which may involve critical thought and analysis); and the other concerns the practical application of reason in respect of things to be done. The impulse to action, however, comes not from the intellectual faculties but from the non-rational part of the psyche, or the emotions. In terms of the *Abhidhamma* analysis, these twin intellectual and emotional operations would seem to be embraced by the group of six 'specific' (*pakiṇṇaka*) psychic functions (*cetasikas*), namely: 'applied thought' (*vitakka*), 'sustained thought' (*vicāra*), 'resolution' (*adhimokkha*), 'courage' (*viriya*), 'joy' (*pīti*) and 'desire' (*chanda*).[16] Thus the process of practical reasoning involves deliberation, which embraces initial attention to the matter in hand (*vitakka*), reflection upon it (*vicāra*), and an intellectual decision or resolution (*adhimokkha*). The implementation of the resolution depends upon an impetus from the affective faculties to bring about the end envisaged through commitment or courage (*viriya*), joy or eagerness (*pīti*) in the endeavour, and the desire or will to realisation (*chanda*). These two complementary processes are fused in *cetanā*, the compass-needle of moral choice which is deflected in accordance

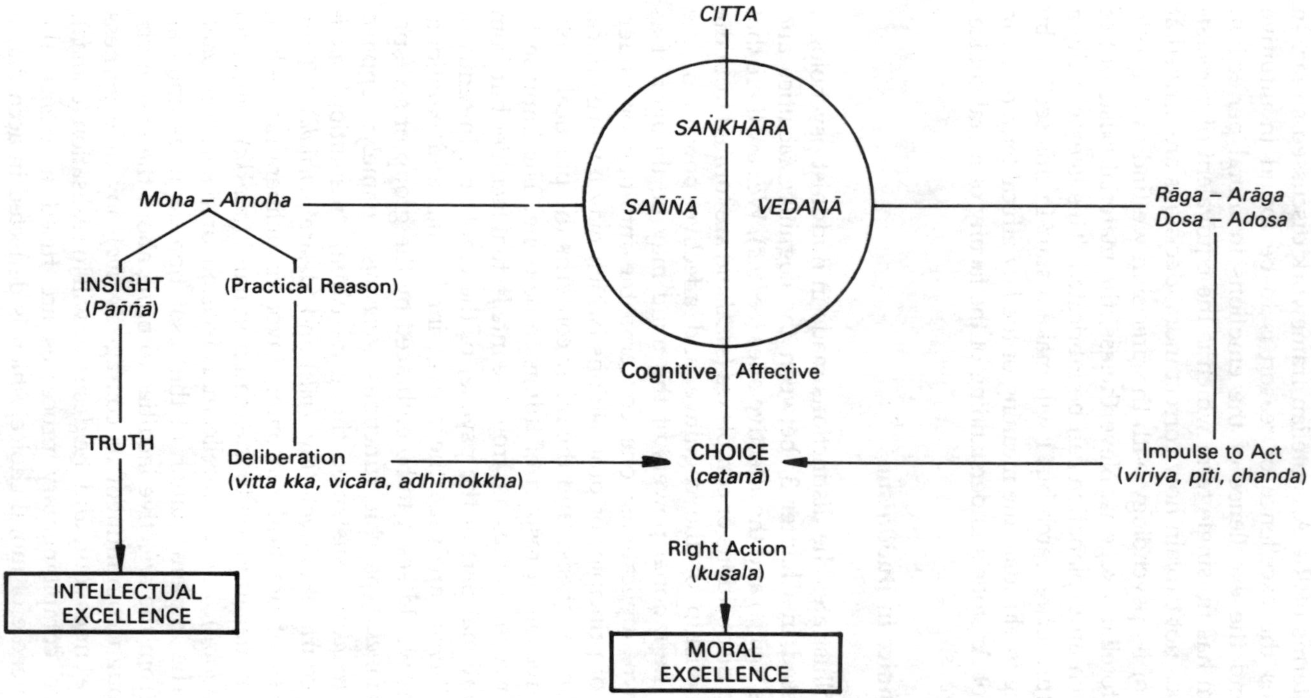

Figure 3. The powers of *Citta* and their functions

with the psychic field created around it. Assuming that one both understands what is good and also desires it, the moral course will lie towards virtue (*kusala*) and final perfection (nirvana).

Cetanā

The outcome of the process described above is choice (*cetanā*). *Cetanā* is very much like *prohairesis* and stands at the crossroads of reason and emotion. *Cetanā* is often regarded as a purely cognitive function, as the translation of it by 'intention' and 'volition' indicate. This narrowing of its meaning has been criticised by Poussin and Guenther.[17] Instead, *cetanā* is best pictured as the matrix in which the push and pull of the rational and emotional aspects of the psyche are funnelled in the direction of moral choice. It is therefore a function of the total personality and not merely its cognitive operations. This might be expected in view of its identification with *kamma*: if *cetanā* was merely cognitive then all kammic evil would be intellectual (*moha*). We know, however, that it is not, since craving (*rāga*) and hatred (*dosa*) also play an important role. Conversely, without the thrust of emotional commitment the appreciation of good ends remains static or takes the form of a vague and diffuse benevolence. In this sense 'meaning well' or having 'good intentions' is merely the counterfeit of moral character. 'Thus', writes Phillipa Foot, 'it seems right to attribute a kind of moral failing to some deeply discouraging and debilitating people who say, without lying, that they mean to be helpful' (1978: 4). Generosity and the other virtues involve not merely the bare realisation that a practice is good, but also the instantiation of the practice. The implementation depends upon a personal commitment which involves more than purely intellectual assent to its goodness. In short, *cetanā* describes not merely intention but the total posture of the personality, both cognitive and affective.

Cetanā, then, is not distinct from thought and feeling – it is the particular configuration or deployment of psychic potential which is found within the individual human subject. The *Expositor* defines it as follows: '*Cetanā* is that which intends: the meaning is that it arranges the associated (mental) states as objects in line with itself.'[18]

Cetanā describes the general moral stance or posture adopted by the psyche and its orientation with respect to ends. In this sense it is synonymous with *saṅkhāra*[19] and is both conditioned and conditioning. In all the major Abhidharmic classifications it is given as one of the basic and omnipresent factors of psychic life (*mahābhūmika-dharma*) and its influence is felt in all aspects of mentation. It may be thought of as referring to the underlying, perhaps unconscious as well as conscious, motivations and drives inherited in the form of predisposing complexes (*saṅkhāras*). These inherited attitudes and dispositions will carry through to influence specific moral choices and decisions made in the present, which will in turn predispose the subject further in line with the pattern of choices made. The imagery used to describe *cetanā* illustrates its organisational and directional function. In the *Expositor* (ibid.) it is compared to a landowner who takes fifty-five strong men (meaning the other mental forces or *cetasika-dhammas*) into the fields to reap, where he supervises them and energetically works alongside them. It is also said to be like a chief disciple, head carpenter or general who takes the initiative in action and is followed by the other students, carpenters or soldiers (*Asl.*111f.). Again it is said that *cetanā* is exceedingly energetic (*atireka-vāyāma*) and makes a double effort (*diguṇa-ussaha*) and a double exertion (*diguṇa-vāyāma*) (*Asl.*111). It both initiates and sustains activity and focuses the whole personality upon the task or object in hand. In this respect it is both dispositional and operational – it predisposes to action and leads to a result.

The Will

If the above is a correct account of *cetanā*, then it should not to be confused with the Western concept of the will as a faculty distinct from the intellect and the emotions. This is neither a Greek nor an Indian idea, and its origin in Western intellectual history can be found in the writings of St Augustine. 'It is generally accepted', writes Dihle, 'in the study of the history of philosophy that the notion of will, as it is used as a tool of analysis and description in many philosophical doctrines from the early Scholastics to Schopenhauer and Nietzsche, was invented by St Augustine' (1982: 123). Augustine's purpose in elaborating the concept of will (*voluntas*) was to forge a link between his trinitarian theology and his anthropology such that the power of the will became the subjective reflection in human psychology of the creative energy of the divine *logos*. The will, as a distinct spiritual faculty ultimately independent of sensuous and intellectual life, becomes the seat of choice between good and evil. Dihle writes:

> From St Augustine's reflections emerged the concept of a human will, prior to and independent of the act of intellectual cognition, yet fundamentally different from sensual and irrational emotion, by which man can give his reply to the inexplicable utterances of the divine will (1982: 127).

It is likely that the origination of the philosophical concept of the will by Augustine was influenced and facilitated by the Latin language and its comparative lack of psychological refinement.[20] Greek recognises no such faculty as the will in its psychological terminology. There is no Aristotelian expression for 'freedom of the will', and Aristotle is sometimes criticised for failing to develop an adequate theory of the will although, as Hardie notes, 'he did not do badly without it' (1980: 163). Kenny replies to this charge as follows:

> This criticism of Aristotle depends upon a certain view of the nature of the will. According to a view familiar in modern philosophical tradition, the will is a phenomenon of introspective consciousness. Volition is a mental event which procedes and causes certain human actions: its presence or absence makes the difference between voluntary actions. The freedom of the will is to be located in the indeterminacy of these internal volitions. The occurrence of volitions, and their freedom from causal control, is a matter of intimate experience (1979: vii).

Neither *prohairesis* nor *cetanā* are pure, abstract volitions. A theory of the will as defined above is not to be found in Aristotle or Buddhism, and perhaps for good reason. Kenny continues:

> It is true that this account of the will is not to be found in Aristotle. This is not to Aristotle's discredit, for this whole conception of volition and freedom has been subjected, in our own time, to decisive criticism by philosophers such as Ryle and Wittgenstein. Philosophers who accept the criticisms of this school have attempted to build afresh a philosophical theory of the springs of human action which will be free of the confusions involved in the theory familiar in modern philosophical tradition. The resulting new structures bear a remarkable resemblance to what we find in Aristotle's *Ethics* (1979: viif.).

Buddhism is similar in not relying on a theory of the will to support its notion of moral responsibility. Karunaratna writes:

> The expression 'freedom of *will*' or its equivalent is not found in the *suttas* or other authentic texts recording the teachings of the Buddha and its use in modern expositions only reflects an unstated wish to interpret Buddhist thought in terms of the categories of Western thought.[21]

Responding to the charge that the possibility of developing a positive psychology of will has been neglected by Buddhist scholars, De Silva writes:

> This certainly is an important area to be explored. But the word 'will' is semantically troublesome . . . The semantic position here is important: the term 'will' is so vague that it cannot be identical with the more diversified, specific and analytical Buddhist terms' (1979: 78).[22]

In an article on the concept of the will in early Buddhism, Matthews brings out the complex interaction of the psychic faculties involved in volitional action:

> In my investigation of a concept of will in the *Nikāyas*, I have found that the most meaningful and useful definition is one that straddles the traditional conative, affective and cognitive 'roles', that embraces such terms as *viriya* (energy, striving), *chanda* (desire, intention), and *dvārāni-sugguttāni* (guarding the doors of the senses) (1975: 152).[23]

Here *cetanā* is not the central focus of the discussion and Matthews concentrates rather on the affective inputs to volition (what he refers to as 'the positive characteristics of the early Buddhist concept of will') in order to rebut the assertion that all desire is thought wrongful and to be extirpated. At the same time he is clear that if the concept of will is to be used in Buddhism at all it must be understood as embracing both emotional and rational faculties. Matthews draws a distinction between the impetus to action and the rational canalisation of the impetus into a moral course:

> I justify this definition by arguing that if 'will' is characterized as

simply 'energy' or 'striving', much of its moral and essentially ethical nature is lost, and likewise if it is characterized only in ethical terms, it loses that sense of positive drive so apparent in much of the Buddhist *magga*, or soteriological path (1975: 153).

Poussin draws attention to the breadth of meaning of *cetanā*:

> We have said that an act is essentially *cetanā*, and translated this as 'volition'. But the notion that the word *cetanā* covers is complex and it is only recently that the translation as 'volition' has been proposed. Buddhist language, in addition to *cetanā*, has a rich terminology. The Sarvāstivādins believe that: 1. *Chanda*, 'wish' defined as 'desire to act', 2. *manasikāra*, the 'act of attention' by which we ply or bend thought towards the object, and also 'judgement', 3. *adhimokṣa*, which is something like approbation or approval, are simultaneous with *cetanā*. Add *vyāma* 'effort', *niśraya* 'decision', as much in an intellectual as a volitional sense, *adhyavasāya*, 'resolution'. Add *vitarka* which, following 'wish', triggers off 'effort', which the schools sometimes make into a certain sort of *cetanā*, volition, and sometimes a certain sort of *prajñā* or 'knowledge'. The list is not complete, and its mere extent points to the absence of a term which exactly covers the idea of the will (1927: 135f.).

As may be seen from the following statement, Poussin was clear that *cetanā* was neither an exclusively intellectual nor emotional faculty. However, he does not consider that it may be an interaction of the two and concludes instead that it is a separate power of the mind corresponding to the Augustinian notion of the faculty of the will:

> The relations between intelligence, passion and volition are mysterious, and the Buddhists did not give a methodical exposition of them. We are sure, at least, that *cetanā*, which is action, is not confused with desire or passion; it is not of the emotional order. On the other hand, if it belongs to the understanding, it is not confused with 'view' or opinion. Our doctors know that the will, although they name it badly, is distinct from motives of an intellectual order, from desires and from aversions' (1927: 138).

There is no English term which satisfactorily includes all the meanings of *cetanā*. Guenther suggests that 'stimulus, motive or drive' are the most appropriate equivalents (1976: 42f.). However, while this expresses well the participation of the emotions it falls into the other extreme of ignoring the role of the cognitive faculty which 'volition' and 'intention' capture rather better. Many English terms have been suggested for *cetanā*,[24] but bearing in mind the psychological continuum it covers it is unlikely that any single term will capture the full range of meanings. In Figure 3 we have not assigned a specific Buddhist term to 'Practical Reason', but *cetanā* may be a suitable candidate when understood in an expanded goal-seeking sense. In Buddhaghosa's imagery *cetanā* knows the end as well as the means, like a landowner or general who organise their subordinates for a specific purpose. *Cetanā* would then not be just the specific faculty of choice which comes at the end of deliberation, but also be present from the start as the faculty which originally intuits the good ends in connection with which practical choices will subsequently need to be made. *Cetanā* would thus embrace a continuum which runs from predisposition through choice to action. The orientation of *cetanā* and the choices and actions it leads to will be determined by the interrelation of cognitive and affective potential on both conscious and unconscious levels. Thus Karunaratna:

> *Cetanā* or the will which is conditioned by affective and cognitive elements (*vedanā, saññā*) may either function as the closely directed effort on the part of the individual or it may function, as it often does, without conscious deliberation by him.[25]

Prohairesis similarly involves the co-operation of reason and desire. Aristotle says that *prohairesis* is 'either desireful reason (*orektikon nous*) or reasonable desire (*orexis dianoetike*)' (*NE*.VI.2, 1139b4–5). Echoing this Kenny states that '*Prohairesis* is at one and the same time desiderative thought and deliberative desire' (1979: 94). According to Gauthier:

> For him [Aristotle], an intention [*prohairesis*] is right when reason has so pervaded desire that this latter is drawn toward the very object that reason prescribes. This pervading of desire by reason is virtue itself, and this is why virtue rectifies intention (1967: 16).

Intention and Action

Hardie distinguishes three ways in which Aristotle uses the term *prohairesis*:

i) the desire to do an action
ii) the decision to do an action
iii) the initiation of an action (1980: 164).

Gauthier understands Aristotle as using the term in this inclusive sense such that the three components occur together:

> It is necessary to recall that for Aristotle an 'intention' necessarily expresses itself in action, for it is identified with 'decision'. Aristotle has only one word, *prohairesis*, to designate both the one and the other. A contradiction has often been seen here – does Aristotle not teach that decision has means for its object, whereas intention is obviously directed towards an end? . . . This is to forget that an Aristotelian 'decision' is only directed to means in order better to be directed to the end. It is a sufficiently powerful desire for the end, so clarified by deliberation to make us take means to reach the end successfully; and if it is distinguished from the wish for the end which is *boulesis*, this is not because wish is directed toward the end, but because this wish is directed toward the end too weakly to take the means to reach it successfully. Indeed, it does not even know if those means exist. Thus what Aristotle means to say in making moral intention a *prohairesis* is that it is an *effective* act; the entirely Platonic wish or *boulesis* is not yet moral intention for him. Only the desire for the end which expresses itself in action is moral intention, and this is why virtue necessarily implies the decisive intention which is *prohairesis* and the exterior act which is *praxis* . . . The first does not occur without the second (1967: 16f.).

It would seem to be true of *cetanā* also that the intention and the *praxis* are constantly conjoined. The *Points of Controversy* (VII.4) widens the meaning of generosity (*dāna*) to include something given as well as the intention to give. Guenther emphasises the dynamic aspect of *cetanā*:

> We see that *cetanā* not only arouses mass activity but also sustains it so that certain definite results appear. This shows beyond

> doubt that the translation of *cetanā* by 'volition' is against all evidence . . . In its most sharply distinguished sense volition designates merely the act of making a choice or decision, but it rarely suggests the determination to put one's decision or choice into effect. Volition is thus the very reverse of *cetanā* which everywhere is said to put something into effect (1976: 43f.).

We may note, however, that what is put into effect need not be physical action, and that the use of the term 'volition' may not always be inaccurate. The Buddha seems to have held the view that the process of *cetanā* was followed by a *praxis* of some kind, and that deliberation (*cetayitvā*) was followed by action (*kammaṃ karoti*). However, he distinguishes three types of *praxis*: bodily (*kayasā*), vocal (*vācāsā*) and mental (*manasā*). *Cetanā*, then, reaches a terminus with moral implications, but the morally determinative *praxis* may be purely mental in form. When *cetanā* is used in this sense the translation of it by 'volition' may not be misleading.

Cetanā is morally determinative, and therefore action without *cetanā* is not ethically charged. This is not an idea which is peculiar to Buddhism. The English criminal law, for example, considers both the mental state of the accused and his overt actions. It draws a distinction between the *mens rea* and the *actus reus*: the latter is the physical action and the former is 'the state of mind which must be present in an accused if his overt action is to constitute a crime, and if he is to be held responsible for it'.[26] Kenny's explanation of *mens rea* brings out a point of possible difference between *cetanā* and *prohairesis*:

> In general, an enquiry into the *mens rea* of an accused is an enquiry into his reasons for acting as he did. When we say that someone acted for a certain reason, we are attributing to him both a cognitive and an affective state: a desire for a certain state of affairs to be brought about, and a belief that a certain manner of acting is a way of bringing about that state of affairs. Cognitive states of mind are those which involve a person's possession of a piece of information (true or, as the case may be, false): such things as belief, awareness, expectation, certainty, knowledge. Affective states of mind are neither true nor false but consist in an attitude of pursuit or avoidance: such things as purpose, intention, desire, volition. Some mental states, of course, are both affective and cognitive: hope and fear, for instance, involve

> both an expectation of a prospective state of affairs and a judgement of the state of affairs as good or evil. Very various cognitive and affective states may constitute *mens rea* in different crimes and in different circumstances (1978: 46).

In law, generally speaking, *mens rea* by itself does not constitute a crime unless accompanied by *actus reus*. *Prohairesis*, too, (which Kenny translates as 'purposive choice') embraces both *mens rea* and *actus reus*. *Cetanā*, however, seems to allow for purely mental states as morally determinative, which means that for Buddhism a covert mental state will satisfy the requirement of *actus reus*, at least as far as moral action is concerned. In monastic jurisprudence, however, an overt *actus reus* is required for there to be a transgression of the *Vinaya*.[27]

On the other hand, motive alone is not the sole criterion of rightness. As Poussin points out, following the *Treasury*, the ritual slaying of animals is not meritorious merely because Brahmins believe it to be so; nor is euthanasia for aged parents morally right even though it is the custom in certain countries (1927: 30). This suggests there is an objective standard of rightness discoverable and attainable through the partnership of reason and right desire. For *cetanā* to be virtuous it must conform to these requirements, and even acts performed from a good motive are wrongful if based on *moha* (*Kośa*.IV.68d).

We have noted that moral responsibility and moral choice are determined by the total personality with its cognitive and affective faculties. *Cetanā, prohairesis*, and *mens rea* are defined with reference to that core of the personality which is the final resort of explanation for moral action and which is ultimately definitive of moral status. To say that reason is involved in this complex is not to say that moral choice is essentially calculative: on the contrary, virtue is seen most clearly in one who chooses promptly and intuitively what is right.[28] In such a person the desire for the good is instinctive and the choice of right means can be made immediately without the distorting influence of egotistical considerations. As Clark notes:

> The Buddhist and the Aristotelian saint alike are not pressed by self-control to do what is right, nor do they accompany their actions with verbal conclusions about what they ought to be doing – the conclusion of the practical syllogism is for them, as

for animals, an action (*De Motu* 701a10f), not as it is for most of us a murmured encouragement to virtue' (1975: 189).

4. THE DESIRE FOR THE GOOD

In Buddhism virtuous choices are rational choices motivated by a desire for what is good and deriving their validation ultimately from the final good for man (nirvana). It may seem odd in a Buddhist context to speak approvingly of 'desire', and I think a comment would not be out of place on the role of the affective faculties in the pursuit of the final good. The failure to distinguish the various senses of 'desire' has led to confusion as to the role which Buddhism envisages for the affective faculties in the religious life. All too often the assumption has been that they have no role at all.[29]

It is an oversimplification of the Buddhist position to assume that it seeks an end of all desire. Such a view, however, is not uncommon. Poussin succumbed to it confessing 'I believed for a long time that a Buddhist should not desire *Nirvāṇa* before coming to recognise that the desire for what is good (*kuśaladharmacchanda*) is necessary and important' (1927: 152). The complete eradication of desire would be a suppression of the affective side of human nature and result only in apathy. In Buddhist terminology it would be an exclusion of the capacity for feeling (*vedanākkhandha*) which is a fundamental part of man's being, and the denial of the opportunity for this capacity to reach its own particular excellence. Buddhism does not seek this suppression of feeling: what Buddhism seeks an end of is desire *for what is not good*, namely things which cripple rather than promote spiritual growth. It seeks the end only of desires which are perverted by ignorance (*avijjā*). Its aim is not to exterminate feeling (*vedanā*) but to liberate it from its attachment to false values (*vipallāsa*). The goal is the replacement of worthless objectives by an orientation of the entire personality towards what is truly good. Even the Buddha was not free of desires, although he was, of course, free from desire motivated by delusion (selfish desire). His desire for the well-being of others remained throughout his life, and he tells us that as far as others are concerned he desires their good, welfare, and salvation.[30] 'Purposeful activity' (*sankheyyakāro*) is said to be one of his characteristics (*Sn*.351), and there can be no effective purpose without affective commitment. Enlightenment itself must be desired like any other goal, and in the Canon (*S*.v.271ff.) Ānanda rejects the suggestion that desire for nirvana is a hindrance to its attainment.[31]

The Meaning of *Taṇhā*

Perhaps it is an obvious point but it is important to bear in mind that it is not 'desire' as such which is condemned in Buddhism, but *taṇhā*, and that the English word 'desire' is only an approximation of the meaning of this term.[32] As Mrs Rhys Davids points out, in the work of the earlier translators the single English word 'desire' is made to do duty for no less than seventeen Pali words including *taṇhā*, 'not one of which means desire taken in its ordinary general sense but rather in that of perverted, morbid, excessive desire' (1898: 54). She characterises this excessive desire as the result of want (*ākaṇkhā*) becoming craving (*taṇhā*), desire (*chanda*) becoming lust (*chanda-rāga*), lusts of the flesh (*kāma-rāga*) and sensual delight (*nandi-rāga*) (1898: 49).

Buddhaghosa distinguishes between desire as *chanda* and desire as *taṇhā*:

> [With regard to] 'desiring' there are two kinds of desire (*patthanā*): desire as *taṇhā* and desire as *chanda*. Desire as *taṇhā* is instanced in the passage 'One who desires has longings and trembles about his expectations' [*Sn*.902]. [On the other hand] right desire (*kusala-cchanda-patthanā*), the will to accomplish (*kattukamyatā*), [is illustrated in the passage] 'The stream of becoming (*pāpimato*) is cut off, broken and destroyed, Rejoice, monks, and desire the good (*khema*)' [untraced]. The second [kind of desire] is the one that is meant here. By 'desiring' is meant 'wishing to reach that good end [Arahatship], leaning, tending, and inclining towards it (*MA*.i.41).[33]

Desire, even in its extreme form of craving (*taṇhā*), is not just a free-floating emotion which attaches itself willy-nilly to a succession of objects. It is desire for things under a certain description, namely that *it would be good* to have, possess and enjoy those things. It is the initial conception of them as good things which provides the stimulus and motivation for pursuing them. It is not that there is simply a quotient of amorphous desire (libido) swilling around in the psyche that can be satisfied by indiscriminate means. On the contrary, things are wanted only in so far as they are conceived of as good. 'Emotions', writes MacIntyre, 'are intentional, that is, they presuppose beliefs and we cannot characterise the emotion except in terms of the relevant object of belief' (1971: 245). The goal of eliminating desire *per se* is unintelligible, since there is no such thing as desire without an object. To aim at the destruction of 'desire' is to tilt at windmills. It is not desire that is to be eradicated but the desire for things mistakenly conceived of as good (desirable) when they are not. There are two aspects to the rectification of desire: first the curbing of its excessive forms through temperance or restraint (*saṃvara*); and second the channelling of desire towards that which is identified as good after a programme of correct rational analysis. What is required to overcome *taṇhā* is the partnership of reason and right desire, involving both insight into the unworthy nature of these objectives and the simultaneous education of the feelings to delight in only worthwhile (good) ends.

There are many and varied conceptions of what is good. The job of practical wisdom (*phronesis*) is to identify what is truly good (and hence truly desirable) and to pursue it intelligently. Virtue (*kusala*) involves both a correct identification of the good and a participation in it, and it is from this participation that arise the feelings of satisfaction and delight in the good. Here the emotional response is quite appropriate. *Taṇhā*, on the other hand, is essentially an incorrect evaluation and inappropriate emotional response – it is the counterfeit of correct emotional participation. *Taṇhā* stands for the kind of desire which is never satisfied, which endlessly seeks gratification yet never reaches a terminus. Its aim is the experience of pleasurable states, but since these are transient it can never find fulfilment. To take a simple example, *taṇhā* is like the desire of a chainsmoker for one cigarette after another whereas right desire is the desire to give up smoking once and for all. In the latter case the desire dissolves upon the attainment of the end and the attainment of the end is accompanied by positive feelings of satisfaction and achievement. When asked by Uṇṇābho the Brahman whether the desire (*chanda*) for nirvana was wrong, Ānanda compared the desire for nirvana to Uṇṇābho's desire to come to the park that day and pose his question: once he had achieved his goal the desire disappeared (*S*.v.272). It would seem that the kind of desire to be avoided is not the desire to achieve good ends but the desire for sensory gratification, a desire which cannot be assuaged and yet refuses to let go of its objective. Buddhaghosa brings out this adhesive quality of wrong desire when he likens *lobha* to 'a lump of meat thrown into a hot pan'.[34] Shortly after his enlightenment the Buddha declared that he was free of desire (*chanda*) for forms, sounds, odours, and tangible objects – all things which delight the mind through sensory experience and celebrate the embodied state of existence.[35]

The Role of the Emotions

If there is *no* emotional involvement in a purpose or objective (and this vacuity is what many mistakenly believe Buddhists to aim at) then a dimension of human experience is arbitrarily denied. Yet Buddhist sources point out the joy and satisfaction of the religious life both in the pre- and post-enlightenment condition (Collins, 1982: 192). The same may be said of all successful action. Thus Finnis:

> Typically, success in the attainment of any goal is itself an experience, indeed an experience which is pleasurable and satisfying. What matters to us, in the last analysis, is not the emotional experience of getting knowledge, but coming to know; not the emotions of friendship, but being a friend . . . But in each case, there is typically an emotional aspect to participation in one or other of these goods, and that emotion or feeling is one aspect of their reality as human goods. True, a participation in these goods which is emotionally dry and subjectively unsatisfying is still good and meaningful as far as it goes. But these goods are not participated in fully unless they are *experienced* as good. That characteristic human experience of good we call emotion or (intensional) feeling. Such full participation in good is the opportunity made possible by our bodily/intellectual nature, given favourable circumstances (1983: 47f.).

Human good cannot be complete if it is only participated in by the intellect; to be fully realised it must be seen as good and *felt* as good, and this involves an appropriate emotional response. Aristotle's doctrine of the mean (which we have not dealt with here) is essentially an attempt to establish where an appropriate emotional response lies. 'I take the doctrine', writes Richard Norman, 'to be a thesis about the proper relation between reason and feeling' (1983:

50). Norman regards the Aristotelian thesis as lying midway between the extreme positions typified by Plato and D.H. Lawrence. For Plato, reason (*logos*) must assert authoritative control over the other two parts of the soul (desire and anger). For Lawrence, on the other hand, 'reason should keep out of the way, and leave room for the free and entirely spontaneous expression of the feelings' (1983: 51). Aristotle adopts a middle position and so, essentially, does Buddhism, although we also find in the latter views closer to both extremes. Thus we find talk in the Theravāda of extirpating the passions as if they had an autonomous life independent of reason; and in the Mahāyāna by the time of Śāntideva *rāga* is spoken of as a virtue and becomes almost a *sine qua non* of enlightenment.[36] Neither Aristotle nor the Buddha accepted these extremes, and Norman can be read as referring to both when he says of the former:

> I want to suggest that we can usefully see Aristotle as questioning the necessity of this antagonism. For Aristotle, feelings can themselves be the embodiment of reason. It is not just a matter of reason controlling and guiding the feelings. Rather the feelings can *themselves* be more or less rational. Reason can *be present in them* (1983: 52 emphasis in original).

To say that feelings are rational means that they are appropriate to the situation. For Aristotle strong emotions such as anger could be appropriate in certain circumstances, and we may notice that 'righteous anger' also has a place in Christianity. For Buddhism, however, this would be an extreme emotional response. So where does the correct response lie? For Aristotle, the correct response (the mean) is to be determined by the man of practical wisdom (the *phronimos*). For Buddhists the *phronimos* is the Buddha, and it is his choice which determines where virtue lies. The record of his important moral choices is contained in Buddhist sources such as the *Tracts* and the preceptual formulae extrapolated from them, as we saw in Chapter 2. The correct role for the emotions in Buddhist ethics is to be found in the sentiments of love and concern which inspired the Buddha to make the choices he did.

In this chapter we have considered the overall ethical structure of Buddhism in the light of the Aristotelian model. Both are teleological systems, and we examined their conceptions of the final goal or *telos,* the starting point in untutored human nature from which one moves towards this *telos,* and the mechanism of moral choice by which progress towards this goal is made. A more detailed investigation of the points of similarity and difference must be the subject of further research.

Conclusion

As statements of the conclusions reached have been updated in the course of the discussion my summary here will be brief. Our three objectives stated in the Introduction were as follows: (a) to enquire into the meaning and content of *sīla*; (b) to relate *sīla* to the overall conception of human good culminating in liberation as expounded by the Buddha; (c) to put forward a hypothesis concerning the formal characterisation of the Buddhist ethical system. These objectives overlap to a degree and to some extent have been touched on in each chapter. Broadly speaking, however, the first received specific attention in Chapters 1 and 6, with separate references to sources from the Small and Large Vehicles respectively. The substantive preceptual content of moral codes and related classifications were examined both as an end in itself and for the light it could shed upon our further objectives. Of particular interest here were the reformulated moral categories elaborated by the Mahāyāna and the pattern of ethical push and pull which seemed to lead in two directions at once. It sought to excel the *śīla* of the *Śrāvakas* both in the rigour of its discipline and in its devotion to the service of others, and this tension found stability of a kind in the tripartite ethical structure consisting of *śīla* as temperance (*saṃvara*), pursuit of the good (*kuśala-dharma-saṃgrāhaka-śīla*), and altruistic concern (*sattva-artha-kriyā-śīla*).

The exploration of our second objective ran thread-like through the first six chapters. The binary pattern of human good consisting of *sīla* and *paññā* was noted in the *Collection on Moral Practices,* and in Chapter 2 we analysed the scholastic presentation of the obstacles to perfection using the concept of a virtue. The ethical and intellectual dimensions of the goal were related to Buddhist psychology, and the role of meditation (*samādhi*) in this scheme was outlined at this point. In Chapter 3 we sought to challenge an alternative conception of Buddhist value-theory which posits a fundamental cleavage between the twin spheres of human good. The relegation of ethics to the 'kammic' and its divorce from the 'nibbānic' was resisted as a distorted representation of canonical teachings and contemporary practice. The commonly adduced support for the 'transcendency thesis' – the Parable of the Raft –

was examined and reinterpreted in a manner more consonant with the context and the overall scheme of Buddhist soteriology. The bilateral scheme of human good was also found to be evident in Mahāyāna sources in the scheme of the Perfections, and in the emphasis on Insight (*Prajñā*) and Means (*Upāya*) as the two essential qualities of a *bodhisattva*.

While noting the bilateral spheres of human good as fundamental our sources also evince a shift in the pattern of emphasis given to each. The historical development of the Buddhist tradition may in fact be regarded as fuelled by the inner dynamic of this synthetic relationship. In the Small Vehicle we see the ascendency of *Paññā*, and in the Large Vehicle the rise of *Karuṇā* to the point where it eclipses the former and achieves the status of a supreme ideal. This development triggers the appearance of antinomian doctrines (*upāya*$_2$) both in a metaphorical and perhaps a prescriptive form.

Our final objective was to put forward a formal characterisation of the Buddhist ethical system, and to this we turned our attention in the final two chapters. We considered first of all the possibility of Buddhist ethics being a member of the Utilitarian family of ethical theory, to which the closest approximation would be NRU. This was rejected as formally incompatible and also irreconcilable with basic Buddhist doctrines and attitudes, and we concluded that the resemblance between Buddhist and Utilitarian ethics could not be maintained on closer investigation. There remains the possibility, however, that a form of the *upāya* doctrine may lend itself to a characterisation as a utilitarian hybrid similar to the Situation Ethics of Joseph Fletcher. Further anthropological and historical research would be needed to assess the grounds for such a claim.

In the final chapter we turned our attention to what seems to be one of the most promising and fruitful candidates for an analogue to Buddhist ethics, namely the ethical theory of Aristotle. Both Aristotle and the Buddha were alike in eschewing metaphysical notions and instead directing their attention to the practical and empirical. The central concern of both is with the *telos* of human nature and the means of attaining it. The abstract similarities of the two systems were explored and we also examined a more specific point of contact concerning the faculties of intention and moral choice. For Aristotle the good for man is something to be participated in but never completely attained, whereas for the Buddha the goal of full perfection was achievable over the course of many lifetimes through the cultivation of the Eightfold Path.

In Chapter 1 I promised to return at this point to the question of the theoretical classification of Buddhist ethics and to summarise my reasons for the conclusions I announced there. I hope that the reasons for the characterisations I advanced will have become apparent in the course of the discussion but we may state them once again as follows. The description of Buddhist ethics as egotistical must be rejected on the basis of the discussion in Chapter 2 where the Buddha's moral perfection was seen to be undergirded by sympathy (*anukampā*) and fraternal concern. This concern is not the prerogative of the enlightened and is commended to all. The view of Buddhist ethics as egotistical stems from an instrumentalist conception of *kamma* and a linear soteriology which regards *sīla* as a step to be 'got over'. The alternative characterisation of Buddhist ethics as altruistic is more appropriate but requires qualification in view of the personal soteriological consequences of ethical development which are not to be lost sight of. Moral development in Buddhism never occurs at the expense of one's own long-term good: it benefits both oneself and others. In terms of the patterns of validation offered by Little and Twiss (1978: 236) we may accordingly strike out the possibiity of 'unqualified intrapersonal teleology' (ethical egoism). The two remaining possibilities of 'qualified intrapersonal teleology' and 'qualified extrapersonal teleology' are each inadequate since the dominant pattern of validation in Buddhism recognises the simultaneity of one's own and the other's good.

On the issue of Relativism and Absolutism we note that Buddhism steers a middle course and acknowledges variation within a structured pattern of the pursuit of human good. The good for man is not arbitrary – it is governed by the facts of human nature and the inalienable characteristics of the world we inhabit, such as impermanence and change. A position of extreme relativism is therefore ruled out. Yet within these confines forms of life may vary to some degree, a fact acknowledged by the Buddha, and the basic goods may be participated in in a variety of ways: the absolutism is, accordingly, attenuated and qualified. This does not mean that none of the precepts are absolutes, only that not all of them are. Since the precepts are derived from and define the conduct of the Buddha (the *phronimos*), and given his consistency in adhering to them over many lifetimes sometimes under extreme conditions, there must be a strong presumption that they are universally binding (I leave to one side here the maverick Mahāyāna sources which promote the doctrine of *upāya*$_2$). By 'universal' is meant 'applying to all rational beings': this excludes those precepts which apply only to monks, which obviously cannot be universal in scope. By 'absolute' is meant 'applicable in all circumstances': there are four precepts which seem to be intended in this sense, namely those forbidding murder, stealing, lying, and sexual misconduct. These are the first four precepts of the *Short Tract* and figure in both the Five Precepts and the Four *Pārājikā*. Describing the precepts as 'absolutes' does not mean it is always easy to apply them in practice. The restriction on 'sexual misconduct' obviously requires further definition. From a legal point of view the precepts are rather imprecisely drawn up, and attempts at clarification have been made from time-to-time in Buddhist sources (Derrett, 1983). Leaving casuistry to one side, however, the general intention of the precepts is clear enough, and I think there is little doubt the Buddha intended these four basic precepts, at least, to be absolutely and universally respected.

Buddhist ethics may be characterised as objectivist and naturalist, a position consonant with the empiricism of the Buddha. Ethical judgements are objective since criteria are provided for an assessment of their rightness and wrongness independently of subjective moral perception or preference (Jayatilleke, 1970b; Weeraratne, 1976: 58–65). And Buddhist ethics is naturalist in view of the account of ethics which can be given in terms of the psychological constitution of the moral subject, for instance by reference to *dharmas* (Chapter 2). My reasons for rejecting consequentialism have been stated briefly above and are fully set out in Chapter 7. Finally, since the moral life in Buddhism has a definite *telos* it is preferable to describe it as teleological rather than deontological in form.

Notes

1 THE STUDY OF BUDDHIST ETHICS

1. On the absence of philosophical ethics in Hinduism see Creel (1977: 20–32).
2. On the characterisation of Buddhism as a 'soteriology' see Matthews (1975: 152n.2).
3. For a comprehensive bibliographic essay on Buddhist Ethics see Reynolds (1979).
4. As to other research work see Stephenson (1970), Anuruddha (1972), Rajapaksa (1975) and Bush (1960).
5. P. Williams (1989: 190).
6. For a discussion of definitional problems in connection with Buddhism as a 'religion' see Little and Twiss (1978: ch. 3). On the analogous problem of the dislocation of *Dharma* from *Mokṣa* in Hinduism see Creel (1977: ch. 3).
7. As far as Mahāyāna ethics is concerned, little has been said. Articles relating to Zen have been written by Brear (1974) and Fox (1971). Only Gomez (1973) has attempted to fill the void in Madhyamika ethics, and the absence of material in this field has been lamented by May (1978: 234).
8. On the 'transcendence of good and evil' in Tantra see Misra (1984: ch. 6). 'Tantra' is such a nebulous concept that it is unwise to make generalisations about it. Much more work needs to be done before it will be meaningful to speak about a 'Tantric' view of ethics. My guess, however, is that ethics is no more transcended here than it is in any other branch of Buddhism.
9. Little and Twiss's promising approach to Theravāda ethics was side-tracked by giving undue prominence to the *anattā* doctrine.
10. I am greatly indebted to J.M. Cooper (1975) whose interpretation of Aristotle in many ways provides the inspiration for the present book.
11. Cf. Thomas (1914: 344); Saddhatissa (1970: 17f., 29); De Silva (1979: 2); Tatz (1986: 1). For occasional brief but intriguing speculations in the reverse direction, i.e. Aristotle elucidated by reference to (Far-Eastern) Buddhism, see Clark (1975), especially Appendix C: 'I conclude that Aristotle may profitably be considered in a Chinese setting: Aristotle can be understood and passages which have hitherto been emended or ignored given a coherent sense if we treat him as something like a Mahāyanā Buddhist' (1975: 216).

2 ASPECTS OF *SĪLA*

1. On the chronology of these 13 *suttas* see Pande (1983: 77–94). For a summary of their contents see Barua (1971: 403–432).
2. The other two sections are the *Mahāvagga* (*suttas* 14–23), and the *Pāṭikavagga* (24–34).
3. For a translation with commentarial extracts see Bhikkhu Bodhi (1978).
4. *'Puthujjano Tathāgatassa vaṇṇaṃ vadamāno vadeyya.'*
5. K.R. Norman (1983: 32).
6. The *Short Tract* is also found at *M*.i.178–80.
7. Cf. Derrett (1983: 12).
8. *'Pāṇātipātam pahāya pāṇātipātā paṭivirato samaṇo Gotamo'* (*D*.i.4).
9. *'Yathā va pan'eke bhonto samaṇa-brāhmaṇā saddhā-deyyāni bhojanāni bhuñjitvā, te evarūpaṃ . . . anuyuttā viharanti, iti evarūpā . . . paṭivirato samaṇo Gotamo ti'* (D.i.5).
10. Wieger (1910: 145ff.) translates a selection of *Vinaya* texts preserved in Chinese in which the order of the final five precepts varies considerably. Despite the reordering the provisions remain substantially the same. Additional prohibitions include marriage, breeding animals and hunting. Cf. Derrett (1983: 7f.).
11. Thus *anabhijjhā* = *alobha*; *avyāpāda* = *adosa*; and *sammādiṭṭhi* = *amoha*. For a commentary on these ten items see *MA*.i.198ff.
12. In the *Fruits of the Religious Life* and subsequently it is the monk (*bhikkhu*) or person following in the Buddha's footsteps who is the subject of the *sīlas*.
13. *'Bhagavaṃ mūlakā no bhante dhammā, Bhagavaṃ nettikā, Bhagavaṃ paṭisaranā'* (*M*.i.309f, 317).
14. Cf. Bastow (1988: 167).
15. On these 13 stages and their conceptual relation to the goal see Bastow (1969). On discourses relating to *Sīla*, *Samādhi* and *Paññā* see Barua (1971: ch. 3).
16. *M*.i.301; *A*.i.291. The Mahiśāsakas maintained that the Path had only five factors and that the category of *Sīla* (right speech, action and livelihood) should not be included since as physical action it was separate from the mind (*cittavippayutta*). The Theravāda contested this and reaffirmed that *Sīla* enjoyed an equal status with the other components. Cf. Bareau (1955: 187, 237).
17. A reference to *sīla*, *dhamma* and *paññā* may be found at M.i.38. Buddhaghosa confirms that *'dhamma'* here stands for the *samādhikkhandha* (*MA*.i.174).
18. *'Ariyo pan'ayye aṭṭhaṅgiko maggo saṅkhato udahu asaṅkhato ti. Ariyo kho avuso Visākha aṭṭhaṅgiko maggo saṅkhato ti. Ariyena nu kho ayye aṭṭhaṅgikena maggena tayo khandhā saṅgahītā, udāhu tihi khandhehi ariyo aṭṭhaṅgiko maggo saṅgahīto ti. Na kho avuso Visākha ariyena aṭṭhaṅgikena maggena tayo khandhā saṅgahītā, tihi ca kho avuso Visākha khandhehi ariyo aṭṭhaṅgiko maggo saṅgahīto'* (M.i.300f.)
19. *'No h'idam bho Gotama sīla-paridhotā hi bho Gotama paññā, paññā-paridhotaṃ sīlam, yattha sīlam tattha paññā, yattha paññā tattha sīlaṃ. Sīlavato paññā paññāvato sīlaṃ, sīla-paññānañ ca pana lokasmin aggam akkhāyati. Seyyathā*

pi bho Gotama hatthena vā hatthaṃ dhopeyya, pādena vā pādaṃ dhopeyya, evam eva kho bho Gotama sīla-paridhotā paññā, paññā-paridhotaṃ sīlaṃ' (D.i.124). Cf.*SnA*.1.237.

20. *'Idha samaṇo vā brāhmaṇo vā kusalaṃ dhammaṃ adhigaccheyya, kusalaṃ dhammaṃ adhigantvā na parassa āroceyya, kiṃ hi paro parassa karissati? Seyyathā pi nāma purāṇam bandhanaṃ chinditvā aññam navaṃ bandhanaṃ kareyya, evaṃ-sampadam idaṃ pāpakaṃ lobha-dhammaṃ vadāmi. Kiṃ hi paro parassa karissatīti'* (*D*.i.224).
21. The Buddha rejects a similar view put forward by Sakka (*S*.i.206). Cf. the proposition in the *Kvu* (18.3) that compassion is rooted in passion.
22. *'Pāpakaṃ ti parānukampā-virahitattā lāmakaṃ'* (*DA*.ii.395).
23. *'Hitānukampī sambuddho yad aññam anusāsati'* (*S*.i.111).
24. *'Sā codanā bhūtā tacchā dhammikā anavajjā.'*
25. On *Paccekabuddhas* and teaching see Kloppenborg (1974: 76ff).
26. *D*.ii.36ff. As to other versions, Katz (1982: 193) points out that in the *Saṃyutta* account (1.136–8) the Buddha hesitates but in the *Majjhima* account (1.330–1) he does not.
27. Cf. Katz (1982: 193): 'There is no one Buddhist canonical attitude, then, towards the Buddha and teaching, and this canonical ambivalence led to some hermeneutical difficulties for the Buddhist commentators . . . The point to note, however, is that the Buddha . . . must and does teach.' A Mahāyāna version of the account may be found in the *Lotus Sūtra*, chs 2 and 7. On the hesitation of the Buddha Vipassi (*D*.ii.35f.) see Saddhatissa (1970: 48ff.). On the division of monastic duties into study and teaching (*ganthadhura*) versus meditation (*vipassānadhura*) see Gombrich (1971: ch. 7); Carrithers (1983: 141).
28. *'Appassuto pi ce hoti sīlesu asamāhito, ubhayena naṃ garahanti sīlato ca sutena ca. Appassuto pi ce hoti sīlesu susamāhito, sīlato nam pasaṃsanti tassa sampajjate sutaṃ. Bahussuto pi ce hoti sīlesu asamāhito sīlato naṃ garahanti, nāssa sampajjate sutaṃ'* (*Vism*. 1.136 tr. Ñāṇamoli). Cf. *M*.ii.154.
29. Cf. *Vism*. 1.154 describing the unvirtuous man. On the sequence of events at death and the 'death-consciousness' (*cuti-citta*) see *Abhs*. tr. 26ff; 72–75; *Vism*. VIII. 1–41. On 'rebirth-linking' (*patisandhi*) *Vism*. XVII 133–145. On the sequence and signs of death *Kośa* 3.42d–44.
30. *'Marane 'pi damātyāgaḥ śīlasyotkṛṣṭir ucyate.'*
31. *Vṛtti* on *Dīpa* v254: *'Etad api śīlamayaṃ puṇyakriyāvastu mahābhogatāphalaṃ mokṣaphalaṃ ca.'*
32. The 40 stanzas praising heaven as a reward for *śīla* are: 2, 3, 4, 7, 9, 20, 21, 24, 29, 30, 31, 32, 33, 34, 39, 40, 41, 42, 43, 44, 46, 47, 48, 49, 50, 51, 52, 55, 56, 57, 58, 59, 66, 67, 68, 70, 75, 77, 78, 85.
33. *SSiddhi Varga* 99 p. 230: *'Śīlasamādhi pratyayavaśāt rūpadhatau utpadyate. Dānaśīlakuśalābhyāsa pratyayena kāmadhātau utpadyate.'*
34. *A*.i.232sq; *M*.i.62f; *A*.ii.136f.
35. *DhSam*. 1.11: *'Dānaśīlavato nityaṃ, sarvasattvānukampinaḥ, sidhyante sarvasamkalpās, tasmāt śīlaparo bhavet.'*
36. *'Na diṭṭhiyā na sutiyā na ñāṇena . . . sīlabbatenāpi na suddhim āha'* (*Sn*. 839).
37. *'Sīla-dassana-sampannaṃ dhammaṭṭhaṃ saccavādinam, attano kamma*

kubbānaṃ, taṃ jano kurute piyaṃ' (*Dh.* 217).

38. *'Prajñāya eva viśuddhi lābhaḥ śīlam tu prajñendriyasya mūlam'* (*SSidhi.* 133). On *śīlavrataparāmāsa* cf. also *Laṅk* 117; *Adhs.* 10; *Dhs.* 1005.
39. *'Sīlanaṭṭhena sīlam. Kim idaṃ sīlanaṃ nāma? Samādhānaṃ vā, kayakammādīnaṃ susīlyavasena avippakiṇṇatā ti attho: upadhāraṇam vā kusalānaṃ dhammānaṃ patiṭṭhānavasena ādhārabhāvo ti attho. Etad eva hi ettha atthadvayaṃ saddalakkhaṇavidū anujānanti. Aññe pana siraṭṭho sīlaṭṭho sītalaṭṭho sīlaṭṭho ti evamādinā pi nayen'ettha atthaṃ vaṇṇayanti'* (*Vism.* 1.19).
40. *'Loke tesaṃ tesaṃ sattānam pakati pi sīlan ti vuccati, yam sandhāya, ayam sukkhasīlo, ayam dukkhasīlo, ayam kalahasīlo, ayam maṇḍanasīlo ti bhaṇanti'* (*Vism.* 1.38).
41. *'Sukham śīlasamādānam tena kāyo na tapyate'* (*Treasury*, IV. 16ab).
42. *Kośa.* IV 47n3 tr. Poussin.
43. *'Yathā mahārāja bījam appakam api samānam bhaddake khette vuttaṃ deve sammā dharaṃ pavecchante subahūni phalāni anudassati, evam eva kho mahārāja yoginā yogāvacarena yathā paṭipāditam sīlaṃ kevalam sāmaññaphalam anudassati evaṃ sammā paṭipajjitabbam'* (*Miln.* 375).
44. *'Yathā mahārāja ye keci bījagāmabhūtagāma vuddhiṃ virūlhiṃ vepullaṃ āpajjanti sabbe te paṭhavim nissāya paṭhaviyaṃ patitthāya evam ete bījagāmabhūtagāma vuddhiṃ viruḷhim vepullaṃ āpajjanti, evam eva kho mahārāja yogāvacaro sīlam nissāya sīle patiṭṭhāya pañc'indriyāni bhāveti: saddhindriyaṃ, viriyindriyaṃ, satindriyaṃ, samādhindriyaṃ, paññindriyan ti.'*
45. *'Yathā mahārāja nagaravaḍḍhaki nagaraṃ māpetukāmo paṭhamaṃ nagaraṭṭhānam sodhāpetvā khānukaṇṭakaṃ apakaḍḍhāpetvā samaṃ kārāpetvā tato aparabhāge vīthi catukka-singhāṭakādi-paricchedena vibhajitvā nagaraṃ māpeti, evam eva . . .'*
46. *'Yathā mahārāja langhako sippaṃ dassetukāmo paṭhaviṃ khanāpetvā sakkhara-kaṭhalakam apakaddhāpetvā bhūmiṃ samaṃ kārāpetvā mudukāya bhumiyā sippaṃ dasseti, evam eva . . .'*
47. *'Seyyathāpi bhikkhave ye keci pāṇā cattāro iriyapathe kappenti kālena gamanam kālena ṭhānam kālena nisajjam kālena seyyam; sabbe te paṭhaviṃ nissāya paṭhaviyam patiṭṭhāya evam ete cattāro iriyāpathe kappenti; evam eva kho bhikkhave bhikkhu sīlaṃ nissāya sīle patiṭṭhāya satta bojjhaṅge bhāveti'* (*S*.v.78).
48. *'Śīlam āsthāya vartante sarvā hi śreyasi kriyāḥ, sthānādyānīva kāryāṇi pratiṣṭhāya vasundharām'* (tr. E.H. Johnston).
49. *'Sīlam nāma sabbesaṃ kusaladhammānaṃ patiṭṭhā, sīle patiṭṭhito kusaladhammehi na parihāyati, sabbe lokiyalokuttaraguṇe paṭilabhati'* (*Madhu.* 106).
50. *'Patiṭṭhāna-lakkhaṇaṃ mahārāja sīlaṃ sabbesam kusalānam dhammānam; . . . sīle patiṭṭhitassa kho mahārāja sabbe kusalā dhammā na parihāyantī ti.'*
51. *'Kāyakammādīnaṃ samādhānavasena kusalānāñ ca dhammānāṃ patiṭṭhānavasena'* (*Vism.* I.20).
52. *'Śīlam hi sarvaguṇānām pratiṣṭhā bhavati'* (*MSA.* XVI.20).
53. PTS tr. 172.
54. *'Saggārohaṇasopānam aññam sīlasamaṃ kuto, dvāraṃ vā pana nibbānanagarassa pavesane'* (I.24).
55. *'Udakasamo sattānam kilesarajojallāpaharane'* (*Miln.* 195).
56. *Vism.* I.24; 1.159; *Thag.* 615; *Miln.* 163; 382; 385.

57. *Miln*. 354.
58. *Miln*. 333.
59. *Vism*. I.24; *Miln*. 195.
60. *Sīla* is said to have four defects: it can be torn (*khaṇḍa*), rent (*chidda*), blotched (*sabala*) and mottled (*kammāsa*). These are likened to the four defects (*khaṇḍa*) in the fertility of a field at *MA*.i.154.

3 ETHICS AND PSYCHOLOGY

1. *'Dharmānām pravicayam antarena nāsti, kleśānām yata upaśāntaye abhyupāya, kleśaiś ca bhramanti bhavārṇave'tra lokaḥ'* (I.3).
2. An equivalent of sorts might be found in Bentham's *The Springs of Action* (A. Goldsworth (ed.) Oxford: Clarendon Press, 1983), which provides an exhaustive classification of states of mind motivating action.
3. *Vism*. I.20.
4. According to W.S. Karunaratna this was the most influential of all the Abhidharmic systems. He writes: 'The classification of *caitasikas* (*caittas*) which gained the widest currency and exercised the greatest degree of impact on all schools of Buddhism of the Hīnayāna and Mahāyāna alike is that of the Sarvāstivādins.' EB *'Cetasika'* 102.
5. To this the Sarvāstivāda add a further category of non-mental forces (*citta-viprayukta-saṃskāra*).
6. *'Cittan ti ārammaṇaṃ cintetī ti cittaṃ, vijānātī ti attho.'*
7. *'Lakkhaṇādito pana vijānanalakkhaṇaṃ cittam, pubbaṅgama-rasaṃ, sandhāna-paccupaṭṭhānam nāmarūpa-padaṭṭhānam'* (*Asl*. 112).
8. EB *'Citta'*, 169, 172.
9. EB *'Citta'*, 169.
10. In the *Abhidharma* formulation the virtues are the 10 'pervasive good states' (*kuśala-mahābhūmika-dharmas*), namely:

1. Faith (*śraddhā*)	6. Non-craving (*alobha*)
2. Energy (*vīrya*)	7. Non-hatred (*adveṣa*)
3. Equanimity (*upekṣā*)	8. Non-injury (*ahiṃsā*)
4. Modesty (*hrī*)	9. Serenity (*praśrabdhi*)
5. Bashfulness (*apatrāpya*)	10. Non-heedlessness (*apramāda*)

And the vices consist of the 18 defilements (*kleśa*), secondary defilements (*upakleśa*), and 'pervasive bad states' *akuśala-mahābhūmika-dharmas*, namely:

1. Ignorance (*moha*)	10. Jealousy (*īrṣyā*)
2. Heedlessness (*pramāda*)	11. Envious Rivalry (*pradāsa*)
3. Torpor (*kausīdya*)	12. Causing harm (*vihiṃsā*)
4. Lack of faith (*aśraddhā*)	13. Malice (*upanāha*)
5. Sloth (*sthyāna*)	14. Deceit (*māyā*)
6. Restlessness (*auddhatya*)	15. Trickery (*śāṭya*)
7. Anger (*krodha*)	16. Conceit (*mada*)
8. Hypocrisy (*mrakṣa*)	17. Shamelessness (*āhrīkya*)
9. Envy (*mātsarya*)	18. Arrogance (*anapatrāpya*)

11. The Cardinal Virtues or 'Roots of Good' have a positive force which is often overlooked. Poussin notes in this connection: '*Alobha*, non-desire, *adveṣa*, non-hatred, are other than the absence of desire, the absence of hatred, the ataraxy of the sage. We are often mistaken about this, forgetting that the 'non-friend' (*amitra*) is the enemy, that the 'non-truth' (*anṛta*) is a lie. In the same way, non-desire and non-hatred are that which opposes desire and hatred (1927: 147). Cf. *MA*.i.205: '*Alobho kusalamūlan' ti ādisu na lobhoti alobho; lobhapaṭipakkhassa dhammass' etam adhivacanaṃ*.' Also *Asl*. 39.
12. Macquarrie (1967).
13. '*Yaṃ kiñci dukkhaṃ sambhoti sabbaṃ taṇhāpaccayā*' (*Sn*. 4).
14. '*Taṇhāya niyati loko, taṇhāya parikissati, Taṇhāya ekadhammassa sabbeva vasam anvagū ti*' (*S*.i.39).
15. '*Taṇhāya jāyatī soko, taṇhāya jāyatī bhayaṃ Taṇhāya vippamuttassa natthi soko kuto bhayam*' (*Dh*.216).
16. '*Saññā ca vedanā ca cetasikā ete dhammā cittapaṭibaddhā, tasmā saññā ca vedanā ca cittasaṅkhāro ti*' (*S*.iv.293).
17. '*Yā c'āvuso vedanā yā ca saññā yañca viññāaṃ ime dhammā samsaṭṭhā no visamsaṭṭhā, na ca labbhā imesam dhammānaṃ vinibbhujitvā vinibbhujitvā nānākaraṇam paññāpetum. Yam h'āvuso vedeti taṃ sañjānāti, yaṃ sañjānāti taṃ vijānāti*' (*M*.i.293).
18. *Miln*. 63f. Cf. *Asl* 42.
19. *Miln*. 87.
20. '*Tatr'āvuso lobho ca pāpako doso ca pāpako, lobhassa ca pahānāya dosassa ca pahānāya atthi majjhimā patipadā cakkhukaraṇī ñāṇakaraṇī upasamāya abhiññāya sambodhāya nibbāṇāya samvattati. Katamā ca sā āvuso majjhimā paṭipadā . . .? Ayam eva ariyo aṭṭhaṅgiko maggo*' (*M*.i.15).
21. '*Maggo hi lobho eko anto, doso eko anto ti ete dve ante na upeti, na upagacchati, mutto etehi antehi, tasmā majjhimā paṭipadā ti vuccati. Etesaṃ majjhe bhavattā majjhimā, paṭipajjitabbato ca paṭipadā ti. Tathā . . . sassatam eko anto, ucchedo eko anto ti*' (*MA*.i.104).
22. '*Vediyatī ti kho bhikkhave tasmā vedanā ti vuccati. Kiñca vediyati? Sukham pi vediyati dukkham pi vediyati adukkhamasukkham pi vediyati*' (*S*.iii.86f.)
23. '*Vediyatī ti vedanā. Sā vedayitalakkhaṇā anubhavanarasā iṭṭhākārasambhogarasā vā cetasika-assāda-paccupaṭṭhānā passadhipadaṭṭhānā*' (*Asl*. 109; Cf. *Vism*. 450).
24. '*Sañjānāti sañjānāti kho . . . tasmā saññā ti vuccati. Kiñca sañjānāti? nīlakampi sañjānāti, pītakampi sañjānāti, lohitakampi sañjānāti, odātampi sañjānāti*' (*M*.i.293).
25. '*Saṃjñā nimittodgrahaṇātmikā. Yāvan nīla pīta dīrgha hrasva strī puruṣa mitra amitra sukha duḥkha ādi nimittodgrahaṇam asau saṃjñāskandhaḥ*' (1.14cd).
26. On *saññā* see e.g. *Vism*. 274; *DA*.iii.1017; *D*.iii.253; *D*.iii.289, 291.
27. '*Bhavanirodho nibbānan ti kho me . . . saññā uppajjati*' (*A*.v.9).
28. For a list of terms used as translations of *vedanā* and *saññā* see Piyananda (1974: 84f.).
29. I am indebted here to Dickwela Piyananda's thesis (1974) on early Buddhist psychology from which this abbreviated account of the process of *saṅkhāra*-formation is taken.

30. *'Avijjāsamphassajena . . . vedayitena phuṭṭhassa assutavato putthujjanassa uppannā taṇhā: tatojo so saṅkhāro.'*
31. *'Cakkhuñ c'āvuso paṭicca rūpe ca uppajjati cakkhuviññāṇaṃ, tiṇṇaṃ saṅgati phasso; phassapaccayā vedanā; yaṃ vedeti taṃ sañjānāti; yaṃ sañjānāti taṃ vitakketi; yaṃ vitakketi taṃ papañceti; yaṃ papañceti tatonidānam purisaṃ papañcasaññāsaṅkhā samudācaranti atītanāgata-paccuppannesu cakkhuviññey-yesu rūpesu'* (*M*.i.3f).
32. Cf. *Dh*.254: 'The Tathāgatas are free from conceptual proliferation' (*nippapañcā Tathāgatā*).
33. *'Pañcakkhandhā pariññātā, tiṭṭhanti chinnamūlakā'* (*Thag*. 90).
34. *'Visaṅkhāragataṃ cittaṃ – taṇhānam khayaṃ ajjhagā'* (*Dh*.153–4).
35. For Aristotle's critique of Socrates on this point see *NE*.VIII.1145b 21–1147b.19; cf.VI.13 1144b.16–1145a.10.
36. For a full-length discussion and defence of this position see R. Beehler (1978). Also Bradley 'Why Should I be Moral?' in *Ethical Studies* (1927).
37. On *anukampā* and friendship see Mrs Rhys Davids (1936: 301–5).
38. For a contrary view see Jones (1979).
39. *'Manasā ce pasannena yad aññam anusāsati na tena hoti samyutto. Sānukampā anuddayā ti.'* On the meaning of *'bahujanahitāya'*, *'bahujanasukhāya'* and *'lokānukampāya'* see *MA*.i.123.
40. Cf. *Kośa* 8.29ab.
41. *DA*.iii.1053; cf. *MA*.i.282 which also lists six ways of counteracting hatred (*vyāpāda*).
42. *'N'āham bhikkhave aññaṃ ekadhammam pi samanupassāmi yena anuppanno vā vyāpādo n'uppajjati uppanno vā vyapado pahīyati yathayidaṃ bhikkhave mettā cetovimutti'* (*A*.i.4).
43. On the role of moral purity in meditation see Paravahera Vajirañāṇa Mahāthera (1975: ch. 6).
44. *'Rājā āha: Bhante Nāgasena, kiṃlakkhaṇo samādhī ti?*
–Pamukhalakkhaṇo mahārāja samādhi, ye keci kusalā dhammā sabbe te samādhipamukhā honti samādhininnā samādhipoṇā samādhipabbhārā ti.
–Opammam karohi ti.
–Yathā mahārāja kūṭāgārassa yā kāci gopānasiyo sabbā tā kūṭangamā honti kūṭaninnā kūṭasamosaraṇā, kūtaṃ tāsaṃ aggam-akkhāyati, evam eva kho mahārāja ye keci kusalā dhammā sabbe te samādhipamukhā honti samādhininnā samādhipoṇā samādhipabbharā ti.' (*Miln*. 38). Buddhaghosa says that *samādhi* is the 'virtuous concentration of the mind' (*kusala citta ekaggatā*) (*Vism. 69*).
45. I disagree with him, however, when he sums up as follows: 'The most convenient way to summarise the *samatha* meditations, of which there are traditionally forty, is that they are preparatory to the real work on the Buddhist path.' The fact that the *samatha* meditations 'inculcate certain desirable character traits' (ibid.) makes the technique as much a part of the 'real work' as *vipassanā*.
46. *'Vyāpādadosaṃ pahāya avyāpannacitto viharati, sabbapāṇabhūta hitānukampī vyāpādadosā cittaṃ parisodheti'* (*A*.iv.437).

4 THE TRANSCENDENCY THESIS

1. Twenty-five years on he is still ploughing the same furrow, as can be seen from his 1989 article. His main stumbling-block is the notion that Buddhism insists that moral deeds be conceived and executed in a desireless vacuum since 'desire of any sort brings rebirth.' However, an indication that he is no longer entirely happy with this position may be found in his comment 'I must in all honesty say that I am not convinced that there *is* total aloofness from *all* desire' (1989: 145).
2. A poll of monks in China taken by Welch suggests that the majority (75%) sought ordination for non-religious reasons. Only 25% were ordained because they felt 'attracted towards Buddhism or its institutions' (Welch, 1967: 260).
3. Saddhatissa (1970: 120); Katz (1982: 181–5) citing Rhys Davids *et al.*; *Miln* 164. Buddhaghosa says there were 500 lay *anāgāmins* in Rājagaha (*DA*.iii.833).
4. The view proposed by King and Spiro is not unprecedented and a similar position seems to have been advocated by the Chinese monk Mahāyāna in his debate with Kamalaśīla in Tibet in the eighth century. His view did not prevail and as Williams points out has been regarded in Tibet as an archetypal 'wrong view' ever since, although finding support in some schools. For a useful summary see Williams (1989: 193ff.).
5. *Vism*. XVI.73; *DA*.iii.899.
6. PTS Dictionary '*Nibbāna*' (emphasis is original). The notion of *nibbāna* as a self-existent state, he suggests, is a product of the scholastic *Abhidhamma* period.
7. Cf. Gudmunsen (1972: 312); Premasiri (1976: 70f.).
8. '*Evam eva kho bhikkhave kullūpamo mayā dhammo desito nittharaṇatthāya no gahaṇatthāya. Kullūpamam vo bhikkhave ājānantehi dhammā pi vo pahātabbā, pāg eva adhammā*' (*M*.i.135).
9. See, for instance, John Ross Carter 'Beyond "Beyond Good and Evil"' in Dhammapala, Gombrich and Norman (eds) (1984).
10. Buddhaghosa confirms that *kulla* is a synonym for the Eightfold Path at *MA*.i.229.
11. '*Kin nu kho bho Gotama orimaṃ tīram, kiṃ pārimaṃ tīran ti? Pāṇātipāto kho brāhmaṇa orimam tīraṃ, pāṇātipātā veramaṇī pārimaṃ tīraṃ. Adinnādānaṃ kho brāhmaṇa orimaṃ tīraṃ, adinnādānā veramaṇī pārimaṃ tīraṃ. Kāmesu micchācāro orimaṃ tīraṃ, kāmesu micchācārā veramanī pārimaṃ tīraṃ. Musāvādo . . . pisunā vācā . . . pharusā vācā . . . samphappalāpo . . . abhijjhā . . . vyāpādo . . . micchādiṭṭhi . . .*' (*A*.v.252).
12. '*Kin nu bho Gotama orimaṃ tīram, kiṃ pārimaṃ tīran ti? Micchādiṭṭhi kho brāhmaṇa orimaṃ tīram, sammādiṭṭhi pārimaṃ tiram. Micchāsaṅkappo – micchāvācā – micchākammanto – micchājīvo – micchāvāyāmo – micchāsati – micchāsamādhi – micchāñāṇam – micchāvimutti.*'
13. '*Tathā 'haṃ Bhagavatā dhammaṃ desitaṃ ājānāmi yathā 'me antarāyikā dhammā vuttā Bhagavatā te patisevato nālam antarayāyati*' (*M*.i.130).
14. '*So vata bhikkhave aññatr' eva kāmehi aññatra kāmasaññāya aññatra kāmavitṭakehi kāme paṭisevissatīti n'etam ṭhānam vijjati*' (*M*.i.133).

15. *'Methunadhamme doso n'atthi'* (*MA*.i.103).
16. *'Idha bhikkhave ekacce moghapurisā dhammaṃ pariyāpuṇanti, suttaṃ geyyaṃ veyyākaraṇaṃ gāthaṃ udānaṃ itivuttakaṃ jātakaṃ abbhutadhammaṃ vedallaṃ; te taṃ dhammaṃ pariyāpuṇitvā tesaṃ dhammānaṃ paññāya atthaṃ na upaparikkhanti, tesaṃ te dhammā paññāya atthaṃ anuparikkhatakaṃ na nijjhānaṃ khamanti. Te upārambhānisaṃsā c'eva dhammaṃ pariyāpuṇanti itivādappamok khānisaṃsā ca, yassa c'atthāya dhammaṃ pariyāpuṇanti tañc'assa atthaṃ nānubhonti, tesaṃ te dhammña duggahītā dīgharattaṃ ahitāya dukkhāya saṃvattanti, tam kissa hetu: duggahītattā bhikkhave dhammānaṃ'* (*M*.i.133f).
17. *'Evam suggahīte Buddhavacane ānisaṃsaṃ dassetvā . . .'* (*MA*.i.108).
18. *'Atha ca pana tvaṃ moghapurisa attanā duggahītena amhe c'eva abbhācikkhasi attānañ-ca khanasi bahuñ-ca apuññaṃ pasavasi'* (*M*.i.132).
19. Buddhaghosa says there is a different name – *uḷumpo* – for a conveyance which is laid out flat as opposed to tied up in a bundle (*MA*.i.109).
20. *'Dhammā pi vo pahātabbā' ti ettha 'dhammā' ti samathavipassanā. Bhagavā hi samathe pi chandarāgaṃ pajahāpeti, vipassanāya pi. Samathe chandarāgaṃ kattha pajahāpesi? "Iti kho, Udāyi, nevasaññānāsaññāyatanassa pi pahānaṃ vadāmi. Passasi no tvaṃ, Udāyi, taṃ saṃyojanaṃ aṇuṃ vā thūlaṃ vā yassāhaṃ no pahānaṃ vadāmi" ti (M.i.456) ettha samathe chandarāgaṃ pajahāpesi. "imañ ce tumhe, bhikkhave, diṭṭhiṃ evaṃ parisuddhaṃ, evaṃ pariyodātaṃ na allīyetha, na keḷāyetha, na dhanāyethā" ti (M.i.260) ettha vipassanāya chandarāgaṃ pajahāpesi. Idha pana ubhayattha pajahāpento "dhammā pi vo pahātabbā, pag eva adhammā" ti āha. Tatrāyaṃ adhippāyo: Bhikkhave, ahaṃ evarūpesu pi santapaṇṇītesu dhammesu chandarāgapahānaṃ vadāmi, kiṃ pana imasmiṃ asaddhamme gāmadhamme vasaladhamme duṭṭhulle odantike, yattha ayaṃ Ariṭṭho moghapuriso niddosasaññī pañcāsu kāmaguṇesu chandarāgaṃ nālaṃ antarayāya ti vadati. Ariṭṭhena viya na tumhehi mayhaṃ sāsane kalalaṃ va kacavaro vā pakkhipitabbo ti evaṃ Bhagavā imina pi ovadena Ariṭṭhaṃ yeva niggaṇhāti'* (*MA*.i.109). There seems no particular reason to identify *dhammā* with meditation here, and meditation does not figure at all as a theme in the Discourse. Buddhaghosa makes the same identification in another place when commenting on *dhammarāgena* and *dhammanandiyā* (*AA*.v.85). Here there is arguably more justification for it since the *jhānas* are mentioned, but it does not strike me in either case as the natural meaning of the text.
21. *'Imaṃ ce tumhe bhikkhave diṭṭhiṃ evaṃ parisuddhiṃ evaṃ pariyodātaṃ allīyetha kelāyetha dhanāyetha mamāyetha, api nu tumhe bhikkhave kullūpamaṃ dhammaṃ desitaṃ ājāneyyātha nittharanatthāya no gahaṇatthāyāti? . . . 'Evam bhante.'*
22. *'Tattha "*diṭṭhiṃ*" ti vipassanā-sammādiṭṭhiṃ. Sabhāvadassanena parisuddhaṃ. Paccayadassanena pariyodātaṃ. "Allīyethā" ti taṇhā-diṭṭhīhi allīyitvā vihareyyātha. "Kelāyethā" ti taṇhā-diṭṭhīhi kīḷamāna vihareyyātha . . . "Nittharanatthāya no gahaṇatthāyā" ti yo so mayā caturoghanittharaṇatthāya kullūpamo dhammo desito no nikantivasena gahaṇatthāya, api nu taṃ tumhe ājāneyyāthā ti'* (*MA*.ii.307f).
23. 'Upamaṃ karonto ca Bhagavā katthaci upamaṃ paṭhamaṃ eva

dassetvā pacchā attham dasseti, katthaci paṭhamaṃ atthaṃ dassetvā pacchā upamaṃ; katthaci upamāya atthaṃ parivāretvā dasseti, katthaci atthena upamaṃ. Tattha . . . "Idha pana, bhikkhave, ekacce kulaputta dhammaṃ pariyāpuṇanti: suttan -pe- Seyyathā pi, bhikkhave, puriso alagadātthiko" ti ādinā pana nayena sakalaṃ pi Alagadasuttaṃ, Mahā-Saropamasuttan ti evaṃ ādīni suttāni atthena upamaṃ parivāretvā dassento āha' (*MA*.i.165f.).

24. In another place in the commentary he remarks that in the *Water Snake* the explanation of false views comes first (perhaps meaning our sections 1–3, followed by the elucidation of the threefold circle of emptiness (our section 4) *MA*.i.176).
25. Candrakīrti comments at *Prasannapaddā* 497. See May (1959: 232).
26. Ed. M. Muller (Oxford, 1881: 23).
27. Ed. B. Nanjio (Kyoto, 1923: 17ff.).
28. For useful references see Lamotte *Traité*, vol.I, p. 64, n. 1. I am grateful to a JIABS reviewer for drawing my attention to this source.

5 ETHICS AND SOTERIOLOGY

1. '*Seyyathā pi nāma Gaṅgodakaṃ Yamunodaka saṃsandati sameti, evaṃ eva . . . saṃsandati nibbānañ ca paṭipadā ca*' (*D*.ii.223).
2. The eighth factor of the Path – *samādhi* – is omitted from the discussion.
3. Cf. *M*.i.196f.
4. '*Katamā ca bhikkhave sammāvācā ariyā anāsavā lokuttarā maggaṅgā? Yā kho bhikkhave ariyacittassa anāsavacittassa ariyamagga-samaṅgino ariyamaggaṃ bhāvayato catūhi pi vācīduccaritehi arati virati paṭivirati veramaṇī - ayam bhikkhave sammāvācā ariyā anāsavā lokuttarā maggaṅgā*' (*M*.iii.74).
5. *VismA*. 464 quoted by Ñāṇamoli *Vism*. tr. 507 n.36.
6. '*Iti kho Ānanda kusalāni sīlāni avippaṭisāratthāni avippaṭisārānisaṃsāni, avippaṭisāro pāmujjāttho pāmujjānisaṃso . . . pīti . . . passaddhi . . . sukhaṃ . . . samādhi . . . yathābhūta-ñāṇa-dassana . . . nibbidāvirāgo . . . vimutti-ñāṇa-dassana iti kho Ānanda kusalāni sīlāni anupubbena aggāya parentī ti*' (*A*.v.2).
7. Ironically, Spiro cites as an allegedly *erroneous* conception of Buddhist soteriology an updated version of this parable supplied by an informant according to which the journey to nirvana is like a train journey from Mandalay to Rangoon calling at stations *en route* (1982: 84).
8. '*Santi Kassapa eke samaṇa-brāhmaṇā sīla-vādā. Te anekapariyāyena sīlassa vaṇṇaṃ bhāsanti. Yāvatā Kassapa ariyaṃ paramaṃ sīlaṃ, nāhaṃ tatha attano sama-samaṃ samanupassāmi kuto bhiyyo. Atha kho ahaṃ eva tatha bhiyyo yadidaṃ adhisīlaṃ*' (*D*.i.174). Cf. S.i.139.
9. '*Ahaṃ kho pana Moggallāna parisuddhasīlo samāno "parisuddhasīlo'mhī" ti patijānāmi, "parisuddhaṃ me sīlaṃ pariyodātam asaṃkiliṭṭhaṃ" ti. Na ca maṃ sāvakā sīlato rakkhanti, na cāhaṃ sāvakehi sīlato rakkhaṃ paccāsiṃsāmi*' (*A*.iii.126).
10. Trans Ñāṇamoli *Vism*. tr. 215 n.9.

11. *'Tīṇi Tathāgatassa ārakkheyyāni. Parisuddha-kāya-samācāro āvuso Tathāgato, n'atthi Tathāgatassa kāya-duccaritaṃ yaṃ Tathāgato rakkheyya "mā me idaṃ paro aññāsīti". Parisuddha-vacī-samācāro āvuso Tathāgato . . . Parisuddha-mano-samācāro āvuso Tathāgato . . .'* (*D*.iii.217).
12. *'Ahaṃ hi Brāhmaṇa jigucchāmi kāyaduccaritena vacīduccaritena manoduccaritena anekavihitānaṃ pāpakānaṃ akusalānaṃ dhammānaṃ samapāttiyā'* (*Vin*.iii.3).
13. *'Sabbe mahārāja pāpakā akusalā dhammā Tathāgatassa bāhitā pahīnā apagatā byapagatā ucchinnā khīṇā khayaṃ pattā nibbutā upasantā, tasmā tathāgato brāhmaṇo ti vuccati'* (*Miln*. 225).
14. *'Abhabbo āvuso khīṇāsavo bhikkhu sañcicca pāṇaṃ jīvitā voropetum . . . adinnaṃ theyyasaṃkhātaṃ ādātum . . . methunaṃ dhammaṃ patisevituṃ . . . sampajānamusā bhāsitum . . . sannidhikārakaṃ kāme paribhuñjituṃ seyyathā pi pubbe agāriyabhūto'* (*D*.iii.235). At D.iii.133 nine items are mentioned and the commentary says that even a stream-winner is incapable of these things (*DA*.iii.913).
15. *'Yāvajīvam arahanto pāṇātipātaṃ pahāya pāṇātipatā paṭiviratā nihitadaṇḍā nihitasatthā lajjī dayāpannā sabbapāṇabhūta-hita-anukampino viharanti'* (*A*.i.211).
16. *'Akusalaṃ bhikkhave pajahatha. Sakkā bhikkhave akusalaṃ pahajituṃ. No ce tam bhikkhave sakkā abhavissa akusalaṃ pajahituṃ nāhaṃ evaṃ vadeyyam akusalaṃ bhikkhave pajahathā ti . . . Akusalañ ca h'idam bhikkhave pahīnaṃ ahitāya dukkhāya saṃvatteyya nāhaṃ evaṃ vadeyyaṃ "akusalaṃ bhikkhave pajahathā" ti. Yasmā ca kho bhikkhave akusalaṃ pahīnaṃ hitāya sukkhāya saṃvattati tasmāhaṃ evaṃ vadāmi "akusalaṃ bhikkhave pajahathā" ti. Kusalaṃ bhikkhave bhāvetha . . .'* (A.i.58).
17. *'Evarūpassa bhikkhave puggalassa lobhajā . . . dosajā, . . . mohajā pāpakā akusalā dhammā pahīnā ucchinnamūlā tālāvatthukatā anabhāvakatā āyatiṃ anuppādadhammā diṭṭh'eva dhamme sukhaṃ viharati avighātaṃ anupāyāsaṃ apariḷāhaṃ diṭṭh'eva dhamme parinibbāyati'* (*A*.i.204).
18. *'Ṭhitiṃ p'ahaṃ bhikkhave na vaṇṇayāmi kusalesu dhammesu pageva pārihāniṃ; vuddhiñca kho 'ham bhikkhave vaṇṇayāmi kusalesu dhammesu no ṭhitiṃ no hāniṃ'* (*A*.v.96).
19. *'Uppannānaṃ kusalānaṃ dhammānaṃ ṭhitiyā asammosāya bhiyyobhāvāya vepullāya bhāvanāya pāripūriyā chandam janeti vāyamati, viriyam ārabhati, cittaṃ paggaṇhāti padahati. Ayam vuccati bhikkhave sammā-vāyāmo'* (*D*.ii.312f).
20. *'Vacanattho pan'ettha kucchite pāpadhamme salayanti calayanti kampenti viddhamsentī ti kusala. Kucchitena vā ākārena sayantī ti kusa. Te akusalasaṅkhāte kuse lunanti chindantī ti kusala. Kucchitānaṃ vā sānato tanukaraṇato osānakaraṇato ñāṇaṃ kusaṃ nāma. Tena kusena lātabbā ti kusalā gahetabbā pavattetabbā ti attho. Yathā vā kusā ubhayabhāgagataṃ hatthappadesaṃ lunanti evam ime te pi uppannānuppannabhavena ubhayabhāgagataṃ saṅkilesapakkhaṃ lunanti tasmā kusā viya lunanti ti pi kusalā'* (*Asl*. 39).
21. *'Sabbākusaladhammapahīno . . . Tathāgato kusaladhamma samannāgato ti'* (*M*.ii.116).
22. *'Aneke pāpake akusale dhamme pahīne . . . aneke ca kusale dhamme bhāvanāya pāripūrikate'* (*Ud*. 66).

23. Buddhaghosa gives a fivefold meaning for *kusala*: health (*ārogya*), blamelessness (*anavajja*), produced by skill (*kosalla-sambhūta*), freedom from distress (*niddaratha*), and happy result (*sukhavipāka*). He indicates that in the *Jātakas* it means 'health', in the *suttantas* it is used with the ethical meaning ('blameless'), and the technical and other senses are found in the *Abhidhamma* (*DA*.iii.883). Cf. *Asl*.62f; *MA*.i.204. On *kusala* in Mahāyāna sources, May (1959: 148, n. 433).
24. I say a 'simple' act to exclude counterfeits of moral acts which have a kind of Machiavellian ulterior motive, which in fact makes them technical or instrumental. For example, a large company makes a donation to the funds of a political party with the calculated aim of furthering its commercial interests. Such a move may be shrewd, astute, timely, and, indeed, 'skilful'. The very fact that it could be characterised in this way, however, distinguishes it from a morally good act. On *dāna* and the motives for it see *D*.iii.258; *DA*.iii.1044f; cf.*D*.ii.395.
25. PTS Dictionary.
26. *D*.i.78.
27. *D*.i.74.
28. *Miln*. 293.
29. Ibid.
30. *Miln*. 48.
31. '*Visesato pan'ettha saddhā-paññānaṃ samādhi-viriyānañ ca samataṃ pasaṃsanti. Balavapañño mandasaddho kerāṭikapakkhaṃ bhajati, bhesajjasamuṭṭhito viya rogo atekiccho hoti*' (*Vism*. IV.47)
32. '*Cittuppādamatten' eva kusalaṃ hoti ti atidhāvitvā dānādīni akaronto niraye uppajjati*' (*MA*.i.291).
33. A Table showing the commentarial definitions of *kusala* may be found in the Introduction to U. Narada's translation of the *Paṭṭhāna* (PTS edn.).
34. '*Mā bhikkhave puññānaṃ bhāyittha; sukhass'etaṃ bhikkhave adhivacanaṃ itthassa kantassa piyassa manāpassa, yad idaṃ puññāni*' (*It*.14–15).
35. *S*.ii.82; *Sn*.520, 790.
36. *Miln*. 45 says that feeling (*vedanā*) cannot be *kusala* and *dukkha* at the same time: '*Yadi bhante kusala na dukkha, yadi dukkha na kusala, kusalaṃ dukkhan ti na uppajjatīti*.' Also MA.i.205: '*Kusalaṃ patvā hi dukkhavedanā n'atthi*.'
37. '*Kusalānaṃ bhikkhave dhammānaṃ samādāna-hetu evaṃ idaṃ puññaṃ pavaddhatī ti*' (*D*.iii.78f).
38. *Critique of Practical Reason* 11.11.i 110–14.
39. Ibid. 110f.

6 ETHICS IN THE MAHĀYĀNA

1. For further listings see: *Śū.Sam*: 26–38; *VNS*. 1.3; *MSA*. ch.16.v.14; *Siddhi*. 620–38 (Poussin tr.). On the *Pāramitās* in general see Dayal (1932: ch. V).

2. On these 10 Perfections see B.C. Law (1934.1. 689); *Vism*. IX.124.
3. *MSA*.100.11ff. The same division is followed by sGam-po-pa (*Jewel*, 1970: 148).
4. Sometimes the 'Thought of Enlightenment' (*bodhicitta*) is included as a third factor, e.g. *M.Av*. 1.1. According to *M.Av*. 1.2 compassion (*karuṇā*) is the seed of Buddhahood since it provides the motivation to gain enlightenment for the benefit of others.
5. Cf. *Jewel*, 149, 170f; *Laṅk*. 119 3–5; *Suhṛll*. v.11; *Aṣṭa*. 71; *M.Saṃgr* iv.7; *Śīlaparikathā* v.11.
6. '*Bosatsukai*' 142.
7. Four translations of this '*Bodhisattva-Prātimokṣa*', as it became known, were made into Chinese, of which Hsuan-Tsang's T'ang version, the *P'u Sa Chieh Pen* (also known as the *Yu Chia Chieh Pen*) seems closest to the present text. See EB '*Bodhisattva-Prātimokṣa*'. A complete English translation with Tsong-kha-pa's commentary is now available in Tatz (1986).
8. *MSA*, Levi (tr.) 190f.v37; *BPMS*, Dutt (tr.) (1931: 269); *Hōbōgirin* '*Bosatsukai*' (listing many Chinese sources); Dayal 1932: 196, n.203; *M.Saṃgr*. VI.2–6; IV.9.
9. Cf. *Śikṣā*. 168.
10. See EB '*Bodhisattva-Prātimokṣa*.
11. Translated in Change (ed.) (1983: 268).
12. The terms *appasāvajja* and *mahāsāvajja* are found (e.g. *DA*.iii.1048f.; *VbhA*. 382), and '*pākaṭaṃ pāpaṃ*' occurs (PTC III.1.3) in the sense of a 'wicked deed' with no special technical meaning.
13. It will be recalled from Chapter One that damage to plants and vegetation is prohibited by *Short Tract* 8, *Pācittiya* 11 and *Sekhiya* 74.
14. That this is the correct interpretation would seem to be backed up by *Miln*. 266f. which speaks of two kinds of defilements (*kilesa*). The first relates to things blameable by the world (*lokavajja*) and the second to things blameable by the *Vinaya* (*paṇṇattivajja*). The first is instanced as the Ten Bad Paths of Action, and the second as improper behaviour for monks such as eating at the wrong time (*vikālabhojana*), damaging vegetation (*bhūtagāma-vikopana*) and playing around in water (*udake hassadhamma*).
15. '*Evaṃ gṛhītvā sudṛḍham bodhicittaṃ jinātmajaḥ; śikṣānatikrame yatnaṃ kuryāt nityam atandritaḥ*.'
16. '*Evam buddhvā parārtheṣu bhavet satatam utsthitaḥ; niṣiddham apy anujñātaṃ kṛpālor arthadarśinaḥ*.'
17. '*Evam anuttaraṃ jñatvā sattvānāṃ hitasukhavidhānāya nityam-ārabdha-vīryo bhavet/ pratiṣiddhārthe pravṛttau kathaṃ na sāpattika iti cet/na/kva cin niṣiddham api sattvārtha-viśeṣam prajñācakṣuṣā paśyataḥ karaṇīyatayā anujñātam bhagavatā/saniḥsaraṇaṃ ca bhagavataḥ śāsanaṃ/ taccāpi na sarvasya/ api tu kṛpāloḥ karuṇā-prakarṣapravṛttitayā tatparatantrasya parārthaikarasasya svaprayojanavimukhasya/ iti prajñākaruṇābhyām udbhūtaparārthavṛtter-upāya-kuśalasya pravartamānasya nāpattiḥ*' (*Pañjika*. 138.16–139.6).
18. '*Atha tato'py adhikaṃ sattvārthaṃ paśyet, śiksāṃ nikṣipet*'.

19. Chang (ed.) (1983: 279n.10). Paul Williams cites other examples from the *Mahāparinirvāṇasūtra* and *Gaṇḍavyūhasutra* (1989: 161f.).
20. *'Saṃcintya gaṇikām bhonti pumsām ākarṣanāya te; rāgāṅkuraṃ ca saṃlobhya buddhajñāne sthāpayanti te'* (*Śikṣā*. 173. 19f).
21. Chang (ed.) (1983: 435).
22. *'Evamanyasmin sattvārthopāye sati rāgajā āpattir anāpattir uktā'* (*Śikṣā*. 94.9).
23. *'Bodhisattvasya tenaivaṃ sarvāpattir garīyasī yasmād āpadyamāno'sau sarvasattva arthahānikṛt'* (*BCA*. IV.8).
24. *'Ekasyāpi hi sattvasya hitaṃ hatvā hato bhavet; aśeṣākāśaparyantavāsināṃ kimu dehinām.'*
25. See *Śiksā* 144.14; 131.13; Poussin (1927: 63f.); Ruegg (1980: 234–41); Kapleau (1983: *passim*).
26. *Bo.Bhū* 261–72. The divisions are enumerated incorrectly by Lamotte (*VNS*. 19.n68).
27. Snellgrove (1989: 10).
28. E.g. *Miln*. 25f.
29. *Prasannapadā* 183–5 May (1959: 147–50).
30. We may see the form it might take as a normative doctrine in the following chapter, section 3.

7 BUDDHISM AND UTILITARIANISM

1. Harris (1980: 38).
2. (1970: ch. 5.2.) The 14 pleasures are of sense, wealth, skill, amity, a good name, power, piety, benevolence, malevolence, memory, imagination, expectation, association and relief. The 12 pains are of privation, the senses, awkwardness, enmity, an ill name, piety, benevolence, malevolence, memory, imagination, expectation, and association.
3. *Collected Works* ii.253 (Sir John Bowring's edition, Edinburgh, William Tait, 1843).
4. Smart (Smart and Williams, 1973: 14–25) attempts to minimise the disagreement between Bentham and Mill on this point by focusing on the 'infecundity' of the lower forms of pleasure, i.e since Bentham would in any event regard Mill's 'lower pleasures' as 'infecund' the two are in fact in agreement.
5. James Mill spent eleven years writing the *History of British India* and was appointed examiner in the East India Company. The younger Mill became an assistant in his father's office at India House at the age of seventeen (Ryan, 1974: 7).
6. The issues here are related to the debate between Bastow (1969) and Gudmunsen (1972) on the relationship between the 'Way' and the 'Goal'. This is not conducted in the context of utilitarian ethical theory but may be illuminated by these considerations.
7. Cf. the discussion in Ryan (1974: 113).

8. David Walker, *The Oxford Companion to Law*, (Oxford: Clarendon Press, 1980); 'intention'; 'motive'.
9. See Lyons (1970).
10. On Smart's electrode-operator argument (Smart and Williams, 1973: 18ff.) cf. Finnis' discussion of Nozick's experience machine (1983: 11.3).
11. It is interesting to recall that specific exoneration is given by the *Bodhisattvabhūmi* in connection with sedition (C.2a).

8 BUDDHISM AND ARISTOTLE

1. The facts concerning the composition of these works are disputed. I am following Cooper (1975: xi). For a more cautious opinion see Hardie (1980: 6, 9), who has more recently admitted that the latest research favours Cooper (Hardie, 1980: 359). Cf. Kenny (1979: ixf). The translations of Aristotle's works I have relied on are in the series edited by Sir David Ross (1908). A useful summary of the central portions of most of the texts relevant to our present enquiry (excluding the *MM*) may be found in Ackrill (1973).
2. The translation of *eudaemonia* as 'flourishing' continues to gain ground over the less satisfactory 'happiness' favoured by earlier translators. 'Happiness' suggests a less enduring condition than the long-term structured participation in virtue which is *eudaemonia*.
3. The notion of *nibbāna* as a collection of basic goods is considered and rejected by Gudmunsen without reference to Aristotle (1973: 42–6). His reasoning seems to be that all nibbānic goods (e.g. nibbānic 'peace') are 'qualitatively' and 'existentially' distinct from their worldly counterparts.
4. The same has happened to Aristotle's *eudaemonia*. Cooper's work (1975) is an attempt to counteract this interpretation.
5. The Buddha stressed the importance of friendship (*kalyānamittatā*) in the religious life (S.v.2). On the duties and obligations of an individual in society see Weeraratne (1976: ch. 3).
6. Allan (1970: ch. 6).
7. On the stages of his development and the dispute concerning the intermediate position see Hardie (1980: ch. V).
8. Cf. Hardie (1980: 72).
9. It is not my purpose here to enter in detail into this intriguing but recondite aspect of Aristotelian anthropology. However, the similarity between the Buddhist and Aristotelian conception of man as a psycho-physical aggregate with a detachable conscious component bears further examination.
10. Cf. Kenny (1979: 13).
11. Allan (1970: 49).
12. Ibid.: 126.
13. Ibid.: 49.
14. For a discussion of the issues here see Hardie (1980) ch. XI, especially

p. 227: 'The end, according to Aristotle, is an object of desire, and it moves us by being the object of thought or imagination. Hence practical wisdom, if it is to be complete and not headless, must include the intuitive thought of the end as well as the intellectual powers required for the discovery of means.'

15. The 'psychic' (*nāma*) faculties are sometimes listed as fivefold, e.g. *S*.ii.3: 'Feeling, cognition, volition, contact of the senses with their objects (*phassa*), and attention: these are the psychic (*nāma*) faculties' (*Vedanā, sañña, cetanā, phasso, manasikāro: idaṃ vuccati nāmaṃ*).
16. On the meaning of these terms see *Asl*.142–5; Govinda (1974: 119); Guenther (1976: 49–60).
17. Guenther (1976: 43n); Poussin *Kośa*.IV.2n. and *infra*. Mrs. Rhys Davids also admits, 'I regret the rendering of *cetanā* by 'volition' in the later editions of my *Buddhist Psychological Ethics* (1923)' (1936: 276).
18. *'Cetayatī ti cetanā: saddhim attanā sampayuttadhamme ārammaṇe abhisandahatī ti attho* (*Asl*.111).
19. 'What, monks, are the formations? There are six kinds of intentions: intentions concerned with form, sound, smell, taste, touch and mental objects' (*katamā ca bhikkhave saṅkhārā? Chayime bhikkhave cetanākāyā, rūpasañcetanā, sadda-gandha-rasa-phoṭṭhabba-dhamma sañcetanā, ime vuccanti bhikkhave saṅkhārā'* (*S*.iii.60).
20. The role of the Latin language in the formation of the concept of the will is discussed at length by Dihle (1982: 132ff.).
21. EB *'cetanā'*, 91.
22. De Silva prefers to analyse the specific conative terminology of Buddhism 'against the background of the concept of *saṅkhāra*' (ibid). He translates *'attakāra'* as 'free will' and *'purisakāra'* as 'personal endeavour' (*op.cit*: 7). Cf. Jayatilleke (1971: 54): 'On this occasion the Buddha says that there is such a thing as "an element of initiative" (*ārabbha-dhātu*) and as a result one can observe beings acting with initiative and this says the Buddha is what is called "the free will of people" (*sattānaṃ atta-kāro*). He also goes on to say that there is an "element of origination" (*nikkama-dhātū*), an "element of endeavour" (*parakkama-dhātu*), an element of strength (*thāma-dhātu*) and an element of perseverance (*ṭhiti-dhātu*) and an "element of volitional effort" (*upakkama-dhātu*), which makes beings of their own accord act in various ways and that this showed that there was such a thing as free will (*A*.iii.337, 338)'. Cf. *MA*.i.284.
23. This useful and thorough material is now more easily available in Matthews, 1983.
24. Karunaratna lists: 'will, volition, intention, motivation, conation, drive, stimulus, disposition, determination, effort, choice, resolve, arrangement, organisation, aspiration, purposive intellection, mental construction and formative tendency' (EB *'cetanā'* 86).
25. EB *'cetanā'* 90.
26. David Walker, *The Oxford Companion to Law* (Oxford: Clarendon Press, 1970).
27. Bareau writes: 'From the point of view of the Buddhist legislator, responsibility is far more closely associated with the execution of the

crime than with criminal intention' (1956: 221). On exonerating conditions in the *Vinaya* see Little and Twiss (1978: 222–5).

28. Cf. Foot (1978: 4f.).
29. Cf. the fruitless debate between A.L. Herman and others in *PEW* (vol. 29, no. 1, 1979; vol. 30, no. 4, 1980) on the so-called 'paradox of desire'. If all desire is wrong, it is suggested, then desire for the *Dhamma* is wrong. cf. Herman (1983: 320–4).
30. *'Puriso atthakāmo hitakāmo yogakkhemakāmo ti kho bhikkhave Tathāgatassa etaṃ adhivacanaṃ arahato sammāsambuddhassa'* (*M*.i.118).
31. On the positive role of desire in the *Nikāyas* see Matthews (1975).
32. This is perhaps another instance of translations leading us astray, as when *paññā* is translated as 'wisdom'. The nature of Buddhist soteriology has been obscured due in no small measure to the unfortunate translation of these two key terms.
33. *'Patthayamāno ti dve patthanā: taṇhāpatthanā ca chandapatthanā ca. "Patthayamānassa hi jappitāni, pavedhitan vā pi pakappitesū" ti (Sn.902) ettha taṇhāpatthanā. "Chinnaṃ pāpimato sotaṃ uddhastaṃ vinaḷīkataṃ, pāmujjabahulā hotha khemaṃ patthetha bhikkhave" ti ettha kattukamyatā kusala-chanda-patthanā. Ayam eva idha adhippetā. "Tena patthayamāno" ti taṃ yogakkhemaṃ pattukāmo, adhigantukāmo, tannino tappoṇo tappabhāro ti veditabbo.'* Five kinds of *chanda* are mentioned at *D*.ii.277. On arousing *chanda* see *MA*.i.140.
34. *'Tattakapāle khitta-maṃsa-pesi viya'*. *Vism*. 396.
35. *'Rūpā, saddā, gandhā, rasā, phoṭṭhabbā ca manoramā/ ettha me vigato chando, nihato tvam asi Antakā'ti'* (*Vin*.1.21).
36. *Śikṣā*.92.4–10.

Bibliography

1. TEXTS AND TRANSLATIONS

An asterisk against a translation (*tr.) indicates that passages cited are from this source throughout.

Abhidhammathasaṅgaha of Anuruddha S.Z. Aung (tr.) *The Compendium of Philosophy* (London: PTS, 1910).
Abhidharmasamuccaya of Asaṅga Prahlad Pradhan (ed.), Visva-Bharati Studies 12 (Santiniketan: Visva-Bharati, 1950).
Abhidharmadīpa, P.S. Jaini (ed.), *Tibetan Sanskrit Works* vol. IV (Patna: Kashi Prasad Jayanwal Research Institute, 1959).
Abhidharmakośa and *Bhāṣya* Swami D. Shastri (ed.) (Varanasi: Bauddha Bharati, 1970); L. Poussin (tr.) 6 vols, new edition E. Lamotte, (tr.) *MCB* XVI (Brussels: Institute Belge des Hautes Études Chinoises, 1980).
Aṅguttara Nikāya E. Hardy (ed.) (London: PTS, 1899); E.M. Hare (tr.) *The Book of the Gradual Sayings* (London: PTS, 1935).
Aṣṭasāhasrikā-Prajñā-Pāramitā with Haribhadra's Commentary called *Āloka*, P.L. Vaidya (ed.) (Darbhanga: The Mithila Institute, 1960); E. Conze, (tr.) (1973).
Atthasālinī E. Muller (ed.) (London PTS, 1897); Pe Maung Tin (tr.) *The Expositor*, Mrs C.A.F. Rhys Davids (ed. and rev.) (London: PTS, 1976 reprint).
Bodhicāryāvatāra, V. Bhattacharya (ed.) *Biblioteca Indica*, vol. 280.
Bodhicāryāvatāra-pañjikā of Prajñākaramati P.L. Vaidya (ed.) *Buddhist Sanskrit Texts*, no. 12.
Bodhisattva Stage see *Bodhisattvabhūmi*.
Bodhisattvabhūmi Unrai Wogihara (ed.) (Tokyo: no publisher provided, 1930–36).
Bodhisattva-Prātimokṣa-Sūtra, N. Dutt (ed.) *IHQ*, 7, 1931, 259–86.
Brahmajāla Sūtra J.J.M. de Groot (tr.) *Le Code du Mahāyāna en Chine* (Amsterdam: Verhandelingen der Koninklijke Akademie van Wetenschappen te Amsterdam, 1893).
Catuḥśataka: *The Catuḥśataka of Āryadeva*, B. Bhattacharya, Visva-Bharati Series, No. 2 (Calcutta: Visva-Bharati 1931); P.L. Vaidya (ed. and tr.) *Études sur Āryadeva et son Catuḥśataka*, chs VIII–XVI (Paris: Paul Guethner, 1923).
Clarifier of the Sweet Meaning see *Madhuratthavilāsinī*.
Compendium of Conduct see *Śikṣā-Samuccaya*.
Compendium of the Law see *Dharma-Samuccaya*.
Compendium of Māhayaña see *Māhayaña-Saṃgraha*.
Compendium of Metaphysics see *Abhidharmasamuccaya*.
De Anima of Aristotle, J.A. Smith (tr.) *The Works of Aristotle*, vol. III, W.D. Ross (ed.) (Oxford: Clarendon Press, 1955 reprint).

Descent to Laṅkā see *Laṅkāvatāra-sūtra*.
Dhamma-Saṅganī E. Muller (ed.) (London: PTS, 1885); Mrs C.A.F. Rhys Davids (tr.) *A Buddhist Manual of Psychological Ethics*, 3rd edn (London: PTS, 1974).
Dharma-Samuccaya, Lin Li Kouang (tr.) *L'Aide Mémoire de la Vrai Loi*, 3 vols (Paris: Adrien-Maisonneuve, 1949).
Dīgha Nikāya T.W. Rhys Davids and J. Estlin Carpenter (eds) 3 vols (London: PTS, 1889–1910); T.W. and Mrs C.A.F. Rhys Davids (eds) *Dialogues of the Buddha* (*Sacred Books of the Buddhists* vols II–IV) (London: PTS, 1977 reprint).
Elders' verses see *Theragāthā*.
Encyclopaedia of Religion and Ethics, J. Hastings (ed.) (Edinburgh: Clark, 1908–26).
Enumeration of Elements see *Dhamma-Saṅganī*.
Entering the Path of Enlightenment see *Bodhicāryāvatāra*.
Expositor see *Atthasālinī*.
Guide, The see *Netti-pakaraṇaṃ*.
Introduction to Madhyamaka see *Madhyamakāvatāra*.
Incremental Discourses see *Aṅguttara Nikāya*.
The Jewel Ornament of Liberation, a *translation of sGam-Po-Pa's *Dam chos yid bzhin gyi nor bu thar pa rin po che'i rgyan zhes bya ba theg pa chen po'i lam rim gyi bshad pa*, H.V. Guenther (tr.) (London: Rider, 1970).
Kathāvatthu A.C. Taylor (ed.) (London: PTS, 1894); S.Z. Aung and Mrs Rhys David (trs) *Points of Controversy or Subjects of Discourse* . . . (London: PTS, 1960 reprint).
Lamp of Metaphysics see *Abhidharmadīpa*.
Laṅkāvatāra-sūtra B. Nanjio (ed.) *Biblioteca Otaniensis* vol. 1 (Kyoto: Otani University Press, 1923); D.T. Suzuki (tr.) (London: Routledge, 1932).
Large Sūtra on the Perfection of Wisdom see Conze, 1975.
Letter to a Friend see *Suhṛllekha*.
Long Discourses see *Dīgha Nikāya*.
Madhuratthavilāsinī I.B. Horner (ed.) (London: PTS, 1946); I.B. Horner (tr.), *The Clarifier of the Sweet Meaning* (London: PTS, 1978).
Madhyamakāvatāra, Tibetan text, L. Poussin (ed.) *Biblioteca Buddhica* IX (St Petersburg: 1912); L. Poussin (partial *tr.) *Le Muséon* 8 (1907), 11 (1910), 12 (1911).
Mahāyāna-Saṃgraha E. Lamotte (ed. and *tr.) *La Somme du Grand Véhicule*: tome I Tibetan and Chinese text, tome II Translation and Commentary (Louvain: Bureaux du Muséon, 1939).
Mahāyāna-Sūtrālaṃkāra S. Lévi (ed. and tr.): tome I text, tome 2 translation (Paris: Librairie Honoré Champlon 1907).
Middle Verses the *Mūlamadhyamika-kārikā* of Nāgārjuna J.W. de Jong (ed.) (Madras: Adyar Library and Research Centre, 1977).
Milindapañha V. Trenckner (ed.) (London: Royal Asiatic Society 1928); I.B. Horner (tr.) 2 vols *Milinda's Questions* (London: PTS, 1963).
Milinda's Questions see *Milindapañha*.
Nanda the Fair see *Saundarananda*.
Netti-pakaraṇam E. Hardy (ed.) (London: PTS, 1902); Ñāṇamoli (tr.) *The Guide* (London: PTS, 1962).

Nichomachean Ethics of Aristotle W.D. Ross (tr.) (Oxford: Clarendon Press, 1925).
Ornament of Mahāyāna Sūtras see *Mahāyāna-Sūtrālaṃkāra*.
Path of Purification see *Visuddhimagga*.
Perfection of Wisdom in 8,000 Lines see *Aṣṭasāhasrikā-Prajñā-Pāramitā*.
Prasannapadā J. May (tr.) *Candrakīrti Prasannapadā Madhyamakavṛtti* (Paris: Adrien-Maisonneuve, 1959).
Points of Controversy see *Kathāvatthu*.
Prātimokṣa-Sūtram A.C. Banerjee (ed.) (Calcutta: J.C. Sarkhel, 1954).
Ratnāvalī J. Hopkins (*tr.) *The Precious Garland and the Song of the Four Mindfulnesses: Wisdom of Tibet Series* 2 (London: George Allen & Unwin, 1975).
Record I. Tsing *A Record of the Buddhist Religion as Practised in India and the Malay Archipelago* J. Takakusu (*tr.) (Delhi: Munshiram Manoharlal, 1966).
Saddharma-puṇḍarīkasūtra H. Kern and B. Nanjio (eds) *Biblioteca Buddhica* 10 (St Petersburg: Imperial Academy of Sciences, 1912); H. Kern (tr.) *The Lotus of the True Law* (Oxford: 1884, *SBE* XXI).
Satyasiddhiśāstra of Harivarman, N.A. Sastri (ed.) (Gaekwad's Oriental Series No. 159, 1975).
Saundarananda E.H. Johnson (ed. and tr.) *The Saundarananda or Nanda the Fair* (London: H. Milford, 1932).
Śikṣā-Samuccaya P.L. Vaidya (ed.) *Buddhist Sanskrit Texts* XI; C. Bendall and W.H.D. Rouse (trs) (Delhi: Motilal Banarsidass, 1981, reprint).
Śīlaparikathā A. Basu (ed. and tr. with Sanskrit reconstruction) *IHQ* March 1931, 28–33.
Sphuṭārtha-Abhidharmakośa-Vyākhyā Unrai Wogihara (ed.) 2 vols (Tokyo: The Publishing Association of Abhidharmakośa Vyākhyā, 1932–).
Suhṛllekha with Mi-pham's commentary L. Kawamura (*tr.) *Golden Zephyr* (Emeryville, Calif.: Dharma Publishing, 1975).
Summary of the Mahāyāna see *Mahāyāna-Saṃgraha*.
Śūraṃgamasamādhisūtra E. Lamotte (tr.) *La Concentration de la Marche Héroïque* (Brussels: *MCB* 11, 1965).
Sutra on Skilful Means, G.C.C. Chang (tr.).
Sutta-Nipāta D. Andersen and H. Smith (ed.) (London: PTS, 1913); E.M. Hare (tr.) *Woven Cadences of Early Buddhists* (*SBB* 15) (London: Oxford University Press, 1947).
Teachings of Vimalaktīrti see Vimalakīrtinirdeśasūtra.
Theragāthā/Therīgāthā H. Oldenberg and R. Pischel (eds) (London: PTS, 1966, 2nd edn); Mrs C.A.F. Rhys Davids (tr.) *Psalms of the Early Buddhists*: Part I, *Psalms of the Sisters*, Part II *Psalms of the Brethren* (London: PTS 1909–13).
Le Traité de la grande vertu de sagesse de Nāgārjuna, E. Lamotte (*tr.) (Louvain: University of Louvain, 1980).
Trance of Heroic Progress see *Śūraṃgamasamādhisūtra*.
Treasury of Metaphysics see *Abhidharmakośa*.
Upāli-Paripṛcchā Vinaya-viniścaya-upāli-paripṛcchā: Enquête d'Upāli pour une exégèse de la discipline P. Python (tr.) (Paris: Adrien-Maisonneuve, 1973).

Vijñaptimātratāsiddh, Louis de la Vallée Poussin (*tr.) 3 vols, (Paris: Paul Geuthner, 1928).
Vimalakīrtinirdeśasūtra E. Lamotte (*tr.) (Sara Boin, English tr.) *The Teachings of Vimalakīrti* (London: Routledge & Kegan Paul, 1976).
Vinaya, The Vinaya Pitakam H. Oldenberg (ed.) 5 vols (London: Luzac, 1964); I.B. Horner, (tr.) *The Book of the Discipline* (*SBB.* vol. X–XV).
Visuddhimagga, The Visuddhimagga of Buddhaghosācariya H.C. Warren (ed.) *HOS* no. 41 1950; Ñāṇamoli (tr.) *The Path of Purification* 2 vols (Boulder and London: Shambhala, 1976).

2. SECONDARY WORKS

ACKRILL, J.A. (1973) *Aristotle's Ethics* (London: Faber & Faber).
ACTON, H.B. (1963) 'Negative Utilitarianism', *Aristotelian Society Supplementary,* 37, 83–114.
ALLAN, D.J. (1970) *The Philosophy of Aristotle,* 2nd edn (Oxford: Oxford University Press).
ANESAKI, M. 'Ethics and Morality (Buddhist)' in J. Hastings (ed.) in *Encyclopaedia of Religion and Ethics* (Edinburgh: Clark, 1908–26) pp. 447–55.
ANURUDDHA, K. (1972) 'Studies in Buddhist Social Thought as Documented in the Pali Nikāyas', PhD thesis, University of Lancaster.
ARONSON, H.B. (1979) 'The Relationship of the Karmic to the Nirvanic in Theravāda Buddhism', *JRE,* 7/1, 28–36.
ARONSON, H.B. (1980) *Love and Sympathy in Theravāda Buddhism* (Delhi: Motilal Banarsidass).
BAREAU, A. (1955) *Les Sectes Bouddhiques du Petite Véhicule* (Saigon: École Française d'Extréme-Orient).
BAREAU, A. (1956) 'The Concept of Responsibility in Ancient Buddhism' *East & West,* 6, 216–23.
BARUA, D.K. (1971) *An Analytical Study of the Four Nikāyas* (Calcutta: Rabindra Bharati University).
BASTOW, D. (1969) 'Buddhist Ethics', *Religious Studies* 5, December, 195–206).
BASTOW, D. (1988) 'An Example of Self Change: the Buddhist Path', *Religious Studies,* 24, 157–72.
BEEHLER, R. (1978) *Moral Life,* (Oxford, Basil Blackwell).
BENTHAM, J. (1970) *An Introduction to the Principles of Morals and Legislation,* J.H. Burns and H.L.A. Hart (eds) (London: Athlone Press).
BISHOP, D.H. (1972) 'Some Notes on Buddhist Ethics', *The Mahābodhi,* May/June, 261–4).
BODHI, Bhikkhu (1978) *The Discourse on the All-Embracing Net of Views* (Kandy: Buddhist Publication Society).
BRADLEY, F.H. (1927) *Ethical Studies,* 2nd rev. edn (Oxford: Clarendon Press).
BREAR, A.D. (1974) 'The Nature and Status of Moral Behavior in Zen Buddhist Tradition', *PEW,* 25, 429–41.

BUNNAG, J. (1973) *Buddhist Monk, Buddhist Layman* (Cambridge: Cambridge University Press).
BUSH, R.C. (1960) 'Foundations for Ethics in the Sacred Scriptures of Hinduism and Early Buddhism', PhD thesis, University of Chicago.
CARRITHERS, M. (1983) *The Forest Monks of Laṅkā* (New Delhi: Oxford University Press).
CARTER, J.R. (1984) 'Beyond "Beyond Good and Evil"', in Dhammapala, Gombrich and Norman (eds), 41–55.
CHANG, G.C.C. (ed.) (1983) *A Treasury of Mahāyāna Sūtras* (Pennsylvania: Pennsylvania State University Press).
CHILDRESS, J. (1979) 'Methodological Issues in Comparative Religious Ethics', *JRE*, 7/1, 1–10).
CLARK, S.R.L. (1975) *Aristotle's man: Speculations upon Aristotelian Anthropology* (Oxford: Clarendon Press).
COLLINS, S. (1982) *Selfless Persons* (Cambridge: Cambridge University Press).
CONZE, E. (1956) *Buddhist Meditation* (London: George Allen & Unwin).
CONZE, E. (1973) *The Perfection of Wisdom in Eight Thousand Lines and its Verse Summary* (California: Four Seasons Foundation).
CONZE, E. (1975) *The Large Sūtra on Perfect Wisdom* (Berkeley: University of California Press).
COOMARASWAMY, A. and HORNER, I.B. (1982) *The Living Thoughts of Gotama the Buddha* (Delhi: Munshiram Manoharlal).
COOPER, J.M. (1975) *Reason and Human Good in Aristotle* (Cambridge, Mass.: Harvard University Press).
CREEL, A.B. (1977) *Dharma in Hindu Ethics* (Calcutta: Firma KLM).
CRUISE, H. (1983) 'Early Buddhism: Some Recent Misconceptions', *PEW*, 33, 2, April, 149–66).
DAHLKE, P. (1908) *Buddhist Essays*, Bhikkhu Sīlācāra (tr.) (London: Macmillan).
DAYAL, H. (1932) *The Bodhisattva Doctrine in Buddhist Sanskrit Literature* (London: Routledge & Kegan Paul).
DEMIÉVILLE, P. (1952) *Le Concile de Lhasa* (Paris: Presses Universitaires).
DE SILVA, P. (1979) *An Introduction to Buddhist Psychology* (London: Macmillan).
DERRETT, J.D.M. (1983) *A Textbook for Novices*: a translation of Jayarakṣita's 'Perspicacious Commentary on the Compendium of Conduct by Śrīghana' (Torino: Indologica Taurinensia).
DHAMMAPALA, G., GOMBRICH, R.F. and NORMAN, K.R. (eds) (1984) *Buddhist Studies in Honour of Hammalava Saddhatissa* (Nugegoda, Sri Lanka: University of Sri Jayawardenepura).
DHARMASIRI, G. (1986) *Fundamentals of Buddhist Ethics* (Singapore: Buddhist Research Society).
DIHLE, A. (1982) *The Theory of Will in Classical Antiquity* (Berkeley: University of California Press).
DUTT, N. (1930) *Aspects of Mahāyāna Buddhism and its Relation to Hīnāyana* (London: Luzac).
DUTT, N. (tr.) (1931) see *Bodhisattva-Prātimokṣa-Sūtra*.

DUTT, N. (1970) *Buddhist Sects in India* (Calcutta: F.K.L. Mukhopadhyay).
FINNIS, J. (1983) *Fundamentals of Ethics* (Oxford: Clarendon Press).
FLETCHER, J. (1966) *Situation Ethics* (London: SCM Press).
FOOT, P. (1978) *Virtues and Vices and Other Essays in Moral Philosophy* (Oxford: Basil Blackwell).
FOX, D. (1971) 'Zen and Ethics: Dogen's Synthesis', *PEW*, 21, 33–41.
FRANKENA, W. (1973) *Ethics*, 2nd edn (New Jersey: Prentice Hall).
GAUTHIER, R.A. (1967) 'On the Nature of Aristotle's Ethics' in J.J. Walsh and H.L. Shapiro (eds) *Aristotle's Ethics: Issues and Interpretations* (Belmont, California: Wadsworth).
GIMELLO, R.M. (1978) 'Mysticism and Meditation' in S. Katz (ed.) *Mysticism and Philosophical Analysis* (London: Sheldon Press, 1978).
GOMBRICH, R. (1971) *Precept and Practice – Traditional Buddhism in the Rural Highlands of Ceylon* (Oxford: Clarendon Press).
GOMBRICH, R. (1984) 'Notes on the Brahminical Background to Buddhist Ethics' in Dhammapala, Gombrich and Norman (eds), pp. 91–102.
GOMEZ, L.O. (1973) 'Emptiness and Moral Perfection', *PEW*, 23, 3, 361–72.
GOVINDA, LAMA (1974) *The Psychological Attitude of Early Buddhist Philosophy* (New York: Samuel Weiser).
GRIFFITHS, P. (1981) 'Concentration or Insight: The Problematic of Theravāda Buddhist Meditation Theory', *JAAR*, XLIX/4, December.
GUDMUNSEN, C. (1972) 'Ethics Gets in the Way: A Reply to David Bastow', *Religious Studies*, 8, 311–18.
GUDMUNSEN, C. (1973) 'Buddhist Metaethics', M. Phil Thesis, University of London.
GUENTHER, H.V. (1976) *Philosophy and Psychology in the Abhidharma* (Berkeley & London: Shambala).
GYATSO, Geshe (1980) *Meaningful to Behold* (Ulverston: Wisdom Publications).
HARDIE, W.F.R. (1980) *Aristotle's Ethical Theory* (Oxford: Clarendon Press).
HARRIS, J.W. (1980) *Legal Philosophies* (London: Butterworth).
HERMAN, A.L. (1983) *An Introduction to Buddhist Thought: A Philosophic History of Indian Buddhism* (Lanham & London: University Press of America).
HINDERY, R. (1978) *Comparative Ethics in Hindu and Buddhist Traditions* (Delhi: Motilal Banarsidass).
HODGSON, D.H. (1967) *Consequences of Utilitarianism* (Oxford: Clarendon Press).
HOLT, J.C. (1981) *Discipline: the Canonical Buddhism of the Vinayapiṭaka* (Delhi: Motilal Banarsidass).
HOPKINS, J. (1975) *The Precious Garland* see *Ratnāvālī*.
HORNER, I.B. (1936) *The Early Buddhist Theory of Man Perfected* (London: Williams & Northgate).
HORNER, I.B. (1950) *The Basic Position of Sīla* (Colombo: Bauddha Sahitya Sabha).
HORNER, I.B. and COOMARASWAMY, A. (1948) *The Living Thoughts of Gotama the Buddha* (London: Cassell).

JAUHARI, M. (1968) *Politics and Ethics in Ancient India* (Varanasi: Bharatiya Vidya Prakashan).
JAYATILLEKE, K. (1970) 'The Ethical Theory of Buddhism', *The Mahābodhi*, 78, July, 192–7.
JAYATILLEKE, K. (1970a) 'The Buddhist Ethical Ideal or the Ultimate Good', *The Mahābodhi*, 78, September, 262–7.
JAYATILLEKE, K. (1970b) 'The Criteria of Right and Wrong', *The Mahābodhi*, 78, May/June, 114–20.
JAYATILLEKE, K. (1971) 'The Basis of Buddhist Ethics', *The Mahābodhi*, 79, Feb./Mar., 50–6.
JOHANSSON, R.E. (1979) *The Dynamic Psychology of Early Buddhism* (New Delhi: Scandinavian Institute of Asian Studies Monograph Series No. 37).
JOHNSTON, E.H. (1937) *Early Sāṃkhya* (London: Royal Asiatic Society).
JONES, R.H. (1979) 'Theravāda Buddhism and Morality', *JAAR*, XLVII/3, 371–87).
KALUPAHANA, D. (1976) *Buddhist Philosophy: A Historical Analysis* (Honolulu: University Press of Hawaii).
KAPLEAU, P. (1983) *A Buddhist Case for Vegetarianism* (London: Rider).
KATZ, N. (1979) 'Does the "Cessation of the World" Entail the Cessation of the Emotions? The Psychology of the Arahant', *Pali Buddhist Review*, 4, 3.
KATZ, N. (1982) *Buddhist Images of Human Perfection* (Delhi: Motilal Banarsidass).
KAWAMURA, L. (1975) *Golden Zephyr* (California: Dharma Publishing).
KENNY, A. (1978) *Free Will and Responsibility* (London: Routledge & Kegan Paul).
KENNY, A. (1979) *Aristotle's Theory of the Will* (London: Duckworth).
KHANTIPALO, P. (1964) *Tolerance: A Study from Buddhist Sources* (London: Rider).
KING, W.L. (1964) *In the Hope of Nibbina* (La Salle: Open Court).
KING, W.L. (1964a) *A Thousand Lives Away* (Oxford: Bruno Cassirer).
KING, W.L. (1980) *Theravāda Meditation* (Pennsylvania & London: Pennsylvania State University Press).
KING, W.L. (1989) 'Motivated Goodness and Unmotivated Perfection', *Anglican Theological Review*, 71, 143–52.
KLOPPENBORG, R. (1974) *The Pratyekabuddha: A Buddhist Ascetic* (Leiden: Brill).
KLOPPENBORG, R. (1983) 'The Earliest Buddhist Ritual of Ordination' in *Selected Studies on Ritual in the Indian Religions*, R. Kloppenborg (ed.) (Leiden: Brill).
LAMOTTE, E. (1980) *Le Traité de la grande vertu de Sagesse de Nāgārjuna* (Louvain: University of Louvain).
LAW, B.C. (1934) 'Buddhist *Pāramitā*', *Indian Culture*, I, 686–91.
LAW, N.N. (ed.) (1940) *Louis de la Vallée-Poussin Memorial Volume* (Calcutta: Calcutta Oriental Press).
LING, T. (1982) *A History of Religion East & West* (London: Macmillan).
LITTLE, D. and TWISS, S.B. (1978) *Comparative Religious Ethics* (San Francisco: Harper & Row).

LYONS, D. (1970) *Forms and Limits of Utilitarianism* (Oxford: Clarendon Press).
McDERMOTT, J.P. (1980) 'Karma and Rebirth in Early Buddhism' in W. O'Flaherty (ed.) *Karma and Rebirth in Classical Indian Traditions* (London: University of California Press).
MACINTYRE, A. (1967) *A Short History of Ethics* (London: Routledge & Kegan Paul).
MACINTYRE, A. (1971) *Against The Self-Images of the Age* (London: Duckworth).
MACINTYRE, A. (1981) *After Virtue: A Study in Moral Theory* (London: Duckworth).
MACQUARRIE, J. (1967) *A Dictionary of Christian Ethics* (London: SCM Press).
MATTHEWS, B. (1975) 'Notes on the Concept of the Will in Early Buddhism', *SLJH*, December, 1, 2, 152–60.
MATTHEWS, B. (1983) *Craving and Salvation: A Study in Buddhist Soteriology* (Waterloo, Ontario: Wilfrid Laurier University Press).
MAY, J. (1978) 'On Madhyamika Philosophy', *Journal of Indian Philosophy*, 6, 233–41.
MAY, J. (1959) see *Prasannapadā*.
MILL, J.S. (1957) *Utilitarianism* (London: Dent).
MISRA, G.S.P.. (1984) *Development of Buddhist Ethics* (Delhi: Munshiram Manoharlal).
ÑĀṆAPOṆIKA THERA (1965) *Abhidhamma Studies* (Kandy: Buddhist Publication Society).
NIELSEN, K. (1973) *Ethics Without God* (London: Pemberton Books).
NORMAN, K.R. (1983) *Pali Literature*, History of Indian Literature Series, J. Gonda (ed.) (Wiesbaden: Otto Harrassowitz).
NORMAN, R. (1983) *The Moral Philosophers* (Oxford: Clarendon Press).
PACHOW, W. (1955) *Comparative Study of the Prātimokṣa on the basis of its Chinese, Tibetan, Sanskrit and Pali Versions* (Santiniketan: Sino-Indian Cultural Society).
PANDE, G.C. (1983) *Studies in the Origins of Buddhism* (Delhi: Motilal Banarsidass).
PIYANANDA, D. (1974) 'The Concept of Mind in Early Buddhism', PhD thesis, The Catholic University of America.
POPPER, K.R. (1962) *The Open Society and its Enemies*, 4th revised edn (London: Routledge & Kegan Paul).
POUSSIN, L. de la VALLÉE (1927) *La Morale Bouddhique* (Paris: Nouvelle Librairie Nationale).
PRATT, J.B. (1928) *The Pilgrimage of Buddhism* (New York: Macmillan).
PREBISH, C. (1980) '*Vinaya* and *Prātimoksa*: The Foundation of Buddhist Ethics' in A.K. Narain (ed.) *Studies in the History of Buddhism* (Delhi: B.R. Publishing).
PREMASIRI, P.D. (1975) 'Moral Evaluation in Early Buddhism', *SLJH*, June, 1, 63–74.
PREMASIRI, P.D. (1976) 'Interpretation of Two Principal Ethical Terms in Early Buddhism', *SLJH*, June 2, 1, 63–74.
PYE, M. (1978) *Skilful Means* (London: Duckworth).

RAHULA, W. (1978) *What the Buddha Taught* (London: Gordon Fraser).
RAJAPAKSA, R. (1975) 'A Philosophical Investigation of the Ethical Hedonism and the Theory of Self implicit in the Pali Nikāyas', PhD thesis, London University.
RAWLS, J. (1980) *A Theory of Justice* (Oxford: OUP).
RAZZINO, A. (1981) '"PAÑÑA" and "KARUṆĀ" in Theravāda Buddhist Ethics Compared to Love in Protestant Christian Ethics', PhD thesis, Northwestern University.
REAT, N.R. (1980) '"Theravāda Buddhism and Morality": Objections and Corrections', *JAAR*, XLVIII, 3, 433–40.
REYNOLDS, F.E. (1979) 'Buddhist Ethics: A Bibliographic Essay', *Religious Studies Review*, 5, 1, January.
REYNOLDS, F.E. (1979a) 'Four Modes of Theravāda Action', *JRE*, 7, 1, 12–26.
REYNOLDS, F.E. (1980) 'Contrasting Modes of Action: A Comparative Study of Buddhist and Christian Ethics', *History of Religions*, 20, 128–46.
RHYS DAVIDS, Mrs C.A.F. (1936) *The Birth of Indian Psychology and its Development in Buddhism* (London: Luzac).
RHYS DAVIDS, Mrs C.A.F. (1898) 'On the Will in Buddhism', *JRAS*, pt.1, Jan., 47–59.
ROSS, D. Sir, (gen. ed.) (1908–) *The Works of Aristotle Translated into English* (Oxford: Oxford University Press).
RUEGG, D.S. (1980) '*Ahiṃsā* and Vegetarianism in the History of Buddhism' in S. Balasooriya *et al.* (eds) *Buddhist Studies in Honour of Walpola Rahula* (London: Gordon Frazer).
RYAN, A. (1974) *J.S.Mill* (London: Routledge & Kegan Paul).
RUPP, G. (1971) 'The Relationship between *Nirvāṇa* and *Saṃsāra*: An Essay in the Evolution of Buddhist Ethics', *PEW*, 21/1, January, 55–68.
SADDHATISSA, H. (1970) *Buddhist Ethics* (London: George Allen & Unwin).
SMART, J.J.C. and WILLIAMS, B. (1973) *Utilitarianism: For and Against* (Cambridge: Cambridge University Press).
SMART, N. (1958) 'Negative Utilitarianism', *Mind*, 67, 542–3.
SNELLGROVE, D. (1956) 'Buddhist Morality' in J.M. Todd (ed.) *The Springs of Morality: A Catholic Symposium* (London: Burns & Oates).
SNELLGROVE, D. (1989) 'Multiple Features of the Buddhist Heritage' in *The Buddhist Heritage* (Tring, UK: Buddhica Britannica I, The Institute of Buddhist Studies).
SPIRO, M.E. (1970) *Buddhism and Society: A Great Tradition and its Burmese Vicissitudes* (Berkeley: University of California Press).
SPIRO, M.E. (1982) *Buddhism and Society: A Great Tradition and its Burmese Vicissitudes* 2nd expanded edn (Berkeley: University of California Press).
STCHERBATSKY, T. (1923) *The Central Conception of Buddhism and the Meaning of the Word 'Dharma'* (London: Royal Asiatic Society).
STEPHENSON, A.L. (1970) 'Prolegomenon to Buddhist Social Ethics', PhD thesis, Claremont Graduate School.
SWEARER, D.K. (1979) 'Bhikkhu Buddhadasa on Ethics and Society', *JRE*, 7/1, 54–64.
TACHIBANA, S. (1926) *The Ethics of Buddhism* (London: Curzon Press).

TAKAKUSU, J. (1956) *The Essentials of Buddhist Philosophy* (Honolulu: Office Appliance Co.)
TATZ, M. (1986) (tr.) *Asanga's Chapter on Ethics with the Commentary of Tsong-Kha-pa, The Basic Path to Awakening, The Complete Bodhisattva. Studies in Asian Thought and Religion*, vol. 4 (Lewiston, New York: The Edwin Mellen Press).
THOMAS, E.J. (1914) 'The Basis of Buddhist Ethics', *The Quest*, 6, 339–47.
VAJIRAÑĀṆA, P. (1975) *Buddhist Meditation in theory and Practice* 2nd edn (Kuala Lumpur: Buddhist Missionary Society).
WANG, S. (1975) 'Can Man go beyond Ethics? The System of Padmasambhava', *JRE*, 3/1, 141–55.
WAYMAN, A. (1961) *Analysis of the Śrāvakabhūmi Manuscript* (Berkeley: University of California Press).
WEERARATNE, W. (1976) '*Role of the Individual in Society according to Buddhism*', PhD thesis, University of Lancaster.
WELCH, H. (1967) *The Practice of Chinese Buddhism* (Cambridge, Mass: Harvard University Press).
WIEGER, L. (1910) *Vinaya, Monachisme et Discipline* (Paris: Cathasia, Serie Culturelle des Hautes Études de Tien-Tsin).
WIJESEKERA, O. (1971) 'Buddhist Ethics' in Ñāṇaponika (ed.) *Pathways of Buddhist Thought* (London: George Allen & Unwin).
WILLIAMS, B. (1965) *Morality and the Emotions* (London: Bedford College Inaugural Lecture).
WILLIAMS, P. (1989) *Mahāyāna Buddhism: the Doctrinal Foundations* (London: Routledge).
WILTSHIRE, M. (1983) 'The Great Hesitation', Unpublished paper.

General Index

Index of Names

BJ 1289 .K44 1992   94 0509

Keown, Damien, 1951-

The nature of Buddhist
ethics

CABRINI COLLEGE LIBRARY
610 KING OF PRUSSIA RD.
RADNOR, PA 19087-3699

DEMCO